Cooking with Herbs and Spices

by Milo Miloradovich

DOVER PUBLICATIONS, INC., NEW YORK

A fountain of gardens, a well of living waters,
and streams from Lebanon. Awake, O north wind;
and come, thou south; blow upon my garden,
that the spices thereof may flow out.

Solomon's Song, IV:15, 16

Published in Canada by General Publishing Company, Ltd., 30 Lesmill Road, Don Mills, Toronto, Ontario.
Published in the United Kingdom by Constable and Company, Ltd.

This Dover edition, first published in 1989, is an unabridged and unaltered republication of the work originally published by Doubleday & Company, Inc., Garden City, N.Y. in 1950, with the title *The Art of Cooking with Herbs and Spices: A Handbook of Flavors and Savors*. The present edition is published by special arrangement with Bryn Mawr College, Bryn Mawr, Pennsylvania 19010.

Manufactured in the United States of America
Dover Publications, Inc., 31 East 2nd Street, Mineola, N.Y. 11501

Library of Congress Cataloging-in-Publication Data

Miloradovich, Milo.
  Cooking with herbs and spices.

  Reprint. Originally published: The art of cooking with herbs and spices. 1st ed. Garden City, N.Y. : Doubleday, 1950.
  1. Cookery (Herbs) 2. Spices. I. Title.
TX819.H4M55   1989   641.6'57   89-25896
ISBN 0-486-26177-8

Appreciation

It is always a privilege to extend appreciation and thanks to friends and relatives, both here and abroad; to all who give unhesitatingly of their store of knowledge and experience that a book such as this may be as complete as possible.

I wish to express my thanks to the personnel of the Agricultural Experiment Stations and Extension Services working in co-operation with the United States Department of Agriculture. Those groups which provided a statistical bulletin or a circular, with suggestions on some of the uses of the more popular herbs, are from all over the United States. They include the Universities of Arizona, Connecticut, Georgia, Illinois, Maine, Minnesota, Vermont, and West Virginia; also the Clemson Agricultural College in South Carolina; Massachusetts State College; New Mexico College of Agriculture and Mechanics Arts; North Carolina State College of Agriculture and Engineering; and Rhode Island State College.

My sincere appreciation to The American Spice Trade Association; to Ida M. Brace, Home Economist and Managing Editor of the *Self-Service Grocer,* and *The Voluntary and Co-operative Groups Magazine;* and to Godfrey Irwin, New York representative of the Wine Institute, for the helpful information which all of them so generously supplied.

Many thanks also to André Prost, considered our best authority on herb honeys, and to his associate, Elmer A. Renner, for so carefully checking with me the botanical and geographical sources of honeys; also to Felix Bado of Joseph Victori & Co., Inc., for his retailing information. And in conclusion much appreciation to John Warren Weiss, of Old Homestead Herbs, for so graciously answering all my questions on the importing and retailing of aromatic herbs and spices.

Milo Miloradovich

Preface

The inspiration for writing this book came out of the many requests and suggestions of friends who were intrigued by the names and uses of the various culinary herbs which are mentioned in my previous volumes on unusual foreign foods and sea foods. They remarked: "We'd use more herbs and spices every day if we only knew more about them." Others questioned: "How and what herbs and spices should we buy when first learning to use them?" And "When and how should we use herbs and spices in everyday cooking?"

Those of my friends who are home economists commented: "There isn't a complete book devoted exclusively to herbs and spices which tells us specifically the exact seasoning qualities of each; how much of what herb or spice to use in everyday recipes to secure those subtle effects and new flavors for which we search constantly." They questioned: "Why don't you write more of what you know about seasoning basic foods with herbs and spices?"

The answer to these and many similar questions is what I wholeheartedly trust is accomplished in this volume. Being a first-generation American gave me the experience of growing up in the environment of a home with a European atmosphere in which even simple meals were made epicurean by the wise and frequent use of aromatic herbs and spices. I have drawn upon that rich background for much of the material included in these pages.

The shelves of our libraries and bookshops are gold mines of highly specialized and basic cookbooks. This volume has been planned so that it may be used in conjunction with these books. For example, if you own a favorite cookbook on eggs, meats, cheeses, game, sea foods, or vegetables, this one will assist you in making more frequent and many more new uses of specific herbs and spices as seasonings for those basic foods.

The amount of herb or spice which you may eventually decide upon as the perfect amount of seasoning for you may differ slightly from the various amounts suggested for average tastes. This is true of any seasoning, even of salt and pepper. However, the addition of an herb or a spice to a favorite basic recipe in no way changes the chemistry of the food. It improves the flavor and makes even the simplest foods more delicious and palatable.

I trust also that this book will help overcome the erroneous idea that foods seasoned with herbs and spices are too pungent or "hot" for daily consumption. If the proper amount of an herb or a spice is used, the result is a delicately subtle one, and the natural flavor of the food is never smothered by too much seasoning. Herb- and spice-seasoned foods are not only more appetizing but more nourishing. Paprika, for example, is an agreeably sweet spice, far richer in Vitamin C than any of the citrus fruits. But we don't go overboard and serve paprika for breakfast in the place of orange juice.

As one learns to use herbs and spices more frequently it is almost second nature to wish to learn more about their cultivation and harvesting. One may even have an urge to grow some of them in a small country garden, or on a city terrace, or perhaps even in a simple window box. An herb garden of one's own may start one dreaming of the gardens of the world with their mysterious legends and romantic histories. A sudden whiff of a deliciously pungent spice can sometimes bring to mind the rise and fall of empires. All this may seem a far cry from cooking with herbs and spices, yet it is all a part of their complete story.

In the legends of the spice caravans and the history of the expansion of the trade routes are narratives far too rich and entertaining to remain buried in ancient history. Because of space, these and other stories which tell of the development of the culinary uses of herbs and spices will be incorporated in a separate volume. It will also include recipes for some of their different fragrant uses in the home.

In this book on flavors and savors may you and all who read find rich enjoyment as you become more intimately acquainted with the unlimited ways in which herbs and spices may be used to season all foods more interestingly.

Milo Miloradovich

Contents

Salt, Sodium Chloride
Definition of Herb Salt and How Prepared
Liquid Herb and Spice Extracts
Using Herb- and Spice-flavored Salts
Tips on Using MSG
Recipes for Using Herb- and Spice-flavored Salts

Cooking with Herbs and Spices

CHAPTER ONE

Savory Herbs

and Spices

"O, mickle is the powerful grace that lies in herbs, plants, stones, and their true qualities." (Shakespeare, *Romeo and Juliet*, II, 3, 15, 1595). For many centuries before these memorable lines were ever penned the savory herbs and spices of the world added flavor and graciousness to the richness of living. The aromatic plants of the earth have played an important part in the development of world commerce; and the pages of ancient history are filled with the magic traditions of their myriad uses.

Just what is an herb? Webster's definition reads: "a seed plant which does not develop woody persistent tissue, as that of a shrub or a tree, but is more or less soft or succulent." This includes all herbs used for many purposes other than to season foods. In this volume the word is used in its culinary sense only. Included are the savory herbs which are easily procurable and readily grown in practically all parts of the world.

The historical pronunciation of the word herb and the best usage of it in the United States is *urb*. This is the articulation to which I am partial. However, there are many persons who prefer to pronounce the word as *hurb* with the *h* aspirate. This latter pronunciation is considered the best usage in England today, though it has been considered such only since the year 1800. In the final analysis the pronunciation can be a matter of personal taste and individual choice since both *urb* and *hurb* are correct.

How shall we define a spice? And when was a spice not a spice? Might not the answer be: "When it was a root, or a piece of bark, or a berry, or a fruit, or even a flower bud?" Specifically, spices are "any of various vegetable productions which are fragrant or aromatic and pungent to the taste."

Most spices are dried or cured under the tropical sun of the countries in which the majority of them grow and are cultivated. For example, the ginger root is dug from the earth and then undergoes a cleaning process before it is dried and exported. Sometimes it is also peeled; then again, some ginger root is boiled in sugar and preserved before it reaches us. Cloves are flower buds; peppercorns are dried berries; and the nutmeg is the dried seed of the kernel of the fruit of a luxuriant and beautiful tropical tree.

USING HERBS AND SPICES
WITH ALL BASIC FOODS

Flavors and seasonings are also matters of personal tastes and choices. We have come a long way in developing new seasonings and flavors since Confucius wrote "Few there are who can distinguish flavors" (450 B.C.). We can certainly take issue with that statement now and replace it with the old nursery rhyme: "Some like it hot, some like it cold; some like it in the pot, nine days old."

The perfect flavor or combination of flavors for you may not be the favorite flavoring or seasoning for another. But this is just where the joy of experimenting and discovering new flavors comes in. Both herbs and spices lend themselves to unlimited imagination when they are used with careful judgment.

Herbs, either singly or in combination, make the most simple, everyday foods more palatable and appetizing. As the real seasoning qualities and aromas of the individual herbs and spices become more familiar through daily use, it becomes quite easy to develop new flavor combinations. Art in any activity is achieved only through sincere and repeated doing. Just reading about something never made anyone an expert; but a little faithful effort pays tremendous dividends.

Though there can be no rigid and set rules in the art of using herbs effectively there are a number of suggestions which will serve as guideposts to attaining an ease and skillfulness in their use. They will assist you in securing more delicious and delectable results with all foods, ranging from the simplest everyday dishes to the most complicated creations of prima donna chefs and sophisticated gourmets.

Some will say that a beginner's list of herbs and spices should be followed. However, I feel that such lists are inhibiting to the creative and experimental homemaker. I believe that any and all herbs and spices may be used by everyone at all times *if* two of the most important seasoning fundamentals are observed. *First:* Use only *fresh* seasonings. A spice or a dried herb which has stood on a shelf until it has lost all its flavor can't possibly give flavor or seasoning to a food. *Second:* Too much of any flavoring is not good.

The aromatic and volatile oils inherent in herbs and spices are often stronger than the natural flavors of most foods. When too much of the herb or spice is used, the real flavor of the food is destroyed and lost. All seasoning is meant to add to the deliciousness of food flavor and not to overpower it.

For the most effective results

—Use freshly dried or fresh herbs and spices sparingly and always carefully.

—Always use less of the dried herb than of the fresh. For example, about ½ teaspoon of dried herb or ¼ teaspoon of powdered herb is equal to 2 scant teaspoons of the freshly minced herb.

—Fresh herbs may be used in recipes calling for dried herbs and vice versa.

—When using dried herbs in salads, sauces, et cetera, the herb will become more naturally aromatic if it is warmed in hot butter, or steeped in hot milk cr water, or lemon juice for a few minutes before it is added to the recipe.

—Never season every dish of a meal with the same herb.

—Fresh leaves and seeds may be minced or crushed by placing them in a fine white cloth before applying the pressure; or they may be crushed with a mortar and pestle.

—Cutting, crushing, or mincing fresh herbs before using brings out the volatile oils and true flavors.

—Either dried or fresh herbs may be tied in small cheesecloth bags when cooking soups and stews; or if placed directly in the liquids, they may be strained through a fine sieve before serving. If not, allow the herbs to remain in the liquids.

—Tradition says that certain herbs are best with certain foods; but *herbs with similar characteristics may be interchanged in a recipe.*

—So it is good to become familiar with the basic flavors and principles of each herb or spice and

—*have the courage to experiment judiciously.*

Some homemakers and cooks will suggest that dried herbs should only be added to the food about a half-hour before it has finished cooking, otherwise the true flavor will be lost. I cannot agree with this school of thought, since my experience has been in savoring the delicious results and delectable tastes of foods in which the dried herbs have been blended and included at the beginning of cooking. It is the release and the blending of the volatile oils of the herbs with the other seasonings and food, during the cooking processes, which give the delicate aromas and unusual flavors.

Through judicious and frequent use one learns the pungency of certain herbs in comparison to the delicacy of others; and experimenting with them can be a never-ending source of delight.

The following suggestions include some of the essential foods and a list of specific herbs and spices which add delicate and appetizing aroma and flavor to foods when the seasonings are carefully blended during the preparation. *See also* other suggestions and detailed recipes included under each chapter devoted to each specific herb or spice.

Herbs and Spices especially good with DESSERTS (*Cakes, cookies, custards, fruits, and pies. For specific suggestions, see under each herb or spice; also Spiced Recipes and Blends.*)

Allspice	Cassia	Mints
Anise seed	Cinnamon	Nutmeg
Basil, sweet	Coriander seed	Poppy seed
Bay leaf	Cumin seed	Rosemary
Borage flowers	Fennel seed	Saffron
Caraway seed	Ginger	Savory
Cardamom seed	Mace	Sesame seed

Herbs and Spices especially good in BEVERAGES (*Fruit drinks, teas, vegetable cocktails. For specific suggestions, see under each herb or spice; also Herb Teas.*)

Allspice	Cardamom seed	Nutmeg
Anise seed	Cinnamon	Rosemary
Basil, sweet	Cloves	Sage
Bay leaf	Ginger	Savory
Bergamot, wild	Mace	Tarragon
Borage	Mints	Thyme

Herbs and Spices especially good with CHEESES (*For specific suggestions, see under each herb or spice; also Herb Blends.*)

Anise seed	Coriander seed	Orégano
Basil, sweet	Curry powder	Paprika
Caraway, fresh	Dill, fresh	Parsley
Caraway seed	Dill seed	Pepper
Cayenne	Fennel seed	Peppermint
Celery	Garlic salt	Rosemary
Celery salt	Marjoram	Saffron
Celery seed	Mustard plant	Sage
Chervil	Mustard seed	Sesame seed
Chili powder	Nutmeg	Thyme
Chives	Onion salt	

Herbs and Spices especially good with FISH and SHELLFISH (*For specific suggestions, see under each herb or spice; also Herb Blends.*)

Basil, sweet	Garlic	Orégano
Bay leaf	Garlic powder	Paprika
Cayenne pepper	Garlic salt	Parsley
Celery	Horseradish	Pepper
Celery salt	Lovage	Rosemary
Celery seed	Marjoram	Saffron
Chervil	Mint	Savory
Chives	Mustard	Tarragon
Curry powder	Onion	Thyme
Dill seed	Onion salt	Water cress
Fennel seed		

Herbs and Spices especially good with MEATS   *(For specific suggestions, see under each herb or spice; also Herb Blends.)*

Allspice	Curry powder	Parsley
Anise seed	Dill, fresh	Pepper
Basil, sweet	Dill seed	Pickling spice
Bay leaf	Fennel seed	Poultry seasoning
Caraway seed	Ginger	Rosemary
Cayenne pepper	Horseradish	Saffron
Celery	Mace	Sage
Celery salt	Marjoram	Savory
Celery seed	Mints	Sesame seed
Chervil	Nutmeg	Shallot
Chili powder	Onion	Tarragon
Chives	Onion powder	Thyme
Cloves	Onion salt	Water cress
Coriander seed	Orégano	
Cumin seed	Paprika	

Herbs and Spices especially good with SALADS and SALAD DRESSINGS   *(For specific suggestions, see under each herb or spice; also Herb and Spice Salad Dressings.)*

Basil, sweet	Dill, fresh	Paprika
Bay leaf	Dill seed	Parsley
Borage	Fennel	Pepper
Burnet	Garlic	Poppy seed
Caraway seed	Garlic powder	Rosemary
Cardamom seed	Garlic salt	Saffron
Celery	Horseradish	Savory
Celery salt	Lovage	Scallions
Celery seed	Marjoram	Sesame seed
Chervil	Mints	Shallot
Chili powder	Mustard, dry	Tarragon
Chives	Mustard seed	Thyme
Coriander seed	Nasturtium	Water cress
Curry powder	Orégano	

Herbs and Spices especially good in SAUCES and STUFF-INGS, see Chapter Ten.

Herbs and Spices especially good with VEGETABLES   (*For specific vegetables, such as asparagus, beets, carrots, et cetera, see under each herb or spice.*)

Anise seed	Curry powder	Orégano
Basil, sweet	Dill seed	Parsley
Bay leaf	Fennel, fresh	Pepper
Borage	Fennel seed	Poppy seed
Caraway seed	Lovage	Rosemary
Celery	Marjoram	Saffron
Celery salt	Mints	Sage
Celery seed	Mustard seed	Savory
Chili powder	Nutmeg	Sesame seed
Coriander seed	Onion	Tarragon
Cress, land	Onion powder	Thyme
Cumin seed	Onion salt	

Herbs and Spices especially good with EGGS   (*For specific suggestions, see under each herb or spice; also Herb Blends.*)

Basil, sweet	Curry powder	Parsley
Caraway, fresh	Marjoram	Pepper
Caraway seed	Mustard plant	Rosemary
Celery	Mustard seed	Saffron
Celery salt	Nutmeg	Sage
Celery seed	Onion	Savory
Chervil	Onion salt	Scallions
Chives, fresh	Orégano	Tarragon
Chive salt	Paprika	Thyme
Cumin seed		

Herbs and Spices especially good with GAME and POULTRY (*For specific suggestions, see under each herb or spice; also Herb Blends.*)

Anise seed	Curry powder	Parsley
Basil, sweet	Garlic	Rosemary
Bay leaf	Garlic salt	Saffron
Caraway seed	Horseradish	Sage
Celery	Lovage seed	Savory
Celery salt	Marjoram	Shallot
Celery seed	Onion	Tarragon
Chives	Onion salt	Thyme
Cumin seed	Orégano	Water cress

Herbs and Spices especially good in SOUPS and CHOWDERS
(*For specific suggestions, see under each herb or spice; also Herb Blends.*)

Anise seed	Cumin seed	Paprika
Basil, sweet	Dill, fresh	Parsley, fresh
Bay leaf	Dill seed	Parsley salt
Caraway	Fennel seed	Poppy seed
Cardamom seed	Garlic	Poultry seasoning
Celery	Garlic powder	Rosemary
Celery salt	Garlic salt	Saffron
Celery seed	Leek	Sage
Chervil	Mace	Savory
Chive salt	Marigold	Sesame seed
Chives, fresh	Marjoram	Sorrel
Cloves	Mint	Tarragon
Coriander seed	Mustard seed	Thyme
Cress, land	Orégano	Water cress

CHAPTER TWO

Culinary
Herb Leaves
and Flowering Tips

ANGELICA, *Angelica archangelica officinalis*

Candied roots, stems, and leaf stalks imported from France; purchased at drugstores; also from herb dealers.

Fresh leaves and stems during summer months from herb gardens.

Fresh roots from herb gardens.

Angelica is a beautiful, hardy biennial which grows more than 6 feet tall. Its hollow stems are often 2 or 3 inches in diameter and the white flowers are large cymes of myriad tiny white blossoms.

This herb, which belongs to the parsley, *Umbelliferae,* family, was called *Archangelica,* the Herb of the Angels, because it was supposed to have dispelled the plague and protected from harm all those who used its leaves. Today, because of its culinary uses, it is known quite simply as GARDEN ANGELICA. The native species, *Angelica atropurpurea,* is commonly known as AMERICAN ANGELICA.

All parts of the herb are unusually aromatic and quite sweet; and the flavor is somewhat like licorice.

Using: The fresh stems and leaf stalks are eaten as celery and used also as a garnish for foods, especially fish. Both the leaves and the stems are used to flavor liqueurs such as absinthe, anisette, Benedictine, chartreuse, and sometimes gin.

Angelica adds a most unusual taste to jams and jellies. See also chapter on Herb Jellies. The candied angelica stems are usually colored a pale green. Sliced thin, and used as decorations on candies and cakes, they are both delicious and attractive. See also chapter on Herb Teas.

CANDY: See Candied Angelica Roots.
COOKIES: See Anise Squares.
GARNISH: Use tender leaves and blanched stems as garnish for baked or broiled fish, as desired.
SALADS: *Fruits, mixed.* Use 1 or 2 leaves finely chopped. Sprinkle lightly over top before serving.

For 4 servings use approximately:

Blanched stems in preferred amounts, when eaten as celery.
2 to 4 chopped leaves in salads.
Leaves and blanched stems in preferred amounts, as garnish.

Angelica Liqueur   TIME: Variable; Age 6 weeks

½ lb. fresh angelica leaves   1½ pts. pure-grain alcohol
2 lbs. sugar   2 qts. water
12 whole cloves   2 4-inch cinnamon sticks

Select fresh young leaves with tender stems. Wash thoroughly under cold running water; dry well on absorbent paper. With sharp knife mince leaves fine; place in wide-mouthed jar; add sugar, cloves, alcohol, water, and cinnamon sticks; mix well; cover tightly. Stand in cool, dark place 6 weeks or more; shake occasionally. Filter through French filter paper; bottle liqueur; cork tightly. Serve as sweet cordial with demitasse. Yield: 6 pints.

Candied Angelica Roots   TIME: 2½ hours

1 lb. angelica roots   2 cups water
2 cups sugar   1 tbs. lemon juice

Scrub and peel roots. Boil in water 20 minutes, or until tender. Drain. Set aside in heavy bowl.
    To prepare syrup: Pour water in saucepan placed over medium flame; add sugar and lemon juice. Cook 20 minutes, or until liquid is a thin syrup. Remove from flame.
    Place roots in syrup. Let stand 1 hour. Replace over flame;

boil gently 30 minutes, or until syrup candies. Drain off syrup. Place roots on waxed paper to dry (warm place at side of stove is good). When perfectly dry, store candied roots in small jars.

ANISE, *Pimpinella anisum*

Fresh leaves during summer months from eastern and Middle West herb gardens.
See also Anise Seed.

Anise is one of the oldest annuals among herbs and belongs to the parsley, *Umbelliferae,* family. This hardy though delicate-looking plant, native to Crete, Egypt, and Greece, is now widely cultivated in all temperate and hot climates including France, Germany, India, Italy, Mexico, South America, and Syria. In the United States its cultivation is limited to the Middle West and eastern states; chief among them is Rhode Island.

The light green foliage, unlike most of the members of the *Umbelliferae* family, is not feathery and fine, but its lacy leaves are divided into three deeply notched leaflets. The yellowish-white flowers of this 2-foot plant form a beautiful heavy cyme at the end of the spreading stems.

The flavor of the fresh leaves is sweetish, like the seeds. When available, the tiny leaves add a most unusual flavor to fruit salads and cakes.

Using: Both the dried and the fresh leaves are used to flavor foods, and the fresh leaves especially will give a slightly sweet flavor to fruit and vegetable salads. They are also a tasty addition to shellfish when the leaves are placed in the boiling water in which the shellfish are being prepared. Mussels, hardshell crabs, and shrimps will have a most unusual sweetness when they have been boiled with fresh anise leaves.

The dried leaves may always be used in place of the fresh, and their aromatic fragrance adds sweetness and scent to sachet combinations. See also chapter on Herb Teas.

SALADS: *Fruit, apple, mixed fruits.* Sprinkle lightly with 1 teaspoon chopped fresh leaves just before serving.
Vegetable, cauliflower, cucumber, lettuce, mixed-green. Sprinkle lightly with 2 teaspoons minced fresh leaves just before serving.

SAUCES: *Cream, white.* Blend 1 tablespoon chopped leaves with sauce just before serving.

SHELLFISH: *Crabs* (hard-shell), *mussels, shrimps, boiled.* Add 4 or 5 leaves to water in which shellfish is being boiled.

SOUPS: *Vegetables, mixed.* Add 2 fresh leaves to other ingredients before cooking.

STEWS: *Lamb, veal.* Add 1 teaspoon fresh chopped leaves just before serving.

For 4 servings use approximately:

¼ to ½ teaspoon dried leaves.
1 to 2 teaspoons chopped fresh leaves.
4 to 6 whole leaves.

BALM or **LEMON BALM,** *Melissa officinalis*

Dried leaves in ½ ounce containers at groceries and markets; also in bulk from herb gardens and herb dealers.
Fresh leaves from herb gardens.
Wild in the waste places, thickets, and woods from Maine to Georgia, Missouri, and Arkansas; also in Oregon and California.

Balm, the well-known lemon-scented perennial, is practically always called LEMON BALM, because its perfumed aroma and flavor are so lemonlike.

The broad, almost round, dark green leaves and the clusters of pale yellow flowers of this herb native to Switzerland and southern France are a lovely sight to see. The plant, found growing in all temperate climates throughout the world, reaches a height of more than 2 feet and blossoms from June to October when kept from seeding. The lemon-minty scent and flavor of the flowers and foliage are as attractive to bees as is thyme.

Using: The fresh leaves or tender sprigs add charm to fruit cups and salads. Like mint, the balm may be crushed in a cup of hot tea as added flavor. Another attractive use is to place a sprig in iced tea and fruit drinks. Try it in plain lemonade or in a cooling claret lemonade and hear the exclamations of praise and pleasure.

DRINKS: *Brewed tea, fruit drinks, lemonades, wine cups.* In *cold* drinks, garnish with sprig of balm inserted in top. For *hot* drinks, crush 1 or 2 leaves in bottom of glass or cup.

MEATS: *Roast lamb.* Rub meat lightly with crushed dried or fresh balm before placing in oven. Serve with traditional Mint Sauce.

SALADS: *Fruits, mixed; tossed-green.* Add 1 teaspoon chopped fresh leaves before adding dressing. If mayonnaise is used, blend in ¼ teaspoon minced balm.

SAUCES: *Cream,* served with fish. Add 1 teaspoon chopped fresh leaves to sauce just before serving.

SOUPS: *Asparagus, cream.* Sprinkle lightly with minced leaves just before serving.

Vegetable. Add 1 sprig to vegetable soups before cooking.

STUFFINGS: Add ¼ teaspoon crushed dried leaves to traditional *sage stuffings* for meats and poultry, especially pork and turkey.

See also Sage Stuffing.

TEA: See Herb Teas.

For 4 servings use approximately:

¼ to ½ teaspoon dried leaves.
2 teaspoons chopped fresh leaves.
1 small sprig fresh leaves.

BASIL or SWEET BASIL, *Ocimum basilicum*

Dried leaves and flowering tips all year in ½ ounce containers at groceries and markets; also in bulk at herb dealers.

Fresh leaves and flowering tips all year from herb gardens when herb is taken indoors during winter months; otherwise, during spring, summer, and autumn.

Honey in groceries in limited quantities.

Basil or sweet basil is a strongly aromatic annual which belongs to the mint, *Labiatae,* family. Native to the Near East, sweet basil is known and grown in practically all countries of the globe today. Some say its flavor is slightly like that of licorice and others will describe it as something like cloves, but the subtle effect of basil in seasoning foods is really indescribable.

There are fifty or sixty species of basil differing in height, color, and taste. Among five or six of the varieties most generally used in America are two tall varieties of SWEET BASIL, *Ocimum basilicum;* two varieties of DWARF BASIL, *Ocimum minimum;* and ITALIAN or CURLY BASIL, *Ocimum crispum;* and a LEMON BASIL, *Ocimum citriodora.* When the leaves of a dwarf variety are purple, the herb is usually referred to as PURPLE BASIL.

The leaves of all the basils have a peppery clovelike scent and taste. The Italian or curly basil is much stronger than the sweet varieties in both aroma and taste; and the lemon basil has a fruity flavor. Basil honey is truly epicurean and resembles a faint, delicate taste of cloves.

Using: The secret of many a delicious tomato dish or sauce lies in the use of sweet basil. The Italians, Portuguese, and Spanish all use basil in preparing native dishes and especially their unusually appetizing tomato sauces. However, basil has many other uses and will add a new tang to practically all foods. Many sausages are flavored with basil. Eels and other fat fish are more than delicious when broiled with crushed sweet basil. Also try using ¼ teaspoon of the dried crushed herb in the water in which peas, string beans, or potatoes are boiled. See also chapters on Herb Butters and Herb Vinegars.

EGGS: *Soufflés; scrambled.* Mix ¼ teaspoon crushed dried basil or 2 teaspoons chopped fresh leaves with eggs before cooking.

FISH: *Eels, fat fish,* broiled. Blend ½ teaspoon crushed dried leaves with melted butter used to baste fish.

GAME: *Hare,* or *venison* casserole. Rub meat lightly with herb before placing in casserole.

MEATS: *Beef, pork,* and *veal roasts; beefsteak casserole* or *pie* (see Beefsteak Pie Boccaccio).
For *roasted meats,* sprinkle lightly with herb before cooking.

POULTRY: *Duck,* roasted. Rub inside of duck lightly with herb before roasting. If *stuffing* is used, flavor with ¼ teaspoon basil and do not rub inside of duck.

SALADS: *Carrot, cauliflower, cucumber, lettuce, mixedgreen,* or *tomato.* If *French dressing* is used, mix dried herb with oil; or toss fresh herb with salad greens. If *mayonnaise* is used, blend herb with dressing before serving.

SHELLFISH: *Lobster, mussels, shrimp,* boiled or steamed. Add ¼ teaspoon dried herb to water before boiling or steaming.

SOUPS: *Bean, beef, pea, tomato, turtle.* Place herb in soup before cooking. See approximate amounts below.

STEWS: *Beef, lamb, veal.* If dried herb is used, place in stew before it begins to boil. If fresh herb is available, use sprig (do not chop) and place in stew pot at same time as meat.

STUFFINGS: *Fish, meat,* and *poultry.* Use ⅛ to ¼ teaspoon basil with 2 or 3 other herbs. See also chapter on Herb Blends and Bouquets.

VEGETABLES: *Eggplant, peas, potatoes, spinach, tomatoes, boiled* or *stewed.* Add herb to water. If *baked,* sprinkle vegetable lightly with herb before placing in oven.

For 4 servings use approximately:

⅛ to ¼ teaspoon dried leaves and tips.
2 to 3 teaspoons chopped fresh leaves.
1 small sprig fresh leaves.

Beefsteak Pie Boccaccio　　　　　TIME: 45 minutes

2 lbs. beefsteak
1 tbs. cooking oil or fat
2 cups boiling water
2 tsp. chopped fresh basil, or
　¼ tsp. dried basil,
　crushed
2 tsp. chopped fresh thyme,
　or ¼ tsp. dried thyme

1 medium-sized onion, sliced
¾ tsp. salt
⅛ tsp. pepper
1 tsp. Worcestershire sauce
⅛ tsp. nutmeg
1 Flaky Pie Crust
2 tsp. flour

Purchase chuck or round steak cut 2 inches thick and cut into squares. Heat fat in fireproof casserole placed over medium flame; add meat cubes; brown quickly on all sides to seal in juices. Season with salt and pepper. Add boiling water; cover. Simmer 10 minutes. Add basil, thyme, and onion; cover. Simmer 10 minutes, or until meat is almost tender. (Round steak requires more time than chuck.)

Blend flour in cup with very little cold water. Add enough hot liquid from casserole to make smooth, thin mixture. Add

Worcestershire sauce. Pour mixture into casserole and stir well. Sprinkle ingredients lightly with nutmeg. Cover with Flaky Pie Crust. Bake in preheated moderately hot oven (375° F.) 30 minutes. Serve piping hot from casserole. Serves 4.

If desired this recipe may be varied by adding 6 small peeled potatoes just before casserole is placed in oven to bake. In which case use only 1 teaspoon flour to thicken liquid. If potatoes are added, pie serves 6.

Flaky Pie Crust   TIME: 10 minutes

1½ cups flour	*½ tsp. salt*
½ cup butter	*3 tbs. cold water*

Sift flour and salt on pastry board; gently blend in butter. Gradually add enough water to hold ingredients together. Form into small ball. Roll out pastry to desired thickness on lightly floured board. Shape crust to cover casserole. Makes one 8- or 9-inch crust.

BAY LEAF or **LAUREL LEAF,** *Laurus nobilis*

Dried whole leaves in ½ and 1 ounce containers at groceries and markets; also in bulk from herb dealers.
Ground in 1⅛ ounce containers at groceries and markets; also from herb dealers.

The bay leaf is the leaf of a large evergreen shrub or small tree grown mostly in the Mediterranean countries and Asia Minor. It is also cultivated in Greece, Portugal, Spain, and Central America.

The spreading branches of this evergreen are filled with smooth, waxy leaves which vary in size from 1 to 3 inches long and ½ to 1 inch wide. They are elliptical and taper to points at the base and the tips, and the undersides of the leaves are a pale, yellowish green.

The aromatic, sweet bay tree found in southern Europe is the LAUREL of the *Lauraceae* family, and is the same plant which the Greeks call the Daphne tree. But the bay tree which grows in California is much larger and is known as the *Umbellularia californica.* Its leaves are used chiefly for their yield of a volatile oil.

The dried leaf remains shiny on top and rather dull underneath, where the tiny veins stand out clearly. The edge of the stiff, brittle leaf is often slightly wavy even though it has been pressed for about 10 days after having been dried in the sun. By the time it is ready for market, each leaf has turned a yellowish green.

The pleasant odor of bay leaf is familiar to many of us, and its characteristically strong, pungent, and almost bitter flavor becomes more apparent as the brittle leaf is crushed. Like most herbs, it is wise to use bay leaves cautiously until one grows familiar with the particular tastes of those for whom the food is being prepared.

Using: One bay leaf, either whole or broken, will give a wonderful flavor to a can of tomato soup, and when crushed and added to tomato juice or aspic, the result is temptingly delicious. A bay leaf placed in the water in which vegetables are boiled will add a subtle interest. For example, try it in beets, onions, and potatoes. Old-fashioned vegetable soup takes on a new taste when a bay leaf is added. Bay leaves are used extensively in pickling spices and vinegars, but the amounts vary with the formula of each manufacturer who prepares them. See also chapter on Spiced Recipes.

FISH: *Chowders, court bouillon, kabobs.* Add 1 bay leaf to ingredients.

GAME: *Venison steak.* Place 1 bay leaf on steak before broiling.
Venison stew. Add 1 bay leaf to ingredients.

MEATS: *Beef, mutton. Pot roast* or *oven roast.* Place 2 bay leaves in bottom of roasting pan.
Pickled meat, such as *corned beef.* Add 1 bay leaf to water in which meat is boiled.
Smoked, such as *ham* and *tongue.* Add 2 bay leaves to water in which meat is boiled. See also Tongue Herb Boiled.

PICKLES: See Dill Pickles.

POULTRY: *Chicken, duck pie.* Add 1 broken bay leaf to ingredients.
Chicken, duck, roasted. Place 2 bay leaves in bottom of roasting pan.
See also Chicken South American Style.

SALADS: *Sea food in Aspic.* Add 1 crushed bay leaf to gelatine.
Tomato. Add 1 crushed bay leaf to salad dressing.

SAUCES: *Meat, tomato.* ½ to 1 leaf crushed and cooked with sauce.

SOUPS: *Beef, lamb, mutton,* stock. Place 1 whole leaf in pot with other ingredients, or add to *bouquet garni.*

STEWS: *Beef, lamb, mutton, poultry, veal, venison.* Add 1 bay leaf to ingredients.

STUFFINGS: *Poultry.* Add 1 crushed bay leaf to ingredients.

VEGETABLES: *Artichokes, beets, carrots, potatoes, tomatoes.* Add 1 bay leaf to water in which vegetables are boiled.

For 4 servings use approximately:

1 to 2 crushed leaves.
1 to 3 whole leaves.

Smoked Tongue Herb Boiled   TIME: 2 hours

1 smoked tongue (3½ to 4 lbs.)	*2 bay leaves*
	1 large-sized onion
1 stalk celery	*8 peppercorns*

Select firm, well-smoked, but moist tongue. Wipe with damp cloth. Place tongue in large, deep kettle; cover with water; add celery, bay leaves, onion, and peppercorns. Bring to boiling point over high flame. Lower flame. Boil moderately 2 hours, or until tender. With fork test only occasionally near small bones at base of tongue to prevent juices escaping. Allow tongue to stand in hot stock for ½ hour before serving piping hot. When ready to serve, remove skin and small bones at base of tongue. Slice in thickness desired. Serve with horseradish or preferred Herb Sauce. Serves 6.

BERGAMOT or WILD BERGAMOT, *Monarda fistulosa*

Dried leaves from herb dealers; also from herb gardens.
Fresh leaves from herb gardens.
Wild in western states north to British Columbia and across the continent to Quebec; also in North Carolina.

Bergamot or wild bergamot is the species native to our own hemisphere and belongs to the mint, *Labiatae,* family. This beautiful perennial with soft, cottonlike foliage and dense clusters of purple flowers with brilliant red corollas grows 2 to 3 feet tall. Its leaves have a pleasantly scented lemon odor. During the entire month of August its flowers of a soft lilac shade tint the plains with their delicate haze as the heather covers the hills of Scotland with warm, misty shades of light.

Another species of bergamot, called LEMON BERGA-MOT, *Monarda citriodora,* grows wild in the mountains of North Carolina. It is hardy enough to grow well under cultivation as far north as Connecticut. By the second year it will have attained its full height of about three feet.

The RED BERGAMOT, *Monarda didyma,* is found in most of our eastern states and has many common names. The one best known is OSWEGO TEA, since the Oswego Indians use it so extensively as a tea. Other common names are FRAGRANT BALM, INDIAN'S PLUME, BEE BALM, and RED BALM.

Using: Bergamot or the wild bee balm was the only tea used by our patriotic colonists during the time they were boycotting British tea. Its dried leaves make a delightful drink, and bergamot tea may be served today in place of other teas. See also chapter on Herb Teas. The fresh leaves and tender sprigs make a delicious addition to tall wine drinks and lemonades.

For 4 servings use approximately:

4 to 5 teaspoons dried leaves in tea.
4 fresh sprigs in tall drinks.

BORAGE, *Borago officinalis*

Dried leaves and flowers from herb dealers; also from herb gardens.
Fresh leaves and flowers from herb gardens, principally in the East.
Wild along the Mediterranean coasts and in Sicily.

Borage, a sturdy annual herb, is one of the most beautiful of plants in spite of its coarse foliage with its stinging, hairy surface. The leaves are large ovals of grayish green. The plant grows to a height of 2 feet or more and the bees love the borage flowers which form drooping clusters of heavenly sky-blue five-pointed stars.

Native to Asia Minor, Greece, Italy, the Mediterranean

coasts, Persia, and Sicily, borage grows in many parts of the
world. In America it is found chiefly in the eastern states. The
tender young leaves of the borage plant taste fresh and cool,
like the flavor of cucumbers.

Using: The dried leaves of borage may be used as well as
the fresh to flavor soups and stews in place of the usual
parsley. A few fresh leaves tossed with a green salad are
delightful; and when cooked with other vegetables they add a
new taste interest. This is so especially with green peas, beans,
and salsify or oyster plant. Simply place a few leaves of
borage in the water in which the vegetables are cooking.

The western Europeans cook young borage leaves as we
cook spinach; and the English often mix the herb with other
greens and serve it plain or creamed as a principal vegetable.
The dried flowers are particularly aromatic and can be used
alone or blended with other herbs to prepare a tea.

Flowering tips and leaves give delightful flavor to many
iced drinks. The flowers may also be candied or crystallized
and then eaten as a confection or used to decorate cakes and
cookies. See also chapter on Herb Teas.

CAKES and COOKIES: Decorate cakes and cookies with
candied borage flowers when icing.
See Crystallized Borage Flowers.
DRINKS: *Iced-tea, fruit,* and *wine* drinks, and *lemonades.*
Place sprig of flowers and leafy tips in glass just before
serving.
SALADS: *Cabbage, cucumber, lettuce, mixed-green.* Blend
2 tablespoons chopped borage with vegetables.
Raw spinach and *borage,* half and half, is exotic when
served with *French Mustard Dressing.*
TEA: See Herb Teas.
VEGETABLES: Cook borage leaves with other greens, using
half and half; such as half spinach and half borage; half
borage and half beet tops.
See also Florence Fennel with Borage.

For 4 servings use approximately:

4 to 5 teaspoons dried leaves in teas.
1 cup fresh flowers when candied.
4 to 5 fresh leaves in cooked vegetables and salads.

Crystallized Borage Flowers　　　　　　TIME: 30 minutes

1 cup fresh borage flowers　　*1 egg white, beaten*
½ tsp. water　　　　　　　　 *Granulated sugar*

Pick flowers in early morning when wet with dew. Wash carefully in cold water; allow to dry on absorbent paper.

Add ½ teaspoon cold water to white of 1 egg; beat well. Dip flowers in egg white, then in sugar. Place on waxed paper to dry. May be eaten immediately. To keep crisp, place in tightly covered jar.

Large leaves of peppermint and spearmint, also rose petals may be crystallized or candied in same way.

BURNET or **SALAD BURNET,** *Sanguisorba minor*

Dried leaves in ½ ounce containers and in bulk at drugstores; also at herb dealers.

Fresh leaves practically all year from herb gardens. Wild in the eastern states.

Burnet or salad burnet is a hardy perennial with several species. Two belong to the rose, *Rosaceae,* family, and one to the carrot, *Daucus.* The species of salad burnets known as the *Sanguisorba minor* is widely cultivated in our southern states, especially in North Carolina. In southern Europe and western Asia the GREAT BURNET, *Sanguisorba officinalis,* grows wild and is not to be had in America.

All burnets look very much alike; and the attractive, lacy, light green foliage makes a lovely border plant in any herb garden. The plant forms small mats or clumps of pinnate, feathery foliage about 8 inches long, and the rose-colored or white flowers grow in a flat umbel at the end of the tall stems.

The tender young leaves have a distinct, delicate flavor resembling that of cucumbers.

Using: Both the dried and the fresh leaves may be used in preparing herb teas and herb vinegars. The delicate flavor of the young tips of the salad burnet is especially delicious in all vegetable salads; and the dried leaves are just as useful as the fresh, for they may be blended in with the salad dressings. A sprig of the delicate-looking foliage is a most attractive addition to the appearance of an iced drink as well as to its flavor. See also chapters on Herb Teas and Herb Vinegars.

SALADS: *Beet, cabbage, carrot, celery, lettuce, mixed-green,* or *tomato.* If French Dressing is used, mix *dried herb* with oil. If *fresh herb* is used, toss it with the other salad greens. If mayonnaise or other thick dressing is used, *blend either dried* or *fresh herb* with the dressing *before* serving.

SOUPS: *Asparagus, celery, lima* (fresh) *bean, mushroom.* Place herb in soups at beginning of cooking.

For 4 servings use approximately:

¼ to ½ teaspoon dried leaves.
2 teaspoons chopped fresh leaves.
1 small sprig fresh leaves.

CAMOMILE or CHAMOMILE, *Anthemis nobilis*

Dried flowers at drugstores; also in bulk from herb dealers and herb gardens.

Camomile has never been an herb for the kitchen, but, like catnip, has become such a popular garden herb because of its usefulness and beauty that I have included it in this volume. The species called *Anthemis nobilis* is known as either ROMAN or ENGLISH CAMOMILE. This is the hardy European perennial which is grown chiefly in our herb gardens because it thrives so well along walks and paths and between stones.

It is a low plant which spreads and creeps as it runs along the ground. Its white daisy-shaped flowers grow upward on long, thin stems and the herb blossoms all summer long until the frost arrives. The dark green, pinnate foliage is about 2 inches long and smells like a sweet ripe apple. Perhaps this is why the Greeks called the herb "camomile," which means *apple of the earth.*

The GERMAN CAMOMILE, or *Matricaria chamomilla,* is an annual which resembles the Roman camomile; and the fragrance of the flowers is warm and sweet.

Using: Today, all over Europe, camomile tea is widely used in place of regular tea and coffee. Here, too, the dried flower heads are used chiefly in Herb Teas.

CAPERS, *Capparis spinosa*

Dried in bulk at some markets; also at herb dealers.

Pickled in brine in 1½ ounce to 3 ounce bottles at groceries and markets; also at herb dealers.

Wild along the mountainsides in Africa, Italy, France, Spain, and along the southern Mediterranean coast.

Capers are the flower buds of a wild bushy plant with close, heavy foliage. It grows about 3 feet high. In Europe it is widely cultivated for its flower buds alone.

The tiny buds open when the sun rises and close when it sets, so the capers are usually gathered at daybreak or very early on the summer mornings before they have had a chance to open. Once cut, they remain closed.

The capers are graded on copper sieves, and the smaller the bud the higher the grade. Usually they are cured and prepared in salt and shipped to America in large kegs. Here they are put in a vinegar brine and packed in very small, dark green, tightly corked bottles so the capers retain their original astringent flavor. The bitter salty taste is epicurean, and very few capers are necessary to give the added flavor sought for.

Using: Capers are used most expertly by many European cooks, and we Americans are learning to utilize the caper flavor with equal imagination. Fish and meat sauces are especially delicious with a few capers added; and as a garnish for cold roasts and salads, capers are unequaled in flavor.

The Italians will always place five or six capers on the *antipasto* (appetizer) plate. The bitter salty taste of the caper provides a tangy contrast to the warm, oily flavor of the dressing, the ripe olives, and other foods which comprise the attractive beginning to the Italian meal. See also chapter on Herb Sauces.

CANAPÉS: Place 1 caper on each canapé instead of sliced green olives.

GARNISH: *Roasts, cold; salads.* Scatter 2 teaspoons capers over cold cuts and salads just before serving.

SAUCES: *Fish* and *meats.* See Herb Sauces.

For 4 servings use approximately:

1 to 2 teaspoons capers when used as garnish; vary to taste.

1 tablespoon capers when used in sauces.

CARAWAY, *Carum carvi*

Fresh leaves from herb gardens.
Roots from herb gardens.
Seed. See Caraway Seed.
Wild in northern climates throughout the world, especially in the northern sections of the United States and Canada.

Caraway is a hardy perennial (sometimes an annual) named after the district of Caria in Asia Minor. It grows about 2 feet high and is widely cultivated in many countries, including Bulgaria, Canada, Holland, Japan, Morocco, Poland, Russia, Syria, and various parts of the United States.

The feathery green leaves resemble the foliage of carrots; and the umbels of yellowish-white flowers which blossom the second year are as delicate as "Queen Anne's Lace," which is a wild, poisonous carrot.

There is no danger of confusing caraway with the wild carrot because of the aromatic perfume of the herb and the fact that it blossoms very early in the summer.

The fresh leaves, the seed, and the root of the caraway have distinct flavors of their own. The taste of the root in no way resembles that of the caraway seed. The slender root, about 8 inches long, is very sweet and far more delicate than parsnips. Its yellow color turns almost an oyster white when the root is cooked. The fresh young leaves are as tasty as the seed but more delicate in flavor.

Using: Fresh young leaves may be used to flavor vegetables, soups, salads, and boiled cabbage or potatoes. A few leaves placed in the pan with roast pork will give the meat new flavor.

The roots may be boiled and eaten as a vegetable, either plain buttered or in cream sauce in the same way as parsnips. See also Caraway Seed.

CHEESES: *Cream* and *cottage.* Add 1 teaspoon chopped fresh leaves to ¼ pound cheese. Mix well and serve on crackers.

MEAT: *Pork,* roasted. Place 1 small sprig fresh caraway herb in baking pan before meat is roasted.

SALADS: *Cabbage* (coleslaw), *cucumber, lettuce, potato,* and *tomato.* Toss 2 teaspoons chopped fresh herb with vegetable used.

SOUPS: *Cabbage,* and *cauliflower, cream of; potato.* Sprinkle each portion with very little chopped fresh herb just before serving.

VEGETABLES: *Cabbage, cauliflower, potatoes, turnips* (white and yellow). Add 1 small sprig fresh caraway leaves to water in which vegetables are boiled.

For 4 servings use approximately:

1 to 2 teaspoons chopped fresh leaves.
Allow 1 root for each serving as vegetable.
1 to 2 fresh sprigs only.

CATNIP, *Nepeta cataria*

Catnip bags at pet shops.
Dried leaves in drugstores; also from herb dealers.
Fresh leaves from herb gardens and some herb dealers.

Catnip is no longer considered a culinary herb. However, it was a favorite herb flavoring for soups and stews as early as the fifteenth century. And today it is such a household favorite that a book on herbs really can't omit it with a clear conscience.

This hardly perennial, a member of the mint, *Mentha,* family, is found in all the temperate zones of Asia, Europe, and America. All over the United States catnip occurs as a common weed in the waste places, and in cultivated land from New Brunswick to Minnesota south to Virginia and Arkansas.

The spikes of the pale blue flowers of the catnip are a lovely contrast to the white wooly surface of the whitish-green leaves of minty flavor.

Using: Today this fragrant herb is used chiefly as a sweet treat for "pussy." And though some of our Indian tribes drink catnip tea frequently, and many people brew a catnip tea as a tonic, the herb has remained a favorite primarily because of its pale blue flowers and pleasant mintlike aroma. See also chapter on Herb Teas.

CELERY, *Apium graveolens*

Dried leaves, all year, in ½ to 1½ ounce containers at groceries and markets; also in bulk at herb dealers.

Fresh stalks and bunches practically all year at groceries
and markets.
Salt. See Celery Salt.
Seed. See Celery Seed.
See also Lovage.

Celery is such a well-known biennial that an herb book can
add little to its world-wide reputation. Its inclusion here is to
make a few helpful hints readily available to all homemakers
interested in herb seasonings. Certainly celery, celery salt, and
celery seed have become important and necessary ingredients
in preparing many standard and unusual recipes.

The plant is native to the marshy lands of southern Europe
and Asia and is now widely cultivated in the temperate climates in many parts of the world, including France, Great
Britain, Holland, and India. In central California celery is
also grown for its seed crop for planting. The fragrant aroma
of the celery fields in Texas and Florida perfumes the air for
miles around as one drives past the vast, fertile acres planted
with this deliciously tasty herb. The crinkly, pinnate, pale
green leaves of the celery plant are as tasty and aromatic as the
crisp stalks; and the seeds have the same nutty flavor.

Using: Every particle of the celery plant is edible: the
leaves, stalks, and roots, either raw or cooked. Fresh celery
leaves with their sharp, almost pungent flavor add a sweetness
to stews and soups. The roots also are wonderful in soups, but
care should be taken not to use more than a small piece of the
root, since it is much sweeter than the stalks. In addition to
being a beautiful and useful garnish, the crisp stalks may be
cut and used in fruit and vegetable salads.

In France and Switzerland celery is eaten as a braised
vegetable much more often than raw. See recipe Celery
Braised Parisienne.

APPETIZERS: *Cheese, fish, meats, shellfish,* and *all canapés.*
Add 1 tablespoon minced celery to ingredients. Use
leaves and stalks as garnish.
Stuffed Celery. Use whole stalks; fill with favorite cheese.
Especially good with Roquefort or creamed filling.
EGGS: *Creamed, deviled, stuffed.* Add 1 tablespoon minced
celery to ingredients when preparing.
Omelets. Use 2 to 3 tablespoons minced celery with 4
eggs.

CHEESE: Blend minced celery with *soft cheeses;* serve as canapé or sandwich spread.

FISH: *Court bouillon.* Add 1 stalk celery with leaves to ingredients.
Stuffed fish. Use 1 to 2 tablespoons minced celery as suggested in familiar recipes.

GAME: Use 1 or 2 stalks and leaves as flavoring in all *game ragouts* and *stews.*

GARNISH: Use every part of the celery as garnish for all *hot* and *cold foods,* including *salads.*

MEATS: Season *all meat dishes* with 1 stalk celery. *Beef, lamb, mutton, veal pot roasts,* and *stews.* Place celery in pot with ingredients at beginning of cooking; herb may be removed before serving.

SALADS: *Fruit* and *vegetables.* Blend chopped celery with salads before adding dressings. Usual amount may vary from 1 tablespoon to 1 cup, according to individual taste.

SANDWICHES: *Canned* and *chopped meats, fish, shellfish,* and *tomato.* Use preferred amount minced celery.

SAUCES: *Brown* and *cream.* Add 1 tablespoon to ½ cup minced celery to meat and cream sauces served with meats and vegetables, according to individual taste.

SOUPS: *Cream, fish* and *shellfish chowders, meat, vegetable.* Use as suggested in favorite recipes.

STEWS: *Fish, meats, shellfish,* especially *clam* and *oyster.* Add ¼ cup cooked minced celery to milk when preparing fish and shellfish stews. Add *raw* chopped celery to other stews.

STUFFINGS: Use *raw* minced celery as suggested in stuffings for *meats* and *poultry.*

VEGETABLES: *Mix* chopped celery *with carrots, onions, peas, tomatoes, green peppers,* and other *sweet vegetables.* Serve in combination with 2 or 3 vegetables. See also recipes which follow.

For 4 servings use approximately:

1 teaspoon dried leaves as flavoring.
1 to 2 bunches as cooked vegetable.
1 bunch as raw vegetable.
Variable amounts as garnish; also when stuffed and served as hors d'oeuvre.

Celery Braised Parisienne   TIME: 30 minutes

2 bunches celery   ½ cup boiling water
2 tbs. butter   ⅛ tsp. salt
1 bouillon cube   ⅛ tsp. white pepper
⅛ tsp. dried basil

Select firm, fresh celery. Remove all outside tough stalks and leaves; split bunches lengthwise through middle. (If bunches are extra large, split twice to make convenient serving pieces of ¼ bunch.) Wash thoroughly under cold running water until all sand is removed.

Place 1 tablespoon butter in large skillet; add celery, very little salt, pepper, and basil. Place over low flame and heat slowly.

Dissolve bouillon cube in ½ cup boiling water; pour over celery; add other tablespoon butter. Cover. Simmer gently 25 minutes, or until celery is tender but not mushy. Serve piping hot in pan juices. Serves 4.

If preferred, ½ cup tart red wine may be used instead of bouillon cube and water. Endive and hearts of lettuce may be prepared in same way. Cooking time from 10 to 15 minutes.

Flemish Baked Onion Soup with Celery   TIME: 4 hours
As prepared in Liége, Belgium.

6 medium-sized onions, sliced   2 bunches celery, quartered
3 lbs. beef with bones   ¼ tsp. white pepper
½ tsp. salt   2 large white turnips
12 small potatoes, peeled   2 qts. cold water
1 carrot, whole   1 cup rich milk

Purchase shank beef with bones; have bones cracked.

Peel and slice onions; peel and wash all other vegetables. Place beef, bones, salt, potatoes, carrot, celery, white pepper, and turnips in large oven crock; cover. Bake mixture in pre-heated moderate oven (350° F.) 4 hours; or boil over medium flame 3 hours. Strain, and rub mixture through very fine sieve; add 1 cup rich milk. Bring to boiling point over medium flame; do not boil. Serve piping hot in preheated hot soup bowls. Garnish each serving with chopped chervil or parsley. Serves 6 to 8.

If thinner soup is desired, add more milk to strained mixture before heating.

CHERVIL, *Anthriscus cerefolium*

Fresh leaves from herb gardens.
Dried leaves in ½ ounce containers from herb gardens; also in bulk from herb dealers.
See also Parsley.

Chervil is a well-known European annual which is becoming better known in our American herb gardens. It is a delicate-looking herb with finely cut, lacy, almost fernlike leaves and umbels of tiny white flowers.

The vivid green leaves of chervil have a pleasant aromatic flavor more subtle than parsley. Some describe it as being similar in taste to tarragon and others will say that it resembles licorice. Its actual taste is indescribable, but it is the basis of many mixed-herb seasonings. In the French combination *aux fines herbes* one always finds that chervil is an important ingredient.

Using: In France and Switzerland chervil is used extensively to flavor salads, sauces, and stuffings for poultry, fish, and shellfish. This lovely green herb is also used in soups, stews, and omelets much as parsley is used, either fresh or dried. The fresh leaves also make a beautiful garnish for salads. A tuberous-rooted variety of chervil is grown and eaten as carrots.

CHEESE: *Cottage, cream.* Blend 1 teaspoon chopped fresh chervil with ¼ pound cheese.

EGGS: *Omelets.* Use about 4 teaspoons chopped fresh chervil. Sprinkle omelet lightly with herb just before serving.

GARNISH: Use leaves instead of parsley.

MEATS: *Roast beef, roast lamb, roast veal,* and *steaks.* Sprinkle lightly with 2 tablespoons chopped chervil just before serving; also use leaves as garnish.

SALADS: *Beet, celery, cucumber, lettuce, tomato.* Sprinkle salad with 2 teaspoons chopped chervil just before serving.

SAUCES: *Béarnaise, butter, cream.* See Herb Sauces.

SEA FOOD: See recipe for Piquant Deviled Crabs.

SOUPS: *Spinach, sorrel.* See recipe for Sorrel and Lettuce Soup.

VEGETABLES: *Beets, eggplant, spinach.* Sprinkle lightly with chopped chervil just before serving boiled buttered vegetables.

For 4 servings use approximately:

¼ to 1 teaspoon dried leaves.
1 to 2 teaspoons chopped fresh leaves.
6 to 8 sprigs as garnish.

CHIVES, *Allium schoenoprasum*

Bulbs from herb gardens.
Fresh leaves, all year, in all markets and from herb gardens.
Salt in 2½ ounce containers and bottles at groceries and
    markets and from herb dealers.
See also Onion; Shallot.

Chives, a perennial belonging to the onion, *Liliaceae*, family,
is one of the herbs grown during the ninth century in the herb
garden of that famous Benedictine monastery near the shores
of Lake Constance in Switzerland.

The young, tender, pencil-shaped tubular leaves of this
dark green lavender-flowered herb possess a light, delicate
onion flavor; and it is among the most popular of culinary
seasonings.

Using: Chives are practically always used fresh. However,
in the recent development of numerous Herb Salts the dried
or powdered leaves of chives are among those used in combination with common table salt and other herbs. The herb
salt forms a seasoning for those who wish the convenience and
the new taste thrill of a quick seasoning. The fresh green
leaves are used to flavor all foods in which a mild onion flavor
is desired. The bulbs may be pickled as tiny onions, and have
an infinitely more delicate flavor. See Pickled Chive Bulbs.

CHEESES: *Cottage, cream.* Blend 1 teaspoon chopped chives
    with each ¼ pound cheese.
EGGS: *Deviled, omelets.* Flavor with 1 to 2 teaspoons
    chopped chives, as desired. For *deviled eggs* add chives
    to yolks when seasoning. For *omelets* add to beaten and
    seasoned eggs.
SALAD DRESSINGS: See Herb Salad Dressings.
SALADS: *Cucumbers, lettuce, mixed vegetable,* and *sea foods.*
    Blend 1 to 2 teaspoons chopped herb with vegetables
    before pouring on salad dressing. For *sea foods,* blend
    chopped chives with dressing.

SAUCES: *Creamed, white sauce.* Season with 2 teaspoons chopped chives just before serving. *Tomato sauce:* Add 3 teaspoons chopped chives before cooking sauce.

SOUPS: *Asparagus, bean, cauliflower, cream of; potato,* and *any soup* in which mild onion flavor is desired. Amounts vary according to taste.

VEGETABLES: Sprinkle chopped chives over vegetables as garnish. See Herb Potato Cakes.

For 4 servings use approximately:

1 teaspoon to 2 tablespoons chopped fresh leaves.
6 to 8 whole leaves in herb bouquets.
1 tablespoon to each ¼ pound butter in herb butters.
2 teaspoons to each cup dressing in herb salad dressings.

Chive-broiled Green Tomatoes   TIME: 15 minutes

4 large green tomatoes   *¼ tsp. thyme*
1 cup dry bread crumbs   *Salt and pepper*
2 tbs. chopped chives   *2 ozs. butter*
⅛ tsp. sage

Select firm green or half-ripe tomatoes; cut into slices about ¾ inch thick; sprinkle lightly with salt and pepper. Set aside.

Blend bread crumbs, 1 tablespoon chopped chives, sage, and thyme in mixing bowl. Dip tomato slices in seasoned bread crumbs. Arrange slices in shallow buttered pan; dot each tomato slice with butter. Place in preheated broiler 4 inches below medium flame. Broil 3 minutes, or until well browned on one side; turn, and broil 3 minutes more, or until golden brown. Garnish with other tablespoon chives. Serve piping hot. Serves 4.

Ripe tomatoes may be prepared in same manner. Place 3 inches below flame; broil but 2 minutes on each side.

Herb Potato Cakes   TIME: 40 minutes

4 medium-sized potatoes   *2 tbs. chopped chives, or cher-*
2 tbs. butter   *vil*
¼ cup warm milk   *3 tbs. butter, extra*
                                              Salt and pepper

Wash and scrape or pare potatoes. Place in saucepan; barely cover with rapidly boiling salted water; cover. Boil 20 to 25 minutes, or until tender. Drain; mash well. Add 2 tablespoons butter, salt and pepper to taste. (Very little salt is necessary.) Add milk; mix well. Add 1 tablespoon chopped chives. When cool enough to handle, or cold, shape into round, flat cakes ¾ inch thick.

Place 3 tablespoons butter in skillet; heat 2 minutes over medium flame. Fry potato cakes 2 minutes, or until golden brown and crisp on one side; turn; brown other side 2 minutes. Garnish with other tablespoon chopped chives. Serve piping hot. Serves 4.

Leftover mashed potatoes may be used. Add 1 tablespoon chopped chives to each 2 cups cold potatoes.

Pickled Chive Bulbs

TIME: 2 hours
Marinate 24 hours

2 pts. chive bulbs
1 cup distilled vinegar
1 tsp. sugar
2 tsp. white mustard seed

2 tsp. white peppercorns
2 tsp. whole allspice
½ sweet red pepper cut into strips

BRINE:

¼ cup salt

1 pt. boiling water

Use firm, perfect bulbs. Wash thoroughly; peel carefully. Place bulbs and red pepper in heavy kettle or crock. Blend salt and boiling water to make brine; pour boiling brine over bulbs and pepper. Allow to stand 24 hours at room temperature. Drain. Pour cold fresh water over chives and pepper. Allow to stand 1 hour. Drain well.

Pour distilled vinegar into saucepan placed over medium flame; add sugar, mustard seed, peppercorns, and allspice. Boil mixture 1 minute, stirring well. Pack bulbs and some red pepper strips in small, hot, sterilized jars; cover bulbs with boiling liquid; seal jars carefully. Allow to cool at room temperature. Store in cool, dark place 2 weeks before using. Yield: Approximately 1½ pints.

Serve as *condiment, hors d'oeuvre,* and *in Gibson* (gin) *cocktails.*

COSTMARY, *Chrysanthemum balsamita*

Dried leaves in bulk from herb dealers and herb gardens.
Fresh leaves from herb gardens.
Wild along country roads of the Middle West and eastern
parts of the United States.

Costmary is a tall, luxuriant perennial of the aster, *Asteraceae,*
family native to western Asia. It probably came from Kashmir.

The plants produce large clumps of long, light green, slender
leaves, and the flowers look like yellow buttons or daisies with
yellow centers and a few straggling white petals. The herb
has a very agreeable, minty scent, while the flavor of the leaves
is somewhat bitter. After being dried and infused, the flavor
changes to a slightly lemonlike flavor.

Costmary is also known as ALECOST since at one time it
was used to flavor ales and beer. Another common name is
BIBLELEAF, from the custom of placing one of the leaves
in the Bible as a bookmark.

Using: The fresh, tender leaf is used to flavor certain meats
and poultry. The flavor is very dominant, so care should be
taken not to use more than a leaf, especially for cakes and
jellies. The tea is really a tonic, but today costmary is still a
favorite among herb teas. See also chapters on Herb Jellies and
Herb Teas.

CAKE: *Pound* cake. Place 1 leaf in bottom of baking pan.

GAME: *Venison, wild duck, roasted.* One leaf only placed in
bottom of pan will add sufficient flavor in combination
with other herbs, such as bay leaf and sage.

MEATS: *Beef, roasted;* also *hamburgers.* Sprinkle lightly
with 1 crushed fresh leaf before roasting or cooking; or
use ¼ teaspoon dried herb.

POULTRY: *Chicken, roasted.* Place 1 costmary leaf in bottom
of roasting pan.

For 4 servings use approximately:
⅛ to ½ teaspoon dried leaves.
1 fresh leaf, whole.

CRESS or LAND CRESS, *Lepidium sativum*

Fresh leaves from herb gardens and in some markets. See
also Water Cress.

Cress or land cress is an annual also known by the name of PEPPERGRASS, and belongs to the mustard, *Brassica*, family. Land cress is native to Persia but will grow in any rich, moist soil, and the seeds are readily procured from most seed stores. It's more difficult to secure the seeds for the BELLE ISLE CRESS, *Barbarea verna*, which is much more peppery than water cress. Another species, called ROCKET CRESS, has practically disappeared from American gardens.

The small dark green leaves of the land cress are oval shaped, and the herb should always be eaten before it begins to blossom. The leaves and stems when young and tender have a tangy taste like the mustard plant or nasturtium leaves.

Using: The land cresses, like the water cresses, are used in many ways to make food look more attractive as well as taste better. The dark green, crisp leaves make appetizing garnishes for roast meats, poultry, and game. They may also be finely chopped and mixed with vegetables and salads. See also Water Cress.

SALADS: *Fruit.* As garnish, 1 or 2 sprigs.
   Vegetables, mixed-green. Blend in 1 or 2 sprigs, finely minced.
SANDWICH FILLINGS: See Herb Butters.
SOUPS: *Cream* soup. Chop cress fine; sprinkle over each serving at table.
VEGETABLES: *Cauliflower, peas, potatoes.* Chop fine; sprinkle over vegetables as garnish just before serving.
   Spinach. Mix half spinach and half cress. Boil and prepare as for spinach.

For 4 servings use approximately:

1 teaspoon to 2 tablespoons chopped fresh leaves as garnish.
½ pound fresh leaves and sprigs with 1 pound spinach, as cooked vegetable.
1 fresh sprig or more for each serving, as one uses parsley for garnish.

DILL, *Anethum graveolens*

Fresh leaves and stems in groceries and markets during late summer and early autumn; also from herb gardens.
Wild in Africa and Asia.

See also Dill Seed.

Dill is a hardy, umbelliferous, aromatic annual native to all the Mediterranean countries and southern Russia. Though still growing wild in parts of Africa and southern Asia, dill is widely cultivated on the continent, especially in India, England, Germany, and Rumania.

Recently in North America dill is almost as well known and as popular as parsley and sage. To a large extent dill is grown commercially in the eastern and southern parts of the country, and to a lesser degree in the Middle West.

The flavor of dill is somewhat pungent, and the stems have a bitterness that almost burns. Yet as a seasoning in sweet and bland vegetables it has a most pleasing taste and exceedingly effective flavor.

Using: Whenever possible it is best always to use the fresh dill leaves and stems, for the herb loses some of its flavor when it is dried. The freshly chopped leaves are used with practically all foods except desserts. We always think of pickles at the mere mention of dill, but its uses are legion and the results flavorful and gratifying. The pungent leaves, finely minced and blended with cream or cottage cheese, make a deliciously different spread for canapés and sandwiches. Even the tender tips of the stems are to be utilized, for when they are very finely chopped and added to fish and cream sauces the effect is appetizing and delicious. Freshly minced dill leaves sprinkled over the tops of broiled steaks and chops just before serving not only add to their attractiveness but give a new tang and flavor to an old favorite. See also Dill Seed; chapters on Herb Butters, Herb Salad Dressings, and Herb Vinegars.

CHEESES: *Cottage, cream.* Blend 2 teaspoons chopped leaves with each ¼ pound cheese.

FISH: *Halibut, mackerel, salmon, sea trout.* Sprinkle lightly with chopped dill before broiling.

MEATS: *Beef—corned, steaks, chops, broiled.* Garnish with freshly chopped leaves before serving.

OMELET: Mix 2 teaspoons chopped dill with eggs before cooking.

PICKLES: Stems and all parts of herb used. See recipes.

POULTRY: Spread 1 dill stem over poultry before roasting; also place dill leaves and stem in bottom of roasting pan.

SALAD DRESSINGS: See Herb Dressings.

SALADS: *Cucumber, potato, lettuce, tomato.* Two teaspoons chopped dill mixed with vegetables.

SANDWICHES: See Herb Butters.

SAUCES: *Cream, white.* Use 1 tablespoon crushed or chopped leaves. Serve with boiled or steamed fish.

SOUPS: *Bean, chicken, pea, tomato.* Two teaspoons chopped dill cooked with other ingredients.

VEGETABLES: *Avocados, beans, beets, eggplant, parsnips, potatoes.* Sprinkle vegetables with chopped dill as garnish before serving.

VINEGAR: See chapter on Herb Vinegars.

For 4 servings use approximately:

2 tablespoons chopped fresh leaves as garnish.
1 small sprig with leaves as flavoring in soups and stews.

Mother's Old-fashioned Dill Pickles   TIME: 1 hour
                                            Fermentation: 3 weeks

40 to 50 small cucumbers	*Sprigs of fresh dill*
2 ozs. whole mixed pickling	*2 cups cider vinegar*
spices	*2 cups salt*
2 qts. water	*¼ lb. garlic*

Select firm, small cucumbers 4 to 5 inches long. Wash well and drain. Separate garlic cloves; peel. Set aside. Place a layer of dill, 2 or 3 garlic buds, and half the pickling spices in a 5-gallon crock. Arrange half the cucumbers in crock. Place more dill and garlic buds over cucumbers. Arrange balance of cucumbers in crock to within 6 inches of top.

Blend well vinegar, salt, and water; pour over cucumbers. Place balance of dill, pickling spices, and garlic over top. Cover with large plate and weigh down to hold cucumbers under brine. Place crock in cool, dark place (not cold); remove scum each day as pickles begin to ferment. In about 3 weeks, when pickles are clear and well flavored with dill, they may be placed in a very cold spot, or packed in jars and stored.

If packed in jars use hot, sterilized quart jars. Arrange pickles in jars. Strain pickle brine; heat to boiling; pour hot liquid over pickles; seal tightly. Store in cold, dark place. Yield: 4 to 4½ gallons.

FENNEL or **SWEET FENNEL,** *Foeniculum vulgare,* var. *dulce*

> Fresh leaves and stalks in all markets from California to Connecticut and New York, during early fall and winter months.
> Wild in countries along the Mediterranean coast.
> See also Fennel Seed.

Fennel or sweet fennel and FLORENCE FENNEL are cultivated varieties of the WILD FENNEL found all along the Mediterranean coasts. The herb is also called CAROSELLA and FINOCCHIO.

Fennel is a beautiful, vigorous perennial usually grown as an annual in the colder climates. Its deep green, fernlike leaves resemble those of dill, and the large stems, flattened at the base, look somewhat like celery. The umbelliferous flowers are yellow, but the plants do not blossom until the second season.

Both the foliage and the stems of the fennels have a mild licorice taste.

Using: The fresh, tender leaves and stems are used to flavor sauces, soups, and salads; also as a garnish for foods, much as celery is used. The *blanched* stems and bulbous bases are eaten raw, like celery; or steamed, as is celery and endive by the French and Italians. (See Braised Celery Parisienne.) *Carosella,* young fennel, is a famous delicacy of Naples. The young stems are cut before the herb blooms, and the Neapolitans serve the tender herb with an olive-oil-and-vinegar dressing.

> FISH: *Eels, mackerel,* broiled. Garnish with chopped fresh leaves.
> SALADS: Prepare *mixed green salad;* add grated, shredded, or sliced fennel to salad as one adds celery.
> SAUCES: See chapter on Herb Sauces.
> SOUPS: Add 1 stalk fresh fennel to soup stocks.
> VEGETABLE: Cook fennel as one cooks spinach, celery, or other green vegetable. Serve with cream sauce. Garnish with borage, chives, or parsley. See also Florence Fennel with Borage.

For 4 servings use approximately:

1 teaspoon to 2 tablespoons chopped fresh leaves as garnish.

1 bunch leaves and stalks when cooked.
1 bunch young stems and base, quartered and eaten raw, as celery.

Florence Fennel with Borage   TIME: 20 minutes

1 bunch Florence fennel   *2 tbs. butter, melted*
½ tsp. salt   *Water to cover (about 1½*
⅛ tsp. pepper   *cups)*
4 tsp. chopped fresh borage

Purchase crisp, leafy, Florence fennel. Wash thoroughly under cold running water. Cut off leafy parts; chop coarsely with sharp knife; cut bulbous base or heart into quarters.

Pour water into saucepan over medium flame. Add salt. When boiling, add fennel. Liquid should barely cover fennel. Boil 12 minutes, or until tender but not soft. If necessary, drain off any excess water.

While fennel is cooking, melt butter in saucepan; season with pepper. Just before serving fennel, pour hot butter over top. Sprinkle lightly with chopped borage. Serve piping hot. Serves 4.

If preferred, fennel may be steamed. Time: about 15 minutes. Serve with grated tangy cheese or favorite tomato sauce and cheese.

GARLIC, *Allium sativum*

Dried bulbs in all vegetable markets all year.
Oil in ½ ounce containers wherever herbs and spices are sold.
Powder in ½ ounce containers in markets and groceries; also from herb dealers.
Salt in ½ ounce containers in markets and groceries; also at herb dealers.
See also Onion; Shallot.

Garlic, that humble, bulbous annual which belongs to the lily, *Liliaceae,* family has even been referred to as a god by Homer. The plant is rather attractive with its tall, flat leaves of grayish green and its delicate flowers which form a lovely, round, snowy-white head. The edible part is the bulbous root made up of tiny cloves held together by a film of white skin.

The flavor and aroma of the herb are strong and far more pungent than the onion or the shallot.

Many of us think of Italy at the mere mention of the word garlic, but it is said to have originated in far eastern Mongolia.

Using: Properly cooked and handled with care, one need no longer shun this toothsome herb. Its flavor is not insistent if the tiny clove of seasoning is removed before serving the food in which it has been cooked. To secure the full flavor, the garlic clove should be cut in half before placing it in the saucepan with the food. The paring knife, used for the cutting, may be rinsed in cold water and rubbed with a piece of lemon to remove all odors. The fingertips respond to the same treatment. Wax paper placed on the cutting board will prevent any of the oil penetrating the wood.

Used sparingly, garlic can add to the natural flavor of most foods. Garlic oil, called an odorless garlic, is now on the market and used as flavoring in soups, stews, and pot roasts. The bottled garlic powder and salt impart a very mild flavor, which is preferred by some. Yet the pungent freshness of the garlic cloves themselves cannot be improved upon. Most of us are familiar with that indescribable something which is added to a tossed green salad when the wooden bowl has been lightly rubbed with garlic before the vegetables have been mixed. Garlic may be substituted for onions or may be combined with onions in all foods using them as flavoring. When combined, use from ½ to 1 clove garlic only. See also chapters on Herb Butters and Herb Vinegars.

FISH: *Bouillabaisse* and *chowders* as suggested in recipes.

FORCEMEAT: Blend ½ clove minced garlic with ingredients.

MEATS: *Kidneys.* Sauté 1 clove garlic in butter used in recipe for Herb Sautéed Kidneys.

Lamb Roast. Use generously if pungent flavor is desired. Make 3 or 4 incisions in meat and insert 1 clove garlic in each. Remove garlic before carving. If more delicate flavor is desired, rub lamb with clove of garlic before roasting, or sprinkle lightly with garlic salt.

Liver. Sauté 1 clove garlic in butter in which liver is pan fried.

PICKLES: See Dill Pickles.

POT ROAST: Brown 1 clove garlic in saucepan with fat before searing meat.

POULTRY: Place 1 clove garlic inside *chicken* or *duck* stuffed with Savory Dressing.

SALAD DRESSINGS: See chapter on Herb Salad Dressings.

SALADS: Rub salad bowl with garlic; or rub slice of bread and place in salad as tossed; remove before serving.

SAUCES: See chapter on Herb Sauces.

> *French* and *Italian meat sauces.* Cut clove in half; leave in sauce 20 minutes; remove.

> SOUPS: *All vegetable soups* and *meat stocks.* ½ to 1 clove added to other ingredients.

For 4 servings use approximately:

½ to 1 clove garlic.

Garlic Oil
INFUSE: 10 days to 2 weeks

1 pt. pure olive oil   *6 garlic cloves, halved*

Purchase best quality French or Spanish olive oil. Add 6 halved garlic cloves to oil. Allow to stand at room temperature 10 days. Taste. If stronger flavor is desired, allow to infuse few more days. Remove garlic cloves from oil.

Use garlic oil *in preparing salad dressings* in which a garlic flavor is desired and one does not wish to use the whole garlic clove or the garlic-flavored vinegars. Use best Italian olive oil.

Onion Oil: Use ½ cup minced onion instead of garlic cloves. Follow recipe.

Shallot Oil: Use 1 tablespoon minced shallots instead of garlic cloves. Follow recipe.

Herb Sautéed Kidneys
TIME: 20 minutes; stand 1 hour

1 lb. kidneys   *¼ cup cold water*
2 tbs. butter   *Salt to taste*
2 scallions, minced   *¼ cup sherry wine*
2 cloves garlic, halved   *4 slices buttered toast*
1 tsp. dry mustard

Purchase beef, calf, or lamb kidneys. Wash thoroughly; remove all tissues and membrane. Slice kidneys into 1-inch pieces; place in mixing bowl; cover with salted cold water (1 teaspoon to 2 cups water). Allow to stand 1 hour. Drain.

Melt butter in skillet placed over medium flame; add scallions and garlic; brown lightly 2 minutes only. Add kidneys; brown lightly by stirring gently 3 minutes.

Blend mustard in ¼ cup cold water; pour over kidneys; stir; cover. Simmer gently 15 minutes. Salt to taste; remove clove of garlic; add sherry wine; cover. Simmer 5 minutes longer, or until of desired tenderness. Serve piping hot over buttered toast placed on preheated hot plates. Garnish with scallions if desired. Serves 4.

HOREHOUND, *Marrubium vulgare*

Dried leaves and young stems in bulk at drugstores and herb dealers.

Fresh leaves and tender stems from herb gardens.

Honey in limited quantities at some farmhouses and roadside stands.

Wild herb in waste places, along roadsides and dwellings, in fields from Maine to South Carolina, Texas, and westward to California and Oregon all along the Pacific coast.

Horehound is a hardy perennial belonging to the mint, *Labiatae,* family and is native to northern Europe and North America. Its common name comes from the description of the fuzzy, crinkled, gray-green foliage. The oval leaves grow close to the stalk and the tiny, tubular white flowers form whorls at the same place on the stems which branch out from the ground and spread to form a bush about 18 inches high.

This bitter herb, soon after it was introduced to America by our early colonists, became a prolific weed. The crushed leaves and juices of the horehound have a characteristically bitter taste which we associate with the candy. Today we still find the brown, brittle, bitter horehound candy in practically every drugstore and candy shop throughout the winter months. And the horehound honey is much sought after by gourmets and honey fanciers.

Using: The fresh flowers and tender leaves may be used to flavor beef stews, braised meats, sauces, and hot drinks. Either the dried herb or fresh herb will season cookies, cakes, and the old-fashioned horehound candy. Because of its pungently bitter taste, the herb should be used very sparingly. See also chapter on Herb Teas.

CAKES AND COOKIES: Place 1 fresh leaf in bottom of cake pan; or blend ½ teaspoon dried herb with ingredients.
CANDY: See recipe for Old-fashioned Horehound Candy.
DRINKS: See Herb Teas.
SAUCES: *Beef, braised.* Flavor pan sauce with 1 horehound leaf instead of bay leaf. Remove before serving.
MEATS: *Beef stew.* Use a horehound leaf in stew with other ingredients. Remove leaf before serving.

For 4 servings use approximately:

½ to 1 teaspoon dried herb as flavoring; 4 teaspoons as tea. 1 fresh leaf as suggested.

Old-fashioned Horehound Candy   TIME: 1 hour

2 ozs. dried horehound leaves   *3 cups hot water*
         or   *3½ lbs. brown sugar*
6 ozs. fresh leaves and stems

Rinse porcelain teapot in boiling water; dry thoroughly. Place dried horehound in teapot; pour bubbling hot, not boiled, water over herb. Steep herb 30 minutes; keep hot on back of stove while steeping. Strain through very fine sieve or cheesecloth.

Place brown sugar in heavy porcelain saucepan; pour liquid over sugar; dissolve well. Bring to boil over medium flame; turn up flame. Continue boiling briskly until liquid tested in cold water will harden and snap lightly. This occurs at 292° F.

Drop quickly on buttered board or pour into shallow buttered pan and cut into squares.

If fresh herbs are used, they should be bruised before infusing by crushing in a clean cloth if a mortar and pestle are not available.

Allspice, angelica, anise, bergamot, cinnamon, clove, coriander, cumin, ginger, mace, peppermint, rose, and spearmint candy may be made by dissolving 3 pounds white sugar in 1 cup cold water flavored to taste with 4 to 6 drops of the essential oil of the herbs. Coloring may be added if desired. Prepare same as for horehound candy.

HORSERADISH, *Rorippa armoracia* or *Radicula armoracia*

Fresh leaves from herb gardens and some markets.

Root, ground, in 2 ounce containers at markets, also from herb dealers.

Root whole fresh in all vegetable markets during late fall and winter; cold-storage roots in the early spring.

See also Condiments.

Horseradish is a very hardy perennial native to Europe and Asia and found growing wild on the plains lying at the feet of the Ural Mountains. The plant has large, luxurious dark green leaves which spread as much as 2 feet or more.

All parts of the root are edible, and all those which are at least 8 inches long and as large around as a pencil are saved for planting. The larger root is ground and mixed with vinegar or mustard and has a deliciously hot pungency and at the same time a cooling taste. What a favorite is Boiled Beef with Horseradish Sauce!

Using: During the summer months the young, *tender leaves* may be used chopped or finely minced and mixed with green salads. The *ground root* is used chiefly as a condiment and as flavoring in cocktail sauces for fish and shellfish; also in cream sauces for beef, fish, ham, and other meats. The amounts vary from 1 teaspoon to several tablespoonfuls, according to individual tastes. See also chapters on Condiments, Herb Butters, Herb Salad Dressings, and Herb Sauces.

CONDIMENT: Use pure, *freshly ground root,* as preferred, with meats and sea foods.

FISH: Use *freshly ground root* with cold or cooked fish, as desired.

MEATS: *Beef, lamb,* or *mutton, boiled* or *roasted.* Use as condiment to taste.

SALADS: See Herb Salad Dressings.

SAUCES: See Herb Sauces.

For 4 servings use approximately:

2 to 4 teaspoons freshly ground root as condiment.

1 to 2 tablespoons freshly ground root in sauces.

To Prepare Fresh Horseradish   TIME: 20 minutes

1 large horseradish root   *1 cup distilled vinegar*
1 cup white wine vinegar or

Cider vinegar should never be used in preparing horseradish for table use, since it causes the grated root to turn dark.

Pour white wine vinegar into large bowl. Peel or scrape the root clean and remove all defects; grate root directly into vinegar. Mixture should be moist but not wet. If necessary, add small additional quantity vinegar. Bottle immediately; cork very tightly. Use prepared root as soon as possible after grating, since it loses its flavor after standing 2 or 3 weeks. Yield: Variable, depending upon size of root.

HYSSOP, *Hyssopus officinalis*

Dried flowering tips in bulk from herb dealers.
Fresh flowering tips from herb gardens.
Honey in limited quantities from herb farms.

Hyssop, or BLUE HYSSOP, is a hardy, handsome perennial which belongs to the mint, *Mentha,* family and is native to southern Europe and Asia.

It is a bushy herb and seldom grows more than 2 feet tall. The long, slender, dark-green leaves have a minty taste and odor, and the plants bloom profusely from June to October. The common name, blue hyssop, indicates the color of the flower spikes, which are closely set on the stems. The deep, dark blue of the blossoms is a strikingly lovely sight in the garden.

Two other species of the true hyssop are the PINK HYS-SOP, *Hyssopus rubra,* and the WHITE HYSSOP, *Hyssopus alba.* The pink and white flowers will blossom most of the summer if the herb is carefully cut back.

Using: The fresh flowers and tops are used as a flavoring in some European sausages. The freshly minced leaves are an addition to fish, game, meats, salads, soups, and stews. Some cooks even flavor fruit pies with minced hyssop leaves. If one wishes a slightly different bitter and minty taste, hyssop will be a new adventure for those who have never tried it. Honey from the hyssop flowers is truly delicious. See also chapter on Herb Teas.

COCKTAILS: *Fruit,* especially *cranberry.* Crush 1 or 2 tender young leaves in bottom of container in which cocktail is prepared.

FISH: *All fat fish.* Garnish sparingly with freshly minced leaves.

GAME: *Wild duck, pheasant.* Lightly sprinkle ½ teaspoon minced herb over bird before roasting.

MEAT: *All fat meats.* One half teaspoon minced hyssop cuts grease.

PIES: *Fruits, sweet,* such as *apricot* and *peach.* Sprinkle ¼ teaspoon dried hyssop over fruit before covering pie with top crust.

SALADS: *Vegetable.* Sprinkle ½ teaspoon freshly minced herb over vegetables before tossing.

SOUPS: Add ½ teaspoon minced herb to ingredients of *sweet vegetable soups* while cooking.

STEWS: *Game, kidney, lamb.* Add ¼ teaspoon dried leaves or ½ teaspoon freshly minced at time of cooking.

For 4 servings use approximately:

¼ teaspoon crushed dried hyssop.
¼ to ½ teaspoon minced fresh hyssop.
1 or 2 whole leaves crushed.
¼ ounce dried flowering tips for 1 pint tea.

LAVENDER, *Lavandula vera*

Dried flowers, in bulk and cellophane packages, may be purchased in department stores, at cosmetic counters, and from herb dealers.

Fresh petals and flowering tops from herb gardens.

Lavender honey from le Provence and Chamonix, France, is in the market in limited quantities. This honey is from bees that sip nothing but the sweet nectar of the lavender blossoms. It has a most delicate, flowery taste.

Lavender smelling salts at all drug and department stores.

Lavender is certainly not primarily a culinary herb though the fresh petals may be used and are used in wine cups, jellies, soft drinks, and desserts to add an exotic flavor to them. So no culinary herb book could be quite complete without including this most cherished plant with its sweet, delicious odor. The perfume of the dried herb lasts for months and sometimes even for several years when placed in chests of linens and lingerie. Who among us is not familiar with the delightful sensation of slipping between snowy-white, crisp linen sheets permeated with the smell of warm sunshine and precious lavender?

The *Lavandula officinalis,* or *Lavandula vera,* is only one of the more than eight species of lavender native to the Mediterranean areas. This sweet, lovely perennial grows from 2½ to 3 feet high and is so well loved in England that we have grown accustomed to calling it ENGLISH LAVENDER. Its leaves are a bluish green and the flowers, which grow on spikes, are often more blue than purple.

Then there is the beautiful FRENCH LAVENDER, *Lavandula stoechas,* with its dark purple flowers and very narrow, long, grayish-green leaves. This species thrives better in the warmer climates and is less hardy than its sister, the sturdy, true English lavender.

The most popular and perhaps the hardiest lavender grown in our northern states is a small, shrubby one known as *Lavandula spica,* or SPIKE LAVENDER. Its leaves are very long, and the violet-colored flowers blossom at the tips of the branching stems high above the body of the plant.

Using: The brave culinary souls will flavor a cooling summer drink with a few petals of fresh lavender, or place a petal or two in the bottom of a glass of jelly. Those who are not given to such exotic experimenting will be content to enjoy the aroma of the dried flowering tips tucked among the linens.

BEVERAGES: Place a small sprig of the flowering tips in each glass of iced drinks.

JELLIES: Place a few petals in the bottom of the jelly glass of preferred fruit base.

For 4 servings use approximately:

4 small sprigs flowering tips in iced drinks.
Variable amounts used sparingly in jellies.

LEEK, *Allium porrum*

Fresh, in bunches, at groceries and markets during autumn; also all winter in milder climates.

Wild in England and Wales; also in woodlands in the United States from New Brunswick to Iowa.

See also Chives, Garlic, Onion, Scallion, and Shallot.

Leek is an annual herb which belongs to the lily, *Liliaceae,* family. Its onionlike flavor is mild and sweet. The herb develops long stalks underground and broad, flat green leaves above. Leeks are grown in trenches and piled up with earth to make the upper stalks white and even more tender than they naturally are.

The first known leek was a wild form, *Allium amelophrasum,* found in the southern part of Europe. And there seems to be no doubt but that it was the ancient Egyptians and Chinese who developed the present species of leek. Wild leeks are still found in parts of Britain and Wales and there is another species, *Allium tricoccum,* which grows in the woods of eastern North America and is found as far west as Iowa.

In spite of the fact that the flavor of the herb is very mild, its aroma is exceedingly strong. An example of just how far its fragrance reaches is always a source of an amusing and most happy recollection. Whenever *Le Jongleur de Notre Dame* is sung at the Opéra Comique in Paris, the warm lyric tones of the baritone in the beautiful "Legend of the Sagebrush" are usually accompanied by the strong scent of the leek which he peels as he sings. Beautiful sounds blend with the aroma of leeks as the realistic stage directions are carefully observed. Needless to say, the applause is thunderous as baritone and basket disappear in the wings.

Using: Leeks may be used in many foods in which only a mild onion flavor is desired. As an extra vegetable they are unusually delicious when baked. See Baked Leeks à la Boeuf. Leeks may also be boiled or braised as one prepares celery in the recipe Celery Braised Parisienne. The famous Leek Soup known as Vichyssoise has become an epicurean favorite in the kitchens of the world. The recipe for Soup Sumatra is the way in which the famous Vichyssoise is prepared on that exotic island of the Dutch East Indies.

SALADS: *Tossed, green.* Mince ½ leek; blend with other vegetables.

SOUPS: *Beef, lamb, veal, vegetable.* Use 1 small leek in addition to other vegetables and remove from all soups except vegetable before serving.

VEGETABLES: *Baked, boiled,* and *braised.* One small bunch leeks will serve from 4 to 6.

For 4 servings use approximately:

½ to 1 leek in salads and soups.
1 bunch of 6 leeks for Soup Sumatra or Vichyssoise.
1 bunch or more as cooked vegetable.

Baked Leeks à la Boeuf   TIME: 30 minutes

1 bunch leeks (about 6)   *1 cup beef bouillon*
½ cup butter   *¼ tsp. salt*
¼ tsp. orégano   *¼ tsp. cayenne*

Select firm, fresh leeks. Cut off roots and any faded tips of leaves. Wash leeks thoroughly under cold running water. Drain. Arrange in oblong casserole.

Melt butter in small saucepan over medium flame; blend in orégano, salt, and cayenne. Pour seasoned butter over leeks; add ½ cup beef bouillon. Bake in medium oven (350° F.) 10 minutes; add other ½ cup bouillon. Bake 10 minutes longer, or until leeks are tender but not mushy and vegetable has absorbed most of the bouillon. Serve piping hot. Serves 4.

Soup Sumatra   TIME: 30 minutes

3 leeks, chopped   *½ tsp. salt*
1 medium-sized onion,   *¼ tsp. ground mace*
*   chopped*   *⅛ tsp. black pepper*
¼ cup sweet butter   *1 cup light cream*
1¼ cups diced raw potatoes   *1 tbs. minced chives*
4 cups chicken broth

Use white part of leeks only; chop fine. Melt half the butter in heavy saucepan; add chopped leeks and onion. Simmer lightly 5 minutes over very low flame, being careful not to brown. Add potatoes, chicken broth, and seasonings. Cook 20 minutes over medium flame. Lift potatoes from liquid with small strainer. Press cooked potatoes through very fine sieve to make purée. Return purée to liquid. Add other half of butter; gradually stir in cream. Blend well. Remove from heat. Cool at room temperature. Chill 1 hour in refrigerator. Serve cold. Serves 4 generously.

Soup Sumatra *may also be served hot,* if desired.

LOVAGE, *Levisticum officinale*

Candied stems (as Angelica) at confectionery supply houses.

Dried leaves and roots in bulk from herb dealers.

Fresh leaves in markets in New England and the western states; also from herb gardens.

See also Celery.

See also Celery Seed.

See also Lovage Seed.

Lovage is a native European perennial which belongs to the parsley, *Petroselinum,* family. In fact, it is often called by the common name of LOVE PARSLEY.

The slender stems grow about 5 feet high and the pale green leaves are divided like celery leaves and grow away from the stem at an angle. The greenish-yellow flowers, like little flat umbrellas, appear early in the springtime. The herb has a flavor and odor like celery, but the taste is much stronger than that of celery. The roots are sweetly aromatic when dried.

Using: The dried leaves and tender stems give a strong celery flavor when used sparingly in soups, salads, and stews as one uses celery. They also make a fragrant tea. See also Herb Teas. The fresh leaves and tender blanched stalks may be used as one uses celery in salads, sauces, soups, and stews. In some of our New England states lovage is cooked and eaten as a vegetable much like celery and spinach. Its flavor is also excellent in fish chowders, but because of the strong taste only half the amounts given for celery should be used. The seeds are used chiefly in candy today, and the roots, though available dried, are valuable for the oil which is used as flavoring for some tobaccos and perfumes. See also Lovage Seed.

FISH CHOWDER: Use ½ stalk fresh lovage instead of celery.

FISH SAUCES: *Lovage Cream Sauce.* Use 1 tablespoon minced fresh lovage in white sauce. See recipe for Basic White Sauce.

SALADS: *Tossed, green.* When a very delicate change is desired, rub the salad bowl with crushed fresh lovage leaves. *Vegetable.* Use 1 tablespoon minced green leaves.

SOUPS AND STEWS: Use fresh leaves sparingly instead of celery; or in combination with celery if stronger flavor is desired.

VEGETABLE: Cut blanched stems and leaves into small pieces

and cook as spinach is cooked. Eaten as greens, lovage makes a most intriguing vegetable when cooked separately or in combination with other greens.
See also Celery uses.

For 4 servings use approximately:

½ to 1 teaspoon crushed dried leaves in sauces and soups. Fresh leaves and blanched stalks use as celery.

MARIGOLD, *Calendula officinalis*

Dried flower heads and petals, powdered, in bulk from herb dealers.
Fresh flower heads and petals at florists or from herb gardens.
Honey in 1 pound jars at fancy groceries, markets, and herb dealers; also at health food stores.
See also Saffron.

Marigold is sometimes called POT MARIGOLD, and is much more popular as a garden flower than as a culinary herb. It is a hardy, colorful annual plant native to southern Europe and eastern Asia. Its bright golden petaled flowers may sometimes grow as large around as a small sunflower.

Poets through the centuries have sung of the golden beauty of the marigold. Both the fresh and the dried petals have a rather bitter taste, and when skillfully used impart a subtle flavor as well as beautiful color to the many foods with which the golden powder is blended.

Using: The fresh petals may be used sparingly in salads both for flavor and as a garnish. Both the fresh and the dried petals may be used in broths, soups, and stews to add a subtle flavor. The taste and the effect are so unusual that 1 or 2 fresh petals placed on the bottom of a large pudding or cake dish are sufficient to produce the exotic result.

The secret of the indescribable flavor of many a Dutch soup and stew lies in the skillful use of the pulverized herb. The Dutch will sometimes place a fresh petal in a custard or a pudding, and the result is extraordinary. Ever since the fifteenth century the French and English have used marigold petals to flavor and color drinks. Even today butter and cheese are colored with the golden powder, and who would not try using a dash of the beautiful yellow in buns and cakes? In preparing chicken broth, less than half a teaspoon of pulverized marigold will have an extraordinarily delicious effect upon the final flavor. See also Saffron Uses.

FISH: *Stews* and *chowders*. Add but 2 or 3 petals in combination with other vegetables given in recipes.

GAME: *Venison stew*. Add ½ teaspoon pulverized marigold while cooking.

MEAT: *Beef, braised* or *pot roast*. Flavor sparingly with pulverized marigold; not more than ½ teaspoon.

Use in all instances in place of saffron when saffron is not readily procured.

For 4 servings use approximately:

2 to 3 fresh petals.
½ teaspoon to 1 tablespoon powder, according to specific recipes.

Marigold Rice   TIME: 45 minutes

4 tbs. butter
1 tbs. minced onion
2 tsp. onion powder
1 cup dry rice
3 cups chicken broth

¼ tsp. powdered marigold,
*   or ⅛ tsp. saffron powder*
¼ tsp. salt
1 cup grated Parmesan cheese

Put rice in dry, clean towel (do not wash); rub rice clean with towel.

Dissolve marigold powder with 2 tablespoons broth in cup. Set aside until ready to use.

Melt butter in large skillet over medium flame; add minced onion and onion powder; stirring constantly. Cook only 3 minutes, or until onion is light yellow. Gradually add broth, rice, and dissolved marigold powder. Cook over low flame, stirring constantly, until all broth is absorbed. (Rice should be thoroughly cooked and all broth absorbed in about 40 minutes.) Remove from heat; quickly toss in ½ cup grated Parmesan cheese; stir gently. (This prevents cheese becoming stringy.) Serve piping hot in preheated plates. Garnish each serving generously with more grated Parmesan. Serves 4 to 6.

If desired, sautéed mushrooms and chicken livers may be added to rice just before serving.

MARJORAM or **SWEET MARJORAM,** *Origanum marjorana*

Crushed dried leaves in 1½ ounce containers from groceries and markets; also from herb dealers.

Whole dried leaves in 1½ ounce containers at groceries and markets; also in bulk from herb dealers.

Fresh leaves from all herb gardens.

Pulverized or powdered leaves (dark green color) in 1½ ounce containers at groceries and markets; also from herb dealers.

See also Orégano.

Marjoram or sweet marjoram is a lovely perennial about 12 inches high with very small, grayish-green leaves and tiny, creamy flowers. Grown in our colder climates as an annual, because it is so often winterkilled, the herb is a rather bushy plant with red, delicate, woody stems.

Marjoram is native to the Mediterranean areas but is now widely cultivated all over the earth. The flavor is spicy and exceptionally pleasant, and it is much sweeter than the species called **WILD MARJORAM,** which is better known as **ORÉGANO.**

Since this herb is less pungent than sage, it is often used as a substitute by those who do not care for the strong flavor of sage. The fragrance of marjoram fills the garden with a pleasant odor, and the dried flowers are often used in sachets and potpourris as one uses lavender.

The smaller species, or **POT MARJORAM,** *Origanum onites,* as its name implies, grows well indoors and may easily be grown from a cutting. The light green leaves and tiny, purple-tinted flowers make a beautiful and decorative house plant as well as providing fresh, aromatic leaves all during the winter months.

Using: The dried or fresh leaves are used to flavor innumerable varieties of foods, and marjoram is one of the most useful of all culinary seasonings. The young tender leaves, fresh or dried, may be used with sea-food soups, eggs, fish, meats, poultry, game, stews, vegetables, salads, and sauces. The powdered marjoram is often blended with other herbs in preparing specific herb blends. It is always an ingredient in poultry seasoning, and is used extensively by sausage manufacturers.

EGGS: *Omelets, soufflés, scrambled.* Blend and mix well ¼ teaspoon crushed dried marjoram or ⅛ teaspoon powdered herb in 4 eggs *before* cooking.

FISH: *Baked, broiled.* Sprinkle very lightly with herb *before* cooking.

GAME: *Hare* and *venison, roast* and *stew.* Use approximately ¼ teaspoon with other herbs as suggested.

MEATS: *Beef, pork, lamb, veal, roast.* Sprinkle meat lightly with herb before roasting.

POULTRY: *Chicken, duck, goose.* Rub inside of poultry very lightly with herb before roasting. If goose, outside may be sprinkled with herb also. *If marjoram-flavored stuffing is used, do not rub herb inside or outside poultry,* otherwise flavor will be too strong.

SALADS: *Chicken, tossed-green.* Fresh, tender young leaves may be minced and blended with salads. Use sparingly; less than a teaspoon of the fresh herb.

SAUCES: *Brown* sauces. Use sparingly; less than ¼ teaspoon of the powdered herb.

SOUPS: *Clam, onion, oyster, turtle.* Use ⅛ to ¼ teaspoon marjoram, according to individual taste.

STEWS: 1 very small sprig, tender leaves placed in stew for 20 minutes while cooking; then remove.

STUFFINGS: *Poultry* and *veal.* Use ⅛ to ¼ teaspoon as suggested in recipes.

VEGETABLES: *Carrots, peas, spinach, zucchini.* Place 1 teaspoon powdered herb or several leaves in water in which vegetable is cooked. Remove before serving.

For 4 servings use approximately:

¼ to ½ teaspoon crushed dried leaves.
3 or 4 small fresh leaves.
⅛ to ¼ teaspoon powdered or pulverized herb.

Marjoram Liver Dumplings   TIME: 30 minutes

½ lb. calf's or steer liver	*⅛ tsp. mace*
2 tbs. marrow or butter	*¼ tsp. salt*
Grated rind of 1 lemon	*⅛ tsp. white pepper*
Farina (about 1 cup)	*1 clove garlic, minced*
¼ tsp. powdered marjoram	*(optional)*

Purchase liver in one piece. Dip liver in boiling water. Simmer

2 minutes. Remove from water. Grate or mince liver, removing all fibers. Blend liver, marrow (or butter), lemon rind, and all seasonings in large bowl. Gradually add sufficient farina until mixture may be formed into tiny round dumplings, not too firm. Less than 1 cup farina is usually enough. Cook dumplings in *boiling bouillon, consommé,* or *chicken broth* 10 minutes. *Serve broth and dumplings* immediately. Serves 4.

If stronger marjoram flavor is preferred, use additional amount herb, but never more than ½ teaspoon.

MINT, *Mentha*

> Dried leaves and flowering tops in ⅜ ounce to 1 ounce containers at groceries and markets; also in bulk from herb dealers and herb gardens.
> Fresh leaves and flowering tops from herb gardens and vegetable markets.
> Honeys in 1 pound jars at fancy groceries, markets, and herb dealers; also from herb farms and health-food stores.
> Wild, peppermint, and spearmint in damp places from Nova Scotia to Minnesota and south to Florida and Tennessee.
> See also Wild Bergamot.

Mint is one of the most widely used herbs in the world. There are several varieties of this delicate, aromatic perennial, and the APPLE MINT is a spreading plant which grows in two forms: the *Mentha rotundifolia,* with its round, wooly leaves about an inch wide, and the *Mentha gentilis variegata.* It is the latter form only, of the apple mint, which is used in cooking. Its smooth, gray-green leaves have a most delicate fruity taste; and its purple flowers grow in whorls on the almost square stems.

CURLED or CURLY MINT, *Mentha spicata,* var. *crispata,* is an erect plant about 24 inches high with dull green curly leaves. Its violet-colored flowers grow on spikes.

ORANGE MINT, *Mentha citrata,* sometimes called BERGAMOT MINT, is a decumbent plant with many branches and much broader leaves than the peppermint. Its stems are almost reddish and the leaves have a purple tinge and a fragrance mixed with lavender.

PEPPERMINT, *Mentha piperita,* is the popular herb with rich, deep green, pointed leaves from 1 to 2 inches long and about ½ inch wide. Their edges are sharply toothed; and the small, purplish blossoms encircle the stem and grow up like thick, blunt spikes.

SPEARMINT, *Mentha spicata,* sometimes called GARDEN MINT and LAMB MINT, resembles the peppermint, but its lance-shaped leaves are generally stemless, and the flower spikes are narrow and pointed rather than thick and blunt.

The mints are believed to be native to Hindustan and Asia. From these countries they were taken into Egypt and soon found their way to the temperate zones throughout the world.

Using: The fresh leafy tops of all the mints are used in beverages, fruit cups, applesauce, ice cream, jellies, salads, sauces for fish and meats; also to flavor vegetables and vinegars. Roast lamb and mint jelly have become inseparable companions. See also chapters on Herb Honeys, Herb Jellies, Herb Sauces, Herb Teas, and Herb Vinegars.

CHEESE: *Cream.* Blend 1 teaspoon freshly chopped leaves with ¼ pound cheese. Serve as appetizer.

DRINKS: *Iced beverages;* also *hot teas.* Whole fresh sprigs as garnish; crushed fresh or dried leaves as flavoring.

DESSERTS: *Ice creams, custards, gelatines, fruit compotes, ices, frostings.* Flavor to taste; usually 1 or 2 teaspoons freshly chopped mint in recipe for 4.

FISH: *Baked, boiled,* or *broiled.* Use 2 tablespoons freshly chopped herb as garnish and flavoring.

FRUITS: *Compotes, cups, salads.* Use whole or chopped leaves as preferred; or place 1 leaf in each serving.

JELLIES: See chapter on Herb Jellies.

MEATS: *Lamb, veal roast.* Chiefly sauces.

SALADS: *Fruit.* Use chopped, minced, or whole fresh leaves as preferred.

Vegetable, such as *cabbage, celery.*

SAUCES: See chapter on Herb Sauces.

SOUPS: Split pea. One half teaspoon minced fresh mint as garnish atop each serving.

SYRUP: See recipe Mint Syrup.

VEGETABLES: *Boiled carrots, green beans, peas, potatoes, spinach.* Use 1 to 2 tablespoons fresh herb; boil with vegetable; remove herb before serving.

For 4 servings use approximately:
¼ to 1 teaspoon crushed dried mint.

1 teaspoon to 2 tablespoons chopped fresh mint.
4 sprigs fresh mint.
2 to 8 whole leaves fresh mint.

Minted Hamburger Patties   TIME: 15 minutes

1 lb. chopped beef
2 tbs. minced fresh mint
½ tsp. salt
⅛ tsp. white pepper
⅛ tsp. ground nutmeg

1 egg, well beaten
1 slice white bread, moistened
2 tbs. butter or bacon fat
6 mint sprigs, extra

In mixing bowl combine beef, mint, salt, pepper, and nutmeg; add egg and crumbled slice of bread which has been slightly moistened in milk or water. Shape mixture into patties ¾ inch thick.

Melt butter or bacon in skillet over high flame; brown patties quickly on both sides; turn down heat. Continue frying only 3 minutes if meat is preferred not too well done; otherwise fry 5 minutes, or until well done. Serve piping hot with mint sprigs garnish. Yield: Approximately 12 patties.

Minted Whole Carrots   TIME: 20 minutes

1 bunch young carrots
1½ cups water
½ tsp. salt
2 tbs. butter, melted

2 tbs. minced fresh mint
⅛ tsp. white pepper
Salt to taste, extra

Select small, young, sweet carrots; scrape and wash; leave whole.

Pour water into saucepan over medium flame; add salt; bring to rapid boil; add carrots. Cook uncovered 10 to 15 minutes (depending upon size), or until tender but not soft. Remove from heat. Drain. Season lightly with pepper and more salt if desired. Return to heat. Pour melted butter over carrots; add minced mint; stir gently to coat carrots. Serve piping hot. Serves 4 to 6.

Fresh green peas, potatoes, spinach, and string beans may be prepared in the same manner.

Mint Syrup   TIME: 15 minutes

6 sprigs fresh mint
3 cups sugar

1 cup water

Select fresh, crisp mint. Wash thoroughly; dry on absorbent paper. Crush or bruise leaves and stems in small bowl.

Pour water into heavy saucepan; dissolve sugar in water; add crushed mint. Bring to boil over medium flame. Boil 5 minutes. Remove from heat. Allow to stand at room temperature 15 minutes. Remove mint sprigs. When syrup is cool, pour into bottle; cork tightly. Yield: 1 cup.

Use as flavoring for drinks; also *with fresh fruit cups* and *desserts.*

MUSTARD PLANT, *Brassica sinapis*

Fresh leaves, called Mustard Greens, in groceries and markets of both the East and the West during late August and early September.

See also Dry Mustard, Mustard Seed.

Mustard is an herb native to all Europe and southwestern Asia and is now widely cultivated in Austria, England, Germany, Holland, Italy, India, North Africa, and the western states of the United States; also in parts of Canada and South America.

There are many species of the mustards found wild throughout most of the world today but only several varieties are cultivated for their aromatic seeds. Among those most widely cultivated commercially are the BLACK MUSTARD, *Brassica sinapis nigra,* which bears seeds of a dark, reddish-brown color sometimes called BROWN MUSTARD, *Brassica sinapis juncea;* and the WHITE MUSTARD, *Brassica sinapis alba,* which has seeds of a yellowish shade.

The slightly peppery flavor of the young green leaves of the mustard plant is well known to both Europeans and Americans; especially those who live outside the metropolitan areas. As we become more acquainted with the mustard plant, its sale in our markets will increase.

Using: The tender young leaves are cooked as a vegetable either separately or mixed with other greens. The raw leaves may be used sparingly in mixed-vegetable salads. See Sorrel and Herbs Salad, Sorrel and Lettuce Soup.

SALADS: *Mixed-green, tossed-green, vegetable, raw.* Use 1 tablespoon chopped fresh leaves; toss with other ingredients.

VEGETABLE: Cooked as other greens, such as *spinach, corn salad,* et cetera.

For 4 servings use approximately:

Usually 1½ pounds is sufficient. Amounts vary.

Mustard Greens aux Beurre   TIME: 30 minutes

1½ lbs. mustard greens or   *¼ cup water*
   use 1 pound mustard   *½ cup light cream*
   greens and ½ pound   *Pinch of tarragon herb*
   corn salad   *1 hard-boiled egg, grated*
2 tbs. butter   *Extra salt*
½ tsp. salt

Remove all wilted leaves and tough stems from greens. Wash thoroughly in cold running water until all sand is removed. Place greens in large saucepan with water which clings to them. If necessary, add very little water while cooking. Do not cover. Cook 10 to 12 minutes, or until tender.

While greens are cooking, boil egg hard (about 10 minutes, not more); remove shell and rub egg through sieve. Set grated egg aside. Melt butter in small saucepan over low flame; gradually add cream; season with salt; keep liquid very warm but do not boil.

When greens are tender, remove from flame; drain off water if necessary. Chop greens very fine and return to saucepan. Pour hot liquid over and stir with fork to mix well. When piping hot, transfer to preheated serving dish. Quickly garnish by sprinkling grated egg over top. Season egg lightly with salt, then very lightly with tarragon. Serve immediately. Serves 4.

NASTURTIUM, *Tropaeolum majus*

Leaves, flowers, and pods, all summer in the garden. Seed during autumn.

The nasturtium is a humble plant with brilliantly colored flowers found in many gardens the world over. It is rarely thought of as an herb, yet it has been used as such for centuries.

It was the Spanish physician, Nicholas Monardes (whose name is immortalized in the botanical name for bergamot:

Monarda didyma) who in 1565 first called the *Tropaeolum majus* a nasturtium. While he was writing a report on the plants of the new world he used the word "nasturtium" because the word means "to turn or twist the nose." This most certainly is a vivid description of the peppery pungency of the stems and flowers. The nasturtium was also sometimes called "Indian Cress."

The common form is a tall, climbing herb; but the more recently developed dwarf variety, which grows low and bushy, is the one best known to those who love the brilliant beauty of its flowers.

Using: The exotic custom of eating the petals of flowers and using them for teas and salads has come down to us from the ancient Orientals. For those of us who still are too shy to eat the delicate petals there are the joys of seeing the leaves and stems used as garnishes for foods and dishes that might otherwise be quite ordinary. Much as water cress is used in canapés and salads, the nasturtium leaves and petals may be easily substituted.

CANAPÉS: *Cream cheese.* Chop only the tender leaves and stems of the nasturtium. Blend 2 teaspoons with ¼ pound cream cheese and use for sandwiches and canapés.

SALADS: *Tossed-green* and *vegetable.* Whole, tender young leaves may be tossed with the other green vegetables. *Flowers* may be used as garnish and then eaten if desired.

SEED: Nasturtium seed and pods may be pickled and used as capers.

See Nasturtium Seeds, Pickled.

For 4 servings use approximately:

Flowers and leaves in preferred amounts, as garnish.
2 to 4 teaspoons minced leaves.
½ to 1 tablespoon seed, as capers.

Nasturtium Seeds Pickled   TIME: 15 minutes

1 pt. nasturtium pods   *1 cup distilled vinegar*
½ oz. salt   *6 white peppercorns*

Gather the nasturtium pods during bright sunshine, when they are very dry but not yet open and the seeds are only half ripened, otherwise the seeds will fall from the pods and be lost. Wipe pods clean with soft white cloth; remove seeds. Place seeds in small sterilized dry glass bottles. Blend salt and vinegar; pour over seeds; add 2 peppercorns to each bottle. Cork up bottles; seal with paraffin. Set aside in cool dark place for 6 weeks. Pickled seeds are then ready to use as one uses capers for seasoning. Approximate yield: ½ pint.

Seeds may also be left in pods and pickled. Simply wipe pods clean, pack in bottles, proceed as shown for seeds.

ONION, *Allium cepa*

Dried all year in markets and groceries.
Fresh or green onions (scallions) practically all year in groceries and markets.
Honey in 1 pound jars at fancy groceries, markets, and herb dealers; also at health-food stores.
See also Chives, Garlic, Leek, Onion Powder, Onion Salt, Scallions, Shallots.

The onion is perhaps the most universal herb used for flavoring, and botanists have never been able to establish its original home. This humble biennial of the lily, *Liliaceae,* family is found wild from the shores of the Dead Sea and the dry desert lands of Syria and India to the dreary plains of North America.

There are innumerable varieties cultivated for table use today. All over the world we find the white, yellow, rose, orange, and red bulbs with their many varying shapes and forms. Some are globular and thick, others are shallow and flat, still others are almost elliptical in shape.

The flavor of the white variety is much milder than that of either the yellow or the red species.

Scallions are the tender young seedlings of onions when the bulb has not yet formed and the layers of skin are thin. They taste mild and sweet, and are used in cooking when a more delicate flavor is desired than that which the onion gives.

Using: Young, green scallions are eaten whole as a relish or hors d'oeuvre with salt. They are also exceedingly delicious when sliced and tossed with other green vegetables in a spring salad.

The dried bulbs of the mature plant are used to flavor practically all foods, even some desserts. Their use in cookery is so generally universal and so much is known about those uses that only a suggestion of them can be included in this volume.

As flavoring for meats and poultry, the onion is one of the most useful of all herbs. A whole onion placed inside a roasting chicken before placing it in the oven will add sweetness and pungency. When stewing chicken and meats, a small onion or several scallions may be added to the gravy. When preparing pot roasts, it is good to brown the onions in the fat before the meat is seared.

Onions and scallions with other vegetables, either cooked or raw, can be unusually appetizing. Flavor the melted butter with a teaspoon or more of grated onion or onion juice before preparing the sauce for creamed vegetables. Creamed spinach with an onion-flavored cream sauce is most delicious.

There are innumerable recipes available to the homemaker; and the majority of cookbooks are filled with suggested uses of this flavorful herb. But if there are those who actually dislike onions as a vegetable may I suggest that they try baking or boiling onions with orégano. In combination with this herb the onion no longer tastes like an onion but becomes a vegetable of extraordinary sweetness and flavor. I like to call onions prepared with orégano *oraynion*. See recipe for Oraynion au Four. See also chapters on Condiments, Herb Butters, Herb Honeys, Herb Powder, Herb Salts, and Herb Vinegars.

APPETIZERS: *Caviar, cheese, meat spreads, sea foods.* Garnish to taste with chopped, grated, minced, or thin-sliced herb.

CHEESE: *Fondues, spreads.* Flavor with ¼ to ½ teaspoon juice or minced herb.

EGGS: *Omelets, scrambled, soufflés.* Flavor or garnish to taste with chopped, grated, minced, or thin-sliced onion.

FISH: *Baked, boiled, broiled, lean* and *fat fish.* Season with thin-sliced onion before cooking.

GAME: *Ragouts, roasted, stewed.* Use ½ to 1 whole onion in sauce while cooking.

MEATS: *Baked, broiled, pies, roasted, stewed.* Flavor with thin-sliced or whole onions to taste.

SALADS: *Mixed greens* and most *vegetables.* Add grated or thin-sliced onion to other vegetables.

SAUCES: *Brown* and *meat* sauces, also *tomato.* As suggested in individual recipes.

SEA FOODS: *Boiled, chowders, steamed.* Flavor lightly to taste as suggested in individual recipes.

VEGETABLES: *All sweet* vegetables. Flavor lightly to taste

while cooking. *Potatoes* being boiled for potato salad may be delicately flavored by placing a small onion in water while cooking.

For 4 servings use approximately:

½ to 1 teaspoon chopped, grated, or minced onion.
1 slice to 1 whole onion as seasoning.
4 whole onions as vegetable.

Onions Baked with Orégano   TIME: 1 hour
Oraynion au Four

4 large Spanish onions	*2 tbs. minced fresh parsley*
1½ cups soft bread crumbs	*⅛ tsp. white pepper*
3 tbs. butter, melted	*¼ tsp. salt*
½ cup chopped walnuts	*¼ cup dry bread crumbs*
1 tsp. dried orégano	

Select large, firm onions. Peel; cut thin slice off top; scoop out centers to make shells ½ inch thick. Mince parts which have been removed. Place onion in large mixing bowl; add bread crumbs, 2 tablespoons butter, nuts, orégano, parsley, pepper, and salt; blend well. Fill onion shells with herb mixture; arrange in baking pan.

Blend dry crumbs with other tablespoon melted butter; sprinkle over onions. Bake in preheated moderate oven (350° F.) 40 minutes, or until onions are tender but not soft. Serve piping hot. Garnish with parsley sprigs or fresh orégano leaves. Serves 4.

ORÉGANO or WILD MARJORAM, *Origanum vulgare*

Dried leaves in small glass or cardboard containers of 1½ to 2 ounces, at groceries and markets; also from herb dealers.
Fresh leaves from herb gardens.
See also Herb Butters, Herb Sauces, Herb Vinegars, Marjoram.

Orégano is the Italian and Spanish common name for WILD MARJORAM. It is a beautiful perennial which grows into a leafy bush about 2½ to 3 feet high.

There are really more than two dozen species of the herb

known as *Origanum marjorana,* but the Spanish, Mexican, and Italian homemakers generally use the one called *Orégano.* The flavors, all of which are pleasant and aromatic, are somewhat stronger than the SWEET MARJORAM, *Origanum marjorana,* and they will vary slightly. The species included in this volume are those which are readily purchased in their dried forms in our food stores and markets.

Using: Orégano may be used in all the ways in which sweet marjoram is utilized. But since its flavor is stronger than that of the sweet variety, it should be apportioned carefully to individual tastes. For example: many Italians will flavor some foods with 1 or 2 teaspoons of *orégano,* while some of the French prefer but half a teaspoon. On the other hand, a small pinch of dried orégano in a tomato-juice cocktail is singularly delicious. The herb, either fresh or dried, has a wonderful effect upon the flavor of tomato or bean soup when a small sprig or a half teaspoon is added to the ingredients. Orégano is also used to flavor sausages; and when broiling or roasting pork or lamb, a sweet pungency is added to the flavor. Poultry, game, sauces, and vegetables are all more delicious when a touch of orégano has been added. Sea-food salads are also more unusual and appetizing with a little orégano added.

APPETIZERS: *Tomato, vegetable-juice cocktails.* Add ½ teaspoon finely minced fresh orégano or ¼ teaspoon crushed dried orégano to each pint of juice.

FISH: *Baked, stuffed.* Rub inside of fish with ¼ teaspoon crushed dried orégano before stuffing.

GAME: *Hare, venison marinade.* Use 1 teaspoon crushed dried orégano blended with other herbs in marinade.

MEATS: *Lamb, pork, veal, broiled* and *roasted.* Rub meat gently with dried herb before broiling or roasting, using 1 to 2 teaspoons.

POULTRY: *Chicken, guinea hen, pheasant, roasted.* Rub poultry lightly inside and out with herb before roasting, using 1 to 2 teaspoons.

SALADS: *Potato, Sea food in aspic.* Blend in 3 teaspoons chopped fresh orégano or ½ teaspoon dried in salad, or in aspic when used.

SAUCES: *Cream* sauce. Add ½ teaspoon dried herb to Basic White Sauce.

Plain tomato sauce. Add ½ teaspoon dried herb or 1 teaspoon minced fresh herb.

SHELLFISH: *Clams, lobster, boiled* or *broiled.* Blend 1 teaspoon minced fresh orégano or ½ teaspoon crushed dried herb with butter and pour over shellfish just before serving when boiled; but before placing in broiler if prepared broiled.

SOUPS: *Bean, tomato.* Add ½ teaspoon crushed dried orégano or 1 sprig fresh herb before cooking.

VEGETABLES: *Onions, peas, potatoes, spinach, string beans, plain* or *creamed.* Add ½ teaspoon crushed dried herb to water in which vegetable is boiled. If creamed, add herb to cream sauce.

See also chapters on Herb Butters, Herb Sauces, and Herb Vinegars.

For 4 servings use approximately:

¼ to 2 teaspoons dried leaves.
1 to 2 teaspoons chopped fresh leaves.
1 small sprig flowering tops and leaves.

Silver Onions Orégano   TIME: 30 minutes

12 small silver (white)	*¾ tsp. dried orégano*
onions	*2 ozs. butter, melted*
½ tsp. salt	*¼ tsp. white pepper*

Purchase small silver onions. Peel carefully.

Place peeled onions in heavy saucepan; barely cover with rapidly boiling water; add salt and pepper. Boil, uncovered over medium flame 10 minutes, or until partially tender. Add orégano. Continue boiling 10 more minutes, or until tender but not soft. Drain. Small particles of orégano will adhere to onions; do not remove. Add melted butter; stir gently. Serve piping hot as side vegetable. Serves 4.

The combination of the onion and orégano flavoring gives a mild, indescribably different taste to the vegetable.

PARSLEY, *Petroselinum hortense*

Dried leaves in small containers of ½ to 1 ounce, at groceries and markets; also from herb dealers.

Fresh leaves at groceries and markets; also from herb gardens.

Parsley salt in ½ ounce glass containers at groceries and
markets; also from herb dealers.
See also Chervil, Winter Savory.

Parsley, a beautiful dark green biennial, is perhaps the best
known and the most generally used of all the herbs. There
are more than thirty forms of this branch of the carrot, *Umbelliferae*, family; and among the best-known varieties are the
DOUBLE-CURLED, the MOSS-LEAVED, the FERN-
LEAVED, and the TURNIP-ROOTED.

The acid-sweet pungency of parsley flavor is known the
world over, and its beauty as a garnish is almost taken for
granted. Many prefer the flavor of the lighter green fern-
leaved variety and say that its taste is superior to the double-
curled variety. But all the parsleys add flavor as well as attractiveness to foods.

Using: Both the dried and the fresh herb have innumerable
uses. Naturally the fresh herb is the one used for garnishing.
Its almost sweet and peculiarly spicy flavor has been a part of
soups, salads, and sauces from ancient times down to the
present day. No doubt the culinary minds of the future will
continue to conjure up new ways to make use of its distinctive
flavor. As an attractive garnish, as well as for flavoring, it is
safe to venture that parsley will continue to be served indefinitely with fish, meats, shellfish, and vegetables.

An unusually delicious use of the herb is made in preparing
biscuits. See Curly-parsley Biscuits. See also chapters on Herb
Butters, Herb Sauces, and Water Cress.

BOUQUET GARNI: 1 sprig of parsley with other herbs.
CANAPÉS: All varieties. Garnish with minced fresh parsley.
CHEESES: *Cottage, cream.* Blend in 1 teaspoon chopped
fresh parsley with ¼ pound soft cheese.
EGGS: *Omelet, scrambled.* Use 1 tablespoon chopped minced
parsley; mix with eggs before cooking; or as a garnish
when done.
FISH: 1 sprig in *Court Bouillon;* minced chopped parsley
may also be sprinkled over top of all kinds of fish just
before serving.
MEATS: *All* meats, *broiled* and *roasted.* Sprigs and minced
parsley to taste, as flavor and garnish. *All* meats, *stews.*
Use 1 sprig parsley with other seasonings; remove parsley
before serving.

POULTRY: *All* poultry. Use sprigs and minced parsley as flavor and garnish after cooking.

SALADS: *Fish, potato,* and *all green vegetables.* Blend in minced parsley; vary amounts to taste.

SAUCES: *Butter, tartar.* See Herb Sauces.

VEGETABLES: *All* vegetables. Use sparingly and sprinkle lightly with minced parsley just before serving.

For 4 servings use approximately:

4 to 8 sprigs as garnish.
1 to 2 teaspoons dried leaves.
1 tablespoon chopped fresh leaves as flavor and garnish.

Macaroni with Blended Herbs   TIME: 40 minutes

*¼ lb. elbow macaroni or spa-
    ghetti*
3 qts. boiling water
2 tsp. salt
1 cup Basic White Sauce
2 tbs. chopped green olives
6 tsp. chopped fresh parsley

2 tbs. chopped pimiento
*1 tsp. chopped fresh orégano
    or ¼ tsp. dried orégano*
2 tbs. olive oil
¼ tsp. cayenne pepper
*1 cup grated sharp cheese
    (American or Cheddar)*

Pour boiling water in large kettle over high flame; add salt; add macaroni or spaghetti. Boil macaroni only 10 minutes, or until tender but not soft. If spaghetti is used, boil 20 minutes. Drain well. Add White Sauce, olives, and all other seasonings except cheese and cayenne pepper to macaroni; mix gently but well; add ½ cup grated cheese. Pour mixture into large buttered casserole. Sprinkle with cayenne pepper then with other ½ cup cheese. Bake in preheated moderate oven (350° F.) 20 minutes. Serve piping hot. Serves 4.

Curly-parsley Biscuits   TIME: 30 minutes

2 cups flour
4 tsp. baking powder
½ tsp. salt
2 tbs. butter or shortening
1 small bunch parsley

*½ cup grated American
    cheese*
¾ cup milk
1 tbs. melted butter, extra

Purchase dark green, double-curled parsley. Wash thoroughly under cold running water. Drain well and dry with paper towel. Chop parsley leaves fine.

Sift flour, baking powder, and salt together in large mixing bowl. With pastry blender, or with 2 knives, or with tips of fingers, cut in 2 tablespoons butter or shortening. Blend in grated cheese, then parsley. Gradually add enough milk to make soft dough, kneading gently. Carefully roll dough on lightly floured board until ½ inch thick; cut with round cutter 2 inches in diameter. Place on biscuit sheet; brush tops lightly with melted butter. Bake in very hot oven (450° F.) 15 minutes. Serve hot. Yield: 14 to 16 biscuits.

To save time: Parsley, cheese, and milk may be blended with 2 cups prepared biscuit mix. Blend well and bake as suggested.

Rosemary Biscuits: Use 2 teaspoons chopped fresh rosemary instead of parsley. Blend well, and bake as suggested.

ROSE, *Rosaceae*

Dried petals in bulk from herb dealers.
Fresh petals wherever there is a garden.
Rose petal honey in 2 ounce to 4 ounce jars at fancy groceries and markets; also from herb dealers.

The myriad exquisite varieties of this most beautiful flower have been derived and developed through the long centuries by repeated hybridization from but three original species. They are the *Rosa chinensis* or China Rose, the *Rosa gallica* or Rose de Provins, and the *Rosa damascena* or Damask Rose.

The whole world of literature and life itself is far richer because of this perfect symbol of life and love. The culinary suggestions given here indicate how rose petals will add an exotic note of flavor and fragrance to our everyday cooking.

Using: Both the dried and the fresh rose petals may be used for flavoring fruit cups, desserts, jellies, and honey; but wherever possible it is usually more satisfactory to use the fresh petals. The candied petals may be prepared in the same manner as mint leaves; and a sweet herb vinegar made with rose petals is unusually delicious with fruit salads. Some imagination and a little time for experimenting will work wonders. See also chapters on Herb Butters, Herb Honeys, Herb Jellies, Herb Teas, and Herb Vinegars.

CANDIES: See recipe for Candied Mint Leaves.

FRUIT CUPS: Crush 1 petal in bottom of each cup.

FRUIT SALADS: *All canned* and *fresh fruits.* Add 1 or 2 fresh petals to each serving.

HONEY: Blend *crushed rose leaves with Orange Blossom Honey.* Several petals will be sufficient to develop a delicate flavoring in 8 ounces honey.

JELLIES: *Fruit* and *mint.* Flavor desired fruit bases with rose petals.

TEAS: Blend dried rose petals with other desired herbs and teas. See also chapter on Herb Teas.

VINEGARS: See chapter on Herb Vinegars.

Rose-petal Syrup   TIME: Variable

Rose petals   *Sugar*   *Cold water*

Select fresh, unbruised petals; carefully separate and spread on clean cloth or screen to dry for 1 or 2 days. When at least a quart of rose petals have been dried, press them tightly together between the palms of your hands. Place the carefully pressed petals in a heavy enamel pan. Measure cold water used; barely cover petals with water; bring to boiling over medium flame; gradually add 3 cups sugar for each cup of water used; boil slowly 10 minutes, or until syrup is formed. Strain through filter cloth; bottle; cork tightly. Keep 2 weeks before using. Yield: Approximately ½ pint.

Syrup may be used to *flavor custards, fruit drinks, puddings,* and *fruit salads* to taste.

ROSE GERANIUM, *Pelargonium capitalum*

Dried leaves in bulk from herb dealers and herb gardens. Fresh leaves from herb gardens.

Rose geranium is perhaps the most popular of the more than 200 varieties of this sweet-scented perennial of herb gardens. As its name implies, this lovely plant tastes and smells of the rose. Originally it came to us from South Africa.

Rose geranium is often thought of as a house plant because of its beautiful foliage, but it will grow from 3 to 4 feet high if given plenty of space in the out of doors. The large, soft, hairy leaves are divided into three main divisions which are deeply cut around the edges. The larger the leaves, the more fragrant their sweet, spicy odor becomes. The tiny pinkish-lavender flowers are not conspicuous but bloom in a graceful, rather loose umbel.

Several other favorite varieties of the geranium bear the name of their fragrance: APPLE, BALM-SCENTED, CAMPHOR-ROSE, LEMON-SCENTED, NUTMEG, ORANGE, PEPPERMINT, and SPICY. The leaves vary in size in the different varieties, but all of them are velvety and soft, though the tiny leaves of the lemon-scented geranium, *Pelargonium crispum,* have edges which feel almost crisp to the touch.

Using: The dried or fresh leaves may be used to give a delicate, flowery rose flavor to many interesting desserts, such as custards, baked fruits, puddings, and ice creams. Most of us know the delicious additional flavor the rose geranium leaves give to jams and jellies. A tiny fresh leaf of the apple or lemon-scented variety in a fruit cup will lend attractiveness to what might otherwise be but a routine, everyday dessert.

The large, fresh leaves are the best for use in the jams and jellies and other desserts. One of the smaller leaves in the bottom of a finger bowl will be a fragrant and attractive change from the usual lemon slice.

The dried leaves are used in some blends of herb teas; also with some of the smaller twigs they are included in old-fashioned bouquets and potpourri jars. Choose your favorite fragrance from among the herb-scented geraniums and place a tiny leaf in the bottom of the pudding dish the next time it is to be the family's dessert. Be prepared for paeans of praise, for it's sure to please their palates. See also chapters on Herb Jellies, Herb Teas, Herb Vinegars, and the uses of Verbena or Lemon Verbena leaves.

CUSTARDS: Place 1 tiny leaf in bottom of individual custard cup before baking.

DRINKS: *Brewed tea, fruit drinks, lemonades, wine cups.* In *cold* drinks, garnish individually with leaf after drink is made. For *hot* drinks, crush 1 leaf in bottom of glass or cup before pouring drink.

FRUIT CUPS: Garnish each cup with ¼ teaspoon chopped fresh leaf; or garnish with 1 tiny whole leaf.

FRUITS: *Baked. Apples, pears, peaches.* Place 1 leaf under each piece of fruit before baking so flavor permeates the pan juices.

ICE CREAM: Place 1 leaf in bottom of tray before freezing.
JAMS AND JELLIES: See chapter on Herb Jellies.
PUDDINGS: Place 1 leaf in bottom of pudding dish before
    baking.

For 4 servings use approximately:

1 teaspoon chopped fresh leaves.
4 whole leaves.

ROSEMARY, *Rosmarinus officinalis*

Dried leaves in 1¼ ounce containers at groceries and
    markets; also in bulk from herb dealers.
Fresh leaves from herb gardens.
Honey in limited quantities from herb farms.

Rosemary is a shrubby, sweet-scented perennial which is often
treated as an annual in the colder climates. This aromatic
herb has tall, erect, branching stems which reach up more
than 3 feet in height. Some plants in the warm sunshine of
Italy often grow more than 6 feet tall. The obtuse, slender,
linear leaves, almost an inch long, are green on top and
grayish green and cottony looking on the underside. They
curve slightly as a pine needle curves.

The small bluish-pink or almost lavender flowers blossom
in clusters at the end of the tall branches. The spicy, blended
aroma and flavor of the leaves, flowers, and stems makes this
shrub of southern Europe one of the best loved of all the
herbs.

Rosemary was called *ros maris* or *dew of the sea* because it
flourished in the salt-sea spray all along the Mediterranean
coast. It is found in profusion today in the moist climates of
North Carolina and Virginia, where it was first planted as a
border plant by our early colonists. Along the Pacific coast
rosemary blossoms all winter long, and its pale blue flowers
delight the eye as does the misty blue of antique porcelain.

Using: The fresh tops of rosemary may be used as garnishes
for fruited summer drinks. The freshly chopped leaves used
judiciously in sauces, stews, soups, and over roasts have a
most delectable effect upon the ultimate flavor. Rosemary
blended with chopped parsley and melted butter and spread
over a capon before roasting makes a delightful change.

Eggs with a dash of the herb, either fresh or dried, are effectively different and coax the appetites of those who sometimes grow tired of eggs. A few tiny leaves of minced fresh rosemary will make a fruit cup or a fruit salad something extraordinarily delicious. The piny flavor of the freshly chopped herb adds an indescribable taste and flavor to jams, sweet sauces, and cream soups. Baking-powder biscuits are more than appetizing when 1 teaspoon or 2 teaspoons of this unusual herb is freshly chopped and blended with the dough. See Curly-parsley Biscuits.

The dried herb has just as exciting a flavor as the fresh leaves, and the unusual tastiness of the Italian and Polish sausages is owing to the amount of rosemary which has been blended in with the other seasonings. The Yugoslavs are also extremely partial to rosemary, and the largest supply of our imported rosemary comes from Yugoslavia. See also chapters on Herb Butters, Herb Honeys, Herb Jellies, and Herb Vinegars.

APPETIZERS: *Fruit cups.* Place 1 fresh rosemary leaf in each cup 5 minutes before serving.

EGGS: *Omelet, scrambled.* Blend in 1 teaspoon minced fresh herb when beating eggs.

FISH: *Eels, halibut, salmon, broiled.* Sprinkle fish lightly with dried or freshly minced herb before placing in broiling compartment. *When boiling fish,* place ¼ teaspoon dried herb or 4 fresh leaves in water in which fish is cooked.

GAME: *Partridge, rabbit, venison, roasted.* Rub lightly with crushed dried rosemary before roasting.

MEATS: *Beef, lamb, pork, veal, broiled* or *roasted.* Rub meats very lightly with crushed herb before placing in oven, using from ½ to 1 teaspoon but not more. See also Lamb Roast Marinated with Sage.

When chopped fresh leaves are used, sprinkle 2 teaspoons over meat ½ hour before removing from oven.

POULTRY: *Chicken, duck, pheasant, quail, roasted.* Sprinkle inside very lightly with crushed herb before placing in oven.

SOUPS: *Chicken, peas, spinach, turtle.* Combine ¼ teaspoon basil, ¼ teaspoon marjoram, and ¼ teaspoon rosemary; add to soup before boiling. Also use fresh rosemary and prepare an herb bouquet of the 3 fresh herbs; *especially delicious in turtle soup.*

VEGETABLES: *Cauliflower, peas, potatoes, spinach, turnips.*
Place herb in water in which vegetable is boiled. Use ¼
teaspoon for all listed vegetables except spinach in which
½ teaspoon may be used. *Mushrooms, broiled* or *sautéed*
in butter: Sprinkle with ¼ teaspoon dried rosemary before cooking.

For 4 servings use approximately:

¼ to 1 teaspoon dried leaves (average taste ½ teaspoon).
½ to 2 teaspoons chopped fresh leaves.
4 leaves in fruit cups.
1 small sprig in summer drinks.

Rosemary Veal Stew   TIME: 1¼ hours

2 lbs. veal rump	*½ tsp. rosemary*
½ tsp. salt	*1 carrot, whole*
½ tsp. cayenne pepper	*6 small white onions*
Juice of ½ lemon	*½ lb. mushrooms, sliced*
1 cup dry white wine	*1 stalk celery, diced*
Herb Bouquet	*Mustard Dumplings*

Select veal rump or leg meat without bone; have meat cut into
2-inch cubes. Place meat in saucepan; add salt, cayenne, and
lemon juice. Cover meat with cold water (about 2 cups). Bring
to boil over medium flame; remove scum with perforated
spoon. Add wine and Herb Bouquet; cover. Simmer gently
45 minutes, or until partially tender. Add rosemary, carrot,
onions, mushrooms, and celery; cover. Simmer gently 20
minutes, or until onions and mushrooms are tender. If more
liquid is desired, add small quantity of wine. Serve piping hot
with Mustard Dumplings. Serves 6.

RUE, *Ruta graveolens*

Dried leaves in bulk at druggists; also from herb dealers.
Fresh leaves from herb gardens.
Wild all over Europe.

Rue is the bitterest herb in the world next to wormwood. But
nature has made up for its peculiarly unpleasant taste by en-
dowing it with a rather delightful flavor when its tiny leaves
are sparingly blended in chicken salad and broth. When rue

is used to make a cheese canapé intriguing, the taste appeal is mysterious.

The beauty of the color of the thick, blue-green leaves is unlike any other in the whole realm of nature. The branching leaves resemble a maidenhair fern with many leaflets that are broader at the tips than near the stem. The herb is a shrubby, hardy evergreen perennial almost 2 feet tall. Its beautiful 4-petaled star-shaped flowers are at least ½ inch across and of a rich golden color. They lie deep within a green calyx and the blossoms grow in a flat corymb. The seed pod looks like a loculated capsule.

Rue is native to the Mediterranean countries, but it is now cultivated in North Carolina and other sections of the southern and eastern United States.

Using: The musty flavor of rue, when used sparingly, is an unusual change for canapés, minced chicken, and mushrooms; or when added to vegetable cocktails, salads, or chicken stew. Its flavor blends well with the slightly bitter taste of Swedish bread; and some *Scandinavians will sprinkle a tiny smidgeon of rue between the slices of the freshly buttered bread,* making a sandwich which defies description. Three or four of the tiny pale green leaves, finely minced, is sufficient for the average taste.

CHEESE: *Cottage* or *cream.* Blend ¼ pound cheese with 1 teaspoon finely minced rue; allow to stand 1 hour; serve in sandwiches or as canapés.

DRINKS: *Vegetable cocktails.* Crush a leaf in bottom of each glass.

RAGOUTS: *Beef* or *lamb.* Add 2 or 3 whole leaves to sauce while cooking.

SALADS: *Chicken, chopped veal, tuna fish, vegetable.* Add ½ teaspoon minced herb to salad dressing.

STEWS: *Beef, chicken, kidney, lamb.* Add 2 or 3 whole leaves to sauce before cooking.

VEGETABLES: *Potatoes, boiled.* Garnish very lightly with minced rue instead of chives.

For 4 servings use approximately:

¼ to 1 teaspoon chopped fresh leaves.
8 whole leaves.

SAFFRON, see Spices.

SAGE, *Salvia officinalis*

> Dried leaves in ½ ounce containers at groceries and markets; also from herb dealers.
>
> Fresh leaves from all herb gardens.
>
> Powdered sage in ½ to 1 ounce containers at groceries and markets; also from herb dealers.
>
> Sage cheese in limited quantities in New England at specialty food shops and cheese markets.
>
> Sage honey in 1 pound jars at fancy groceries, markets, herb dealers, herb farms, and health-food stores.

Sage is a neat, cool, grayish-green perennial which belongs to the mint, *Labiatae,* family and is native to the north Mediterranean countries. Now it is widely cultivated in all the temperate regions of the world.

There are about 500 varieties of this most important culinary herb; and the several mentioned here are among the most popular in use.

The COMMON GARDEN SAGE, *Salvia officinalis,* has spikes of tubular, bluish-purple flowers, and its gray-green leaves are rough to the touch. All the varieties of sage have a similar appearance, but the tastes, the colors, odors, and fragrances of the leaves differ with the different kinds and qualities. The PINEAPPLE SAGE, *Salvia splendens,* has the fruity fragrance of the pineapple; the CYPRUS SAGE leaves are a dark gray when dried, and the aroma is highly fragrant and the taste slightly bitter. The ROSE SAGE, *Salvia officinalis rosea,* and the WHITE SAGE, *Salvia officinalis alba,* are favorites in American gardens.

The dried leaves of the SPANISH SAGE are a dark gray and the flavor is warm and aromatic though the taste is slightly astringent. The best-flavored sage grows wild on the rocky hills of Serbia or Yugoslavia. It is called DALMATIAN SAGE and is considered the best-quality sage to reach our American markets. The aroma of these perfect green leaves is wonderfully aromatic and fragrant. The taste is warm and only slightly bitter.

Today sage is used in greater quantities than many a milder herb. The Swiss and Dutch flavor cheeses with sage, and some of our New England farmers know the secret of preparing

sage cheese. Pork and sage seem to have an affinity; and perhaps this is one of the reasons why the herb is so popular with
us.

Using: There are so many uses for this marvelous herb that
it is little wonder that more than a million and a half pounds
are consumed every year in America alone. Manufacturers of
sausages use tons of sage annually. We all know the delicious
sage dressing with which our Thanksgiving turkeys are stuffed;
and a chicken or a goose is equally tempting when stuffed with
a favorite sage dressing. The next time you're roasting veal,
rub a small quantity of powdered sage over the top of the
roast before placing it in the oven. The flavor of veal seasoned
in this manner will vie with that of the most tender turkey.
The delicate hint of sage in meat loaf will add zest to that good
old standby also.

Fresh sage leaves minced finely and used with caution give
a delicious flavor to cottage and cream cheese canapés. One
or two leaves is sufficient to flavor a quarter pound of either
of these mild cheeses. There are so many recipes listed in the
regular basic cookbooks which suggest the uses of the dried
leaves and powder that this list offers but a few additional
suggestions with some for the use of the *fresh* sage leaves.
See also chapters on Herb Butters, Herb and Tree-blossom
Honeys, and Herb Teas.

CHEESES: *Cheddar* cheese. Blend ½ teaspoon dried sage or
2 fresh leaves minced with soft cheddar; serve as canapés
and sandwiches.
Cottage, cream. Mince 2 fresh sage leaves; blend with
¼ pound cheese; serve as canapés and sandwiches.
FISH: *Baked, all sweet-meated fish.* Place 1 fresh sage leaf
in fish before baking.
Boiled. Use 1 sage leaf in water with other herbs when
boiling fish.
Broiled. Eels and *all fat fish.* Sprinkle lightly with powdered sage before placing under broiler.
GAME: *Hare, rabbit, venison, roasted.* Rub lightly with
crushed fresh sage leaves before placing in oven.
MEATS: *Puddings* and *loaves.* Use either dried or fresh sage;
¼ teaspoon of former; 1 teaspoon minced fresh.
Beef, lamb, mutton, pork, veal, roasted. Rub meat lightly
with powdered sage. See also Lamb Roast Marinated with
Fresh Sage.

POULTRY: *Chicken, goose, turkey.* Use sparingly when poultry is being roasted and stuffed; approximately ¼ to ½ teaspoon is sufficient in stuffing.

SAUCES: *Brown sauces; meat sauces.* Flavor with ¼ teaspoon powdered sage or 1 dried whole leaf; remove leaf before serving.

SOUPS: *Cream soups, fish chowders.* Use 1 fresh sage leaf or ¼ teaspoon powdered sage as seasoning.

STEWS: *Beef, lamb, veal.* Use 1 dried sage leaf instead of bay leaf.

STUFFINGS: *Fish, poultry, meat.* Use from ½ to 1 teaspoon powdered sage in dressing. See Sage Walnut Stuffing.

VEGETABLES: *Eggplant, lima beans, onions, peas, tomatoes.* Place 1 fresh sage leaf in water in which vegetables are *boiled* or *stewed;* or flavor butter with ¼ teaspoon dried sage when vegetables are served plain with melted butter.

For 4 servings use approximately:

1 whole dried leaf.
1 to 4 whole fresh leaves.
¼ to 1 teaspoon powdered sage.
1 to 4 fresh sprigs.

Lamb Roast Marinated with Fresh Sage   TIME: 3 hours
Marinate overnight

1 leg of lamb, 6 to 7 lbs.   *Salt and pepper*
2 small sprigs rosemary   *1 cup hot water*
Fresh sage branches

Have excess fat trimmed from lamb but do not have skin taken off. Wrap lamb with branches of fresh sage and 2 small sprigs rosemary. Cover well with waxed paper. Place lamb in refrigerator overnight. When ready to roast, remove herbs; sprinkle meat lightly with salt and pepper. Place on rack in roasting pan. Roast in preheated hot oven (400° F.) 15 minutes. Remove fat; pour in water. Reduce heat and roast in slow oven (330° F.) 30 minutes for each pound for medium-done roast and 35 minutes each pound for well-done meat.

The English prefer to roast lamb in a hot oven (400° F.) without reducing heat at any time. This takes approximately 2 hours for a 5- or 6-pound roast. Serve piping hot with baked potatoes. Serves 8.

If fresh herbs are not available, use the dried. Rub lamb lightly with ¾ teaspoon powdered sage. Cut 2 gashes in meat with sharp knife; put ⅛ teaspoon dried rosemary in each gash. Season with salt and pepper. Roast as suggested.

Baked Savory English Squares   TIME: 1¼ hours

1 tsp. powdered sage   *2 ozs. oatmeal*
2 tbs. minced scallions   *¼ tsp. salt*
6 ozs. dry bread crumbs   *⅛ tsp. parsley salt*
⅛ tsp. pepper   *Rich milk or cream (about ½*
⅛ tsp. celery salt   *cup)*
2 ozs. finely chopped beef suet

Blend well the sage, scallions, bread crumbs, pepper, celery salt, beef suet, oatmeal, salt, and parsley salt in large bowl. When smooth, add only enough rich milk or cream to make a soft mixture. Spread mixture in buttered baking tin. Bake 1 hour in preheated moderate oven (350° F.). Cut into serving squares. Serve piping hot with favorite fresh herb sauce. Serves 4 to 6.

SAVORY or SUMMER SAVORY, *Satureia hortensis*

Dried leaves in ½ to 1 ounce containers, at groceries and markets; also from herb dealers.
Fresh leaves from herb gardens.
See also Savory, Winter.

Savory or summer savory is an attractive, slender, fragrant annual with tiny tubular, pale-pink and lilac-colored flowers. This herb is a busy, scraggly plant which grows from 16 to 18 inches high in a sunny spot. The aroma of its dark green blunt-tipped leaves is slightly resinous.

The piquant and pleasant flavor of its foliage has become a great favorite in cooking, and many of the marketed herb blends have a goodly share of summer savory in them.

Native to Europe's Mediterranean areas, this colorful member of the mint, *Labiatae,* family is now widely cultivated all over the United States and Europe. Every little garden in Switzerland has a bush of *Bohnenkraut,* as it is commonly called there. The name literally means "herb of the string bean"; and the herb was given that common name because of the delicious flavor it adds to the bean and other green vegetables.

Using: The fresh, tender young leaves and tips may be minced and used to flavor croquettes, egg dishes, meats, and poultry dressings. Fish, salads, stews, sauces, and vegetables take on a new flavor when the tiny leaves of summer savory are used instead of parsley or chives.

APPETIZERS: *Vegetable-juice cocktail.* Season with 1 sprig savory.

EGGS: *Deviled, omelets, scrambled.* Use 3 teaspoons minced fresh summer savory. Blend with eggs before cooking. If fresh herb is not available, use ¾ teaspoon crushed dried herb.

FISH: *Baked, broiled, fresh-* and *salt-water fish.* Sprinkle lightly with about 1 tablespoon freshly minced savory just before serving.

GAME: *Rabbit, venison, stew.* Add 1 sprig to liquid before cooking; remove sprig before serving.

MEATS: *Beef, hamburgers.* Blend 1 teaspoon minced savory to each pound of chopped beef before cooking.

Mutton roast. Sprinkle lightly with minced savory just before serving.

Pies, lamb. Season with ½ teaspoon crushed savory while baking.

Smoked pork, ham, et cetera. Garnish lightly with minced herb just before serving.

Veal roast. Garnish with savory sprigs before serving.

POULTRY: *Chicken, duck, turkey, roasted* and *stuffed.* Use ½ teaspoon dried summer savory with other herbs in dressing.

SALADS: *Tomato, tossed-green.* Blend in 1 teaspoon minced leaves and flowers with salad; garnish with minced leaves just before serving.

SAUCES: *Fish, horseradish cream.* Use 2 teaspoons freshly minced herb; blend with sauce just before serving.

SOUPS: *Bean, consommé, fish chowder.* Use ½ teaspoon dried savory instead of parsley before cooking; or sprinkle freshly minced herb over top just before serving.

STUFFINGS: *Meats, poultry.* Blend in 2 teaspoons minced leaves instead of parsley as flavoring.

VEGETABLES: *Beans, cabbage, peas, sauerkraut.* Place 1 or 2 sprigs in saucepan when cooking.

For 4 servings use approximately:

½ to 1 teaspoon dried leaves.
1 teaspoon to 1 tablespoon chopped fresh leaves.
4 to 8 sprigs as garnish.

SAVORY or WINTER SAVORY, *Satureia montana*

Dried leaves and flowering tops in 1 and 1½ ounce containers at groceries and markets; also from herb dealers.
Fresh leaves from herb gardens.
See also Parsley.
See also Savory, Summer.

Savory or winter savory is another popular species of the more than half-a-dozen dwarf or bushy savories. Like the summer savory, it is native to the Mediterranean areas and is also grown extensively in all parts of the United States and Europe.

The winter variety is a beautiful, hardy perennial with dark green, shiny leaves which have a slightly stronger and more pungent odor and flavor than that of the summer savory. Its lovely pinkish-white and sometimes almost purple flowers resemble the tiny blossoms of the mint, *Mentha*, family. The flowers bloom continuously from midsummer until killed by the frost. In the late autumn the plant is a beautiful sight when still covered with pale blossoms that resemble a soft blanket of pink snow.

Using: Also like the summer savory, the winter variety is a good mixer. The leaves give an added accent to poultry stuffings and some egg dishes. It may be used instead of parsley or blended with it and other herbs. Though not quite so delicate in flavor as the summer savory, it may also be used in place of it and in a bouquet garni for soups and stews.

Winter Savory Soufflé Omelet   TIME: 15 minutes

4 eggs
2 tbs. rich milk or cream
⅛ tsp. salt
1 tbs. minced fresh winter
    savory
⅛ tsp. garlic salt
1 tbs. butter

Separate egg yolks from whites; beat yolks with 2 tablespoons milk or cream, salt, and garlic salt until very light and frothy;

beat egg whites until stiff. Blend minced winter savory with egg yolks; gradually fold in the beaten whites.

Melt butter in frying pan over medium-high flame; when butter sizzles and is golden brown around edges of pan, pour in omelet mixture. Hot butter and steady heat will cause egg mixture to puff up; when light golden brown, in about 2 minutes, lift up gently with fork or spatula and allow balance of mixture to run under; fold over gently. Allow to brown about 3 minutes. Serve piping hot immediately. Garnish with extra winter savory sprigs. Serves 2.

Any preferred sweet-flavored herb may be used instead of winter savory. Mince herb and prepare as suggested.

SHALLOT, *Allium ascalonicum*

> Dried bulbs at groceries and markets; also from herb gardens.
> Fresh from herb gardens.
> See also Chives, Onions.

Shallot is a hardy perennial grown extensively in Europe, especially in England, France, and Switzerland. As the herb has become increasingly popular in American cookery, its cultivation in our eastern and southern states is also expanding.

The shallot has slender awl-shaped leaves, and the angular root produces clusters of small gray bulbs which resemble garlic. The flavor is even more delicate than that of the onion, and the shallot is often substituted for it in European cookery.

Using: Shallots are used so extensively in so many European recipes that here, too, like the suggestions for the onion, its many uses may be only partially indicated. Any meats that are sautéed and cooked quickly, such as beef tenderloin, sirloin, veal, chops, and kidneys are all more unusual and delicious in flavor when sprinkled with chopped or minced shallots. A broiled sirloin steak served with hot melted butter over the top and sprinkled with a mixture of chopped parsley and minced shallots has a deliciousness which defies description. See also chapters on Herb Salad Dressings, Herb Sauces, and Herb Vinegars.

> FISH: *Cod, halibut, whitefish, boiled* or *broiled.* Mix 1 tablespoon chopped parsley and 1 small minced shallot bulb

together; sprinkle fish lightly just before serving with melted butter.

GAME: *Hare* or *rabbit* ragout. Use 1 small shallot instead of onion.

MEATS: *Beef, chops, kidneys, steaks, veal, broiled.* Sprinkle sparingly with minced shallots just before broiling.
Stews: Use 1 or 2 shallots instead of onions.

POULTRY: *Chicken breast, livers, broiled.* Sprinkle sparingly with minced shallots and parsley (chopped fine) just before serving.
Duck, guinea hen, roasted. Place 1 peeled shallot in duck or hen before roasting.

SAUCES: In *butter sauces.* Place 1 peeled shallot in sauce while cooking; remove before serving.
In *wine sauces,* in which recipes suggest onion, use 1 minced shallot instead of onion.

STUFFINGS: *Fish* and *meat stuffings.* Use sparingly instead of garlic or onion, according to desired piquancy.

VEGETABLES: Chopped shallot in *Eggplant Spanish Style* adds an extra subtlety to the flavor.

For 4 servings use approximately:

½ to 1½ teaspoons minced shallot.
1 to 2 whole peeled shallots.

Shallot-broiled Porterhouse　　　　　　　TIME: Variable

1 porterhouse steak	*¼ cup water*
2 tsp. minced shallots	*1 tbs. tarragon vinegar*
½ tsp. salt	*1 tsp. lemon juice*
¼ tsp. celery salt	*1 tsp. meat or vegetable*
⅛ tsp. black pepper	*　extract*
4 ozs. butter	*1 tsp. prepared horseradish*

Have porterhouse or sirloin steak sliced 2 inches thick.

Blend minced shallots, salt, celery salt, and pepper in small bowl; rub seasoned mixture into both sides of steak.

Place steak 3 inches below flame on preheated broiler rack. Broil 5 minutes on one side; turn; broil 5 minutes on other side; reduce flame. Continue broiling 5 more minutes on each side, or until steak is of desired degree of rareness or well done.

Meanwhile, melt 4 ounces butter in small saucepan over

medium flame; add water, tarragon vinegar, lemon juice, meat extract, and prepared horseradish. Simmer gently 5 minutes. Pour piping hot sauce over broiled sizzling steak. Serve with piping-hot baked potatoes and tossed green salad. Allow ½ pound steak or more for each person. Serves 4 generously.

If shallots are not available in market, substitute minced garlic.

SORREL or GARDEN SORREL, *Rumex acetosa*

Fresh leaves at groceries and markets; also from herb gardens.
Wild in meadows of Asia, Europe, and North America.

Sorrel or garden sorrel is native to Asia and Europe, where it still grows wild in the meadows. It is also found wild in many parts of North America.

The herb is sometimes called SOUR GRASS because the large, pale green leaves of this perennial have a sharp acid flavor. The French variety, or *Rumex scutatus,* is less acid or sour than the garden sorrel. The cultivated sorrel is still less sour than that which grows wild. Sorrel is very popular in most of the herb gardens throughout Europe and is growing more so in America.

The garden sorrel has ridged reddish stalks and long, oblong leaves which are arrow-shaped at the base. The round, green-colored flower heads grow on tall spikes. This species may grow almost 3 feet tall. The MOUNTAIN SORREL, growing wild in the Alps, has beautiful flowers of a deep purple shade. The FRENCH SORREL, or *Rumex scutatus,* has larger leaves which are shaped more like a shield, and the plant stands less erect than the garden variety, but even so may reach a height of at least 2 feet. Our American seed catalogues often list the sorrel as a SILVER LEAF highly esteemed as an early spring table green.

Using: Only the very young, fresh leaves are used in salads and as cooked greens; either alone or in combination with other greens, such as spinach, cabbage, and lettuce. In Sweden sorrel is sometimes used in bread, much in the same way in which we prepare parsley biscuits. Many Americans find that minced cooked sorrel alone is much too bitter to the taste. As *Oseille de Belleville,* the French sorrel finds its way to many a table d'hôte luncheon menu in France. I still remember the bitterness of the first mouthful I ever ate; but soon afterward I had acquired a taste for it.

EGGS: *Omelet, soufflé.* Use 2 tablespoons minced *raw* sorrel in omelet soufflé for two. Blend herb with eggs before cooking.

SALAD: *Tossed-green.* Add 1 or 2 minced leaves. See Sorrel and Herbs Salad.

SOUPS: See Sorrel and Lettuce Soup.

VEGETABLES: Prepare boiled or steamed sorrel alone or in combination with other greens.

For 4 servings use approximately:

1 or 2 minced leaves in salads.
½ to 1 pound as vegetable.

Sorrel and Herbs Salad   TIME: 20 minutes

¼ lb. sorrel
1 small head lettuce
4 tarragon leaves or
⅛ tsp. dried tarragon
2 sprigs chervil or ½ tsp.
*   dried chervil*

1 tsp. chopped chives
French dressing made with
*   tarragon vinegar*

Clean and wash sorrel under cold running water; repeat same for lettuce. Break leaves into convenient pieces (not too small). Mince tarragon leaves and chervil sprigs. Toss with sorrel, lettuce, and chives. Place in refrigerator 10 minutes to chill. Just before serving pour generous amount French Dressing over salad; toss gently. Serve immediately. Serves 4 to 6.

If dried herbs are used instead of fresh, blend herbs with French Dressing and allow to stand half-hour before using.

Sorrel and Lettuce Soup   TIME: 1¼ hours

½ cup chopped sorrel
1 head lettuce
¼ lb. butter
½ small leek
1 cup chopped spinach
4 potatoes, quartered

2 tsp. salt
2 qts. boiling water
1 tbs. chopped chervil
4 slices buttered toast
White pepper or paprika

Select fresh, tender herbs and vegetables. Remove tough stems from spinach and sorrel; remove outer leaves of lettuce; peel leek and potatoes. Wash all herbs and vegetables thoroughly under cold running water. Chop sorrel, spinach, and lettuce; slice leek; quarter potatoes.

Place butter in large, deep saucepan over low flame; add leek. Simmer gently 5 minutes, but do not brown. Add potatoes, salt, and boiling water. Turn up flame; boil potatoes 10 minutes; add sorrel, spinach, and lettuce; bring to boil; cover; lower flame. Simmer gently 45 minutes. Mash potatoes in liquid; add chervil. Simmer 5 minutes. Serve piping hot over ½ slice buttered toast placed in preheated bowls. Sprinkle each serving with white pepper or paprika. Serves 6.

If preferred, soup may be strained through very fine sieve before serving. If this is done, be sure to reheat; serve piping hot. Sprinkle each serving with white pepper or paprika, as desired.

Water Cress and Lettuce Soup: Use 1 bunch water cress instead of sorrel; follow recipe above.

TANSY or **FERN-LEAVED TANSY,** *Tanacetum vulgare,* var. *crispum*

Dried leaves at druggist; also from herb dealers.
Fresh leaves from herb gardens.
Wild along the roadsides in the eastern and middlewestern states.

Tansy is a bitter European perennial which at one time was extensively cultivated in the eastern and middlewestern states. In Michigan and Indiana tansy is cultivated on a commercial scale for the volatile oil which is distilled from the plant for use in certain drugs and liqueurs.

Tansy is included in this volume because of its important place in herb history and the fact that in some sections of the country its beautiful foliage is still in culinary use. Not only is tansy used to garnish salad and meat dishes but occasionally a leaf will find its way into a salad as a bit of exotic flavoring.

Using: Izaak Walton mentions tansy as seasoning for very small fish; and in France and England the tender leaves have been used for herb teas ever since the fifteenth century. Later in history tansy leaves were used to flavor egg dishes, cakes, and puddings; but to my knowledge sorrel and chervil have taken the place of tansy in omelets, and we Americans no longer use it in cakes and puddings. However, it still makes a luxuriant garnish, and its spicy bitterness may be just the touch needed to spark a jaded appetite.

CAKES: Flavor with 1 tablespoon tansy juice made by steeping crushed leaves in small quantity of boiling water.

EGGS: *Omelets.* Use from ½ to 1 teaspoon freshly minced tansy with 4 eggs; blend with eggs before cooking.

FISH: *Baked.* Place 1 whole leaf in bottom of baking dish while cooking. Always use tansy cautiously.

GARNISH: *Fish, meats, salads.* The lacy foliage adds attractiveness to all foods. Use as desired.

MEAT PIES: *Beef, lamb, mutton.* One half teaspoon freshly minced tansy will cut the richness of *fat meat;* or 1 whole leaf may be placed in bottom of pie.

TEAS: Prepare as other herb teas, if desired. Tea is somewhat bitter.

For 4 servings use approximately:

¼ teaspoon dried tansy leaves.
½ teaspoon freshly minced leaves.
1 whole fresh leaf.

TARRAGON, *Artemisia dracunculus*

Dried leaves in 1 and 1½ ounce containers at groceries and markets; also from herb dealers.
Fresh leaves from herb gardens.

Tarragon is known to connoisseurs the world over for its unusual, intriguing flavor. Sometimes called FRENCH TARRAGON, this vigorous, fragrant perennial of the aster, *Asteraceae,* family is native to western and southern Asia.

The very slender, pointed, dark green, graceful leaves are widely spaced on stems which are often 18 inches high. When it blossoms, which is rare in the colder climates, the herb has tiny, inconspicuous clusters of greenish-yellow flowers. Today tarragon is widely cultivated in southern Europe and in the temperate zones of the United States as well as throughout the colder New England area.

The flavor of the tender leaves, either fresh or dried, is somewhat astringent, yet it has a sweet, aniselike taste.

Using: Both the fresh and the dried leaves are used to flavor many foods. Minced or chopped finely and spread over steaks, salads, fish, and egg dishes, the herb lends a piquancy to the flavor that is unusually delicious and aromatic. Béarnaise, Hollandaise, and Tartar sauces are often flavored with tarragon. Marinades for fish and meats are improved by the judicious use of this herb. See also chapters on Herb Butters, Herb-flavored Mustards, Herb Salad Dressings, and Herb Vinegars.

APPETIZERS: *Tomato* and *vegetable-juice cocktails.* Use ¼ teaspoon freshly minced herb in each serving.

EGGS: *Omelets, scrambled.* Use 1 teaspoon freshly minced herb with 2 teaspoons parsley; blend in with eggs before cooking.

FISH: *All fish* and *shellfish, baked* or *broiled.* Use whole, fresh leaves (2 or 3 for each serving). Place on fish before cooking.

GAME: *Hare, rabbit, broiled.* Sprinkle lightly with 2 teaspoons freshly minced herb before placing in oven.

MARINADE: When pickling *beef, fish, lamb, mutton, pork,* use 1 teaspoon dried herb or 2 teaspoons freshly chopped herb in pickling liquid.

MEATS: *Steaks; Broiled tenderloin, filet mignon, sirloin.* Blend 2 teaspoons chopped tarragon with butter before pouring over steak.

POULTRY: *Chicken, duck, squab, roasted.* Use 2 teaspoons freshly minced herb; sprinkle lightly over poultry before roasting.

SALADS: *Asparagus, beans, cabbage, cauliflower, chicken, fish, shellfish, tomato, tossed-green.* Blend 2 teaspoons freshly minced herb with ingredients; blend ¼ teaspoon dried herb with dressing.

SAUCES: *Béarnaise, Hollandaise, Mayonnaise, Mustard, Tartar.* Blend ¼ teaspoon dried herb with other ingredients.

SOUPS: *Chicken, consommé, fish chowder, mushroom, tomato, turtle.* Use several whole fresh leaves or ¼ teaspoon dried herb; place in liquid before cooking.

For 4 servings use approximately:

¼ to ½ teaspoon dried herb.

½ to 2 teaspoons chopped fresh leaves.
1 to 4 whole leaves.

Norwegian Fish Soup with Tarragon TIME: 30 minutes

3 lbs. codfish with bones	*1½ tsp. chopped tarragon*
2 large onions, sliced	*1 tsp. chopped chervil*
1 clove garlic	*1 tsp. chopped chives*
Cold water	*¼ tsp. salt, extra*
½ tsp. salt	*⅛ tsp. cayenne pepper,*
⅛ tsp. white pepper	*optional*
2 cups sour cream	

Purchase codfish in one piece with bones. Wipe cod with damp cloth. Place cod in large saucepan; add onions and garlic; pour enough cold water in saucepan to cover cod; add ½ teaspoon salt. Bring to boil over high flame; turn down flame. Simmer gently 12 minutes, or until fish flakes easily when tested with fork. Strain through fine sieve; flake fish. Set aside to cool at room temperature.

Blend fresh chervil, salt, cayenne pepper, and sour cream in large mixing bowl; add flaked fish to seasoned cream; stir gently. Blend fresh tarragon and chives separately. Serve cold soup in deep bowls. Sprinkle each serving with blended tarragon and chives. Serves 6 generously. A most unusual and appetizing luncheon dish when accompanied by a tossed-green salad, crackers, and a mild, rather sweet cheese.

If fresh tarragon and chervil are not available, use 1 teaspoon each of the dried herbs; blend with sour cream ½ hour before adding fish, so herbs may flavor the cream. Sprinkle chopped chives over top of each serving.

THYME, *Thymus vulgaris*

Dried leaves in ½ to 1½ ounce containers at groceries and markets; also from herb dealers.

Fresh leaves from herb gardens.

Ground in 1 ounce containers at groceries and markets; also from herb dealers.

Honey (thyme) at specialty stores and markets in the United States; also abundantly in Sicily.

Wild in the rocky places of Europe, especially England,

Greece, Italy, and Switzerland; in the United States as far north as Greenland and Iceland.

Thyme is native to the Mediterranean areas and Asia Minor. This lovely perennial of the mint, *Labiatae,* family is now extensively cultivated in Canada, England, France, Germany, Italy, Spain, and the United States.

There are more than threescore varieties of thyme. Among some of the better known and most frequently used are the GARDEN and ENGLISH THYME, *Thymus vulgaris;* LEMON THYME, *Thymus citriodorus;* and the WILD THYME, *Thymus serpyllum.*

The garden thyme is a beautiful little herb which grows not more than a foot high. Its grayish-green, warmly aromatic foliage is almost evergreen, and the tiny, pale lavender flowers are a beautiful sight in the garden all during the month of June, as the blossoms cover the herb in profusion.

The lemon thyme, as its name implies, has a distinct lemon fragrance, and its golden-green leaves grow along the ground. In July its pink flowers add to the beauty of this low-spreading variety.

The wild or MOUNTAIN THYME, also called MOTHER OF THYME, varies in height from a low, creeping herb to bushes as high as 9 inches. Its purplish-pink flowers cover the mountain slopes of Greece, Italy, and Switzerland like a carpet of heather during midsummer, and its sweet-smelling leaves fill the air with their fragrance.

Using: The dried or fresh flowers and leaves are used in many foods, and the dried, brownish-green leaves are often ground and blended with other herbs to be used in special stuffings and seasonings. In Switzerland thyme is used to flavor a special creamy goat's-milk cheese, and the famous Benedictine liqueur is flavored with thyme. Creams, custards, croquettes, vegetable cocktails, fish, shellfish, meat, stuffings, chowders, and soups are all improved by the use of this warm, pungent herb. Salads and sauces owe much to thyme; and butters, jellies, and vinegars are intriguing and delicious when flavored with it. See also chapters on Herb Butters, Herb and Tree-blossom Honeys, Herb Jellies, Herb Mustards, Herb Salad Dressings, Herb Teas, and Herb Vinegars.

APPETIZERS: *Sea-food cocktails, vegetable-juice cocktails.* Use ⅛ teaspoon dried herb for each serving; sprinkle on top; then stir just before serving.

BOUQUET GARNI: Use 1 sprig fresh thyme.

CHEESES: *Cottage, cream.* Blend in ½ teaspoon dried thyme with ¼ pound cheese. Serve as sandwich or on canapés.

CHOWDERS: *Clam, fish.* Add 1 teaspoon freshly minced thyme or ¼ teaspoon dried thyme to both cream and plain chowder.

EGGS: *Shirred eggs.* Sprinkle lightly with thyme before placing in oven.

FISH: *All kinds,* both *lean* and *fat, baked, broiled, sautéed.* Lightly sprinkle dried herb on fish before cooking; also serve fish with herb butter.

GAME: *Rabbit, venison, stew.* Use ½ teaspoon dried herb with other ingredients.

MEATS: *Boiled, braised,* or *pot roast,* roast of *beef, lamb, mutton, pork,* and *veal.* Rub meat lightly with herb before cooking.

POULTRY: *Chicken, turkey.* Use in stuffings as suggested.

SALADS: *Aspic, tomato.* Use ¼ to ½ teaspoon dried thyme. *Beets,* pickled. Use ¼ teaspoon; blend dried herb with liquid.
Sea food. Use ⅛ to ¼ teaspoon in dressing for sea food; either mayonnaise or herb dressing. See also Herb and Spice Salad Dressings.

SAUCES: *Creole, Espagnole,* or any *tomato sauces.* Use ½ teaspoon dried herb with other ingredients.

SOUPS: *Beet, clam chowder, gumbo, vegetable.* Use ¼ to ½ teaspoon dried thyme, as suggested.

STEWS: *Lamb, mutton, veal.* Use 1 sprig fresh thyme or ½ teaspoon dried thyme with other ingredients before cooking.

STUFFINGS: *Chicken, goose, turkey, veal.* Use ½ to 1 teaspoon thyme, as suggested in recipes.

VEGETABLES: *Beans, beets, carrots, eggplant, mushrooms, onions,* and *potatoes.* Add ½ teaspoon dried thyme to vegetable *baked, boiled,* or *sautéed;* or blend herb with melted butter to be poured over vegetables just before serving.

For 4 servings use approximately:

⅛ to 1 teaspoon dried herb, as suggested in recipes.
1 to 2 teaspoons freshly minced thyme leaves.
⅛ to ½ teaspoon ground thyme.

VERBENA or LEMON VERBENA, *Lippia citriodora*

Dried leaves whole in bulk from herb dealers.
Fresh leaves whole from herb gardens.

Verbena or lemon verbena is a tender, delicately scented perennial which originally came from Argentina and Chile.

The long, narrow, yellowish-green leaves, pointed at the tip, grow in whorls of 3 or 4 on graceful woody branches. The upper side of the leaves is shiny and the lower is rough and rather dull. The flowers range from a bluish white to a pale lavender, and grow on slender, inconspicuous spikes.

The aroma and fruity flavor of the leaves are like a delicate lime or lemon.

Using: More and more the fresh leaves of the lemon verbena are being used to flavor fruit salads, jellies, fruit and wine drinks, and fruit cups. A lemon verbena leaf in the bottom of a finger bowl adds not only a touch of beauty and imagination to the service but gives a delicate fragrance which is extremely pleasant and different.

The Spanish are especially fond of Lemon Verbena Tea, which is as easily brewed as any tea. The whole dried leaves are infused in boiling water for a few moments and then the tea is sweetened to taste. It is best to use the leaves which have been freshly dried, for they lose their lemony fragrance after about six months. See also chapters on Herb Jellies, Herb Teas, and Rose Geranium uses.

APPETIZERS: *Fruit cups.* Place 1 tiny lemon verbena leaf on top of each serving.

DRINKS: *Cold, fruit, lemonades, wine cups.* Crush 1 leaf in bottom of beverage glass before pouring in drink.

JELLIES: See chapter on Herb Jellies.

SALADS: *Fruits, fresh* or *canned.* Place 1 leaf in bottom of each serving. If stronger flavor is desired, crush leaf in bottom of dish in which fruits are mixed.

TEAS: Whole dried leaves. See chapter on Herb Teas.

WINE CUPS: Crush 1 fresh leaf in bottom of wine cup before serving.

For 4 servings use approximately:

4 to 5 teaspoons dried leaves in tea.
4 whole fresh leaves as flavoring or garnish.

Herb-fruited Wine Cup   TIME: 20 minutes
                                      Chill and steep 8 hours

1 qt. sweet white wine   *4 rose geranium leaves*
1 pt. bottle sparkling water   *Rose geranium leaves, extra*
2 sprigs lemon verbena   *1 pt. strawberries*
2 sprigs pineapple sage   *2 tbs. flower or herb honey*
2 sprigs spearmint   *1 small sprig rosemary*

Sweet white wine is preferred, such as a Bordeaux Blanc or a sweet sauterne.

Pour wine in large bowl which can be covered.

Lightly crush fresh sprigs of lemon verbena, pineapple sage, spearmint, and 4 rose geranium leaves in bottom of large, wide-mouthed jar; pour wine over herbs; seal tightly. Steep for 6 hours at room temperature.

Clean and crush strawberries; sweeten with honey. Chill for 30 minutes in refrigerator. Add sweetened berries to wine.

Chill well in refrigerator. Keep chilled by placing pitcher of shaved ice in center of punch bowl. This also prevents drink becoming diluted. Just before serving pour in sparkling water. *Serve in chilled punch cups with 1 small rose geranium leaf floating on top.* Yield: 3 pints. If preferred, 2 pints sparkling water may be used instead of 1 pint.

WATER CRESS, *Sisymbrium nasturtium aquaticum*

Fresh leaves and stems in small bunches at groceries and markets; also herb gardens.

Wild in running streams throughout the world in all the temperate zones.

See also Cress or Land Cress.

Water cress is a peppery little perennial about 5 or 6 inches high. Native to temperate zones in Europe, it was taken to Africa, England, and America, where it has spread from the streams of Nova Scotia to those of Georgia, Virginia, and Alabama, and as far west as California and Idaho. Now the herb is grown commercially in a number of the southern and western states, including Alabama, California, and Virginia.

The tiny, round, glossy, dark green leaves of the water cress grow at the tips of the paler green stems. The small white flowers with 4 tiny petals blossom in long clusters throughout most of the summer months. The flavor of both the leaves and the stems is pungent and peppery and closely resembles the taste of nasturtium.

Using: Like the land cresses, the water cresses are used with many foods to add flavor, color, and attractiveness. More and more cress is being used in salads, as sandwich fillings, in soups and chowders, and as a cooked vegetable either alone or in combination with other greens. Another unique use of its nutritive value is as an ingredient in biscuit and pastry doughs. See also chapters on Herb Butters, Herb Salad Dressings; also the uses of parsley.

APPETIZERS: *Canapés, sea-food cocktails.* Sprinkle chopped leaves over top just before serving.

BISCUITS: See recipe Curly-parsley Biscuits.

CHEESES: *Cottage, cream, soft spreads.* Mince 4 sprigs water cress for each ¼ pound cheese; blend well.

EGGS: *Omelet, scrambled.* Use 2 tablespoons minced leaves; blend with eggs before cooking. Use sprigs as garnish.

FISH: Minced leaves sprinkled over top of *baked, boiled,* and *broiled* fish; whole sprigs as garnish in amounts preferred.

GARNISH: *Fish, game, meats, poultry, shellfish, baked, broiled, roasted.* Use water cress either minced or whole sprigs in amounts preferred.

MEATS: *All meats, boiled, broiled, roasted.* Minced leaves and whole sprigs from ½ to 1 bunch as garnish.

PASTRY: See recipe for Water Cress Piecrust.

SALADS: *Vegetables, all* either *cooked* or *raw.* Use either minced or whole sprigs, as desired.

SANDWICHES: *Cheese, fish, meat.* Blend minced water cress with ingredients. Use whole leaves and sprigs as lettuce.

SOUPS: *Cream, fish chowders, potato, vegetable.* Mince one-half bunch water cress; add to soup just before serving. Also prepare Herb Soup as Sorrel and Lettuce Soup, using water cress instead of sorrel.

VEGETABLES: *Carrots, cauliflower, potatoes, string beans,* and *all sweet vegetables.* Sprinkle with minced leaves just before serving.

For 4 servings use approximately:

2 tablespoons to ½ bunch minced leaves.
½ to 1 bunch whole sprigs.

Water Cress aux Hollandaise   TIME: 20 minutes

4 bunches water cress
½ cup water, about
1½ cups Hollandaise Sauce

1 hard-boiled egg, minced
½ tsp. salt

Purchase fresh water cress with dark green leaves only. Untie bunches; carefully remove any roots or yellow leaves. Wash thoroughly under cold running water. Place water cress sprigs in large saucepan with water which clings to them. If necessary, add very little water while cooking. Sprinkle with salt. Do not cover saucepan. Cook water cress 5 minutes, or until stems are tender but not soft. Drain well. Serve piping hot with favorite Hollandaise Sauce. Garnish with minced hard-boiled egg. Serves 4 to 6.

Hollandaise Sauce

2 egg yolks
4 tsp. lemon juice
½ cup butter
¼ tsp. salt

¼ tsp. celery salt
⅛ tsp. cayenne pepper
½ cup boiling water

Break egg yolks into top section double boiler; beat eggs lightly with spoon; add lemon juice; beat well.

Cream butter in separate bowl; add to egg mixture, stirring well. Insert top section double boiler into lower section half filled with boiling water. Cook over medium flame 10 minutes, or until butter melts and mixture begins to thicken. Gradually add salt, celery salt, and cayenne pepper. Slowly stir in boiling water until sauce is very smooth. Serve immediately. Approximate yield: 1 cup.

Water Cress Meat or Poultry Piecrust   TIME: 20 minutes

½ bunch water cress, minced
½ bunch water cress, extra
2 cups enriched flour
3 tsp. baking powder
¼ tsp. salt

¼ tsp. celery salt or
¼ tsp. chives salt
½ cup butter
or shortening
¾ cup milk

Purchase fresh water cress with dark green leaves only. Untie bunch; carefully remove any roots or yellow leaves. Wash thoroughly under cold running water; drain well on absorbent paper. Mince half bunch with sharp knife. Set aside. Store other half bunch in tightly covered jar in refrigerator. Use as garnish when pie is served.

Sift flour, baking powder, salt, and celery or chives salt on mixing board; add minced water cress; gradually cut in butter; mix well. By degrees add only enough milk to make a soft dough. Divide mixture in half; gently roll or pat into size of pie casserole. Use as bottom and top of pie. Makes 2 crusts approximately 8 inches in diameter.

Herb Piecrust adds unique flavor to *all fish, meat, poultry,* and *shellfish pies.*

WOODRUFF or SWEET WOODRUFF, *Asperula odorata*

Dried leaves and flowers in 1½ ounce containers at markets, fancy grocers; and from herb dealers.

Fresh leaves and flowers from herb gardens.

Wild along the Rhine River; in the forests of southern Europe and Asia; and in all the temperate climates in the United States.

Woodruff or sweet woodruff is one of the sweetest smelling of perennial herbs. It is sometimes called WALDMEISTER, or *Master of the Woods.*

The fragile, tiny square stems spread like mats to form a blanket of deep green leaves under the shade of trees. The long, oval leaves grow in whorls of 8, and when the sun strikes them they appear lighter and show the tiny hairs on the underside. The clusters of white flowers are like minute, 4-petaled stars, and usually bloom in the forest during June and July, as they grow loosely at intervals along the stems.

Using: Some of the best German wines are flavored with woodruff. In fact, the famous *Maitrink,* or May Drink, called May Wine, originated in the Valley of the Rhine, where Germany's most luxuriant vineyards line the banks of the majestic river. In the springtime many Europeans gather sprigs of fresh woodruff and steep them in a dry white wine. The French will select a choice champagne and the Swiss will steep the herb in Benedictine and cognac to serve them on special occasions. Americans have learned to prepare a May Wine Punch, using a combination of several wines and liqueurs. The fragrant sweetness of the woodruff flavor is usually associated with beverages and fruits. See also chapter on Herb Teas.

DRINKS: *Lemonades, cooling fruit drinks,* and *wine cups.* Garnish with sprig of woodruff before serving. Flavor each beverage as desired by crushing 1 leaf in bottom of glass.

FRUITS: *Mixed fruit cups.* Add 1 leaf woodruff just before serving individual portions.

For 4 servings use approximately:

Variable amounts dried herb in punches and teas.
4 fresh leaves in fruit cups.
4 small sprigs flowering tips in tall drinks.

May Wine Herb Punch   TIME: Variable
                                           Steep 8 hours

½ oz. dried woodruff   *1 bottle champagne*
4 bottles dry white wine   *1 cup sugar*
1 large jigger Benedictine   *1 pt. sparkling water*
2 large jiggers cognac   *6 sprigs fresh woodruff, if*
1 pt. fresh strawberries   *available*

Purchase any good, dry white wine, such as Riesling, Rhine, or very dry sauterne.

Place dried woodruff in wide-mouthed jar; open 1 bottle dry white wine; pour over woodruff; seal tightly. Steep 8 hours.

Hull, wash, and halve strawberries. Chill all liquids thoroughly. Do not place ice in punch. Keep chilled by placing container shaved ice in center of punch bowl.

Pour all wines and liqueurs into punch bowl. Dissolve sugar in sparkling water; add to punch; stir. Add strawberries and fresh sprigs of woodruff. Serve in chilled punch cups. Serves 12 generously.

CHAPTER THREE

Culinary

Aromatic

Herb Seed

ANISE SEED, *Pimpinella anisum*

Ground in 1 to 1½ ounce containers at groceries and markets; also from herb dealers.

Wild on the island of Jamaica.

Whole in 1 to 1½ ounce containers at groceries and markets; also in bulk from herb dealers.

See also Anise.

Anise seed is the dried fruit of the flowering umbels of the anise herb, *Pimpinella anisum*. Most of America's supply comes from the island of Jamaica, though anise is grown commercially quite extensively for its seed in many climates from the temperate to the very warm zones. These include India, Mexico, Spain, Italy, Germany, southern Russia, and the Orient.

The diminutive oval seed, less than ¼ inch long, is a greenish-gray color which sometimes appears almost brown. When seen under a powerful microscope, the tiny hairs which cover the seed are plainly visible.

The seed has a sweet, agreeable odor and the taste is pleasant and aromatic.

Another species, called STAR ANISE, is the seed of an evergreen tree, the *Illicium verum*, of the magnolia family. It grows in China and Japan, where the dried fruit is called

BADIAN ANISE or CHINESE ANISE. The small, round, yellow and white flowers of the plant do not expand fully but conceal the starlike seed in dark brown beaks. Because of its beautiful shape, this species received its popular and lovely name of star anise. The flavor of the seed is sweet and very much like the oriental anise.

Using: The whole seed is used to top rolls, coffee cakes, cookies, and confectionery. Various soups, cheeses, stews, beverages, and candies are flavored with either the ground or the whole seed; and the best licorice candies always have a generous amount of anise in them to increase the palatability and goodness of their taste. The sole flavor of the liqueur called anisette is derived from the anise seed, and many sweet gins contain a certain degree of anise flavoring.

A small round cheese of the Netherlands is sprinkled with anise seed; and here in America many manufacturers of sausages use either ground or whole anise seed as a flavoring. The taste appeal of many canned meats is increased by the use of this sweet seed. The ground anise seed, when used in boiling shellfish, adds a deliciously different and new flavor, especially to mussels, hard-shell crabs, and shrimps. See also chapter on Herb Teas.

APPETIZERS: *Canapés of cheese, shellfish.* Sprinkle lightly with whole seed.

BREADS: *Coffeecakes, sweet* breads. Sprinkle top lightly with whole seed before baking.

CAKES AND COOKIES: Flavor with ½ to 1 teaspoon ground seed; use ground anise instead of cinnamon to top sweet cookies. Also sprinkle lightly with whole seed before baking. See also Anise Squares.

CANDIES: See recipe for Old-fashioned Horehound Candy.

CHEESE: *Cottage.* Blend ½ to 1 teaspoon whole seed with ¼ pound cheese. Serve on canapés, as sandwiches, or salad.

DRINKS: See Anisette; also Herb Teas.

FRUITS: *Apples, raw* or *stewed, compotes, mixed fruits, stewed.* Flavor with ½ teaspoon whole seed. *When eating raw apples,* dip lightly in anise seed for a new-taste sensation.

MEATS: *Beef, veal, stews.* To each pound of meat use ½ teaspoon whole seed tied in cheesecloth and placed in stew before cooking. Remove before serving. *Use in all*

stews with vegetables in which a sweetish flavor is desired.

PIES: *Fruit, all.* Use ground anise or whole seed in all fruit
pies instead of cinnamon; from ¼ to ½ teaspoon, according to flavor desired.

For 4 servings use approximately:

¼ to 1 teaspoon ground seed.
¼ to 2 teaspoons whole seed.

Anise Squares   TIME: 30 minutes
Chill 30 minutes

½ cup butter   *1¾ cups enriched flour*
1 cup sugar   *¼ tsp. salt*
1 egg, beaten   *1½ tsp. baking powder*
1 tsp. ground anise seed or
*   fennel seed*

Cream butter in large mixing bowl; gradually add sugar, stirring constantly until smooth. Add egg; blend well.

Sift together ground anise seed, flour, salt, and baking powder; gradually add to mixture in bowl; blend well by beating
vigorously. When dough is smooth, divide into 3 or 4 sections.
Shape each section into roll about 2 or 3 inches in diameter.
Wrap each roll in waxed paper. Place in refrigerator 30 minutes to chill. Cut into thin slices; shape into squares with
cooky cutter; arrange on greased baking sheet. Bake in preheated hot oven (400° F.) 10 minutes. Yield: 40 to 50
squares.

Anisette Hot Milk   TIME: 5 minutes

1 tsp. ground anise seed   *1 tsp. butter*
2 cups rich milk

Blend anise seed with milk; heat gradually in small saucepan
over low flame until very hot but not boiling. Pour hot milk
into heavy glass; float ½ teaspoon butter on top. Drink immediately. A deliciously tasty and appetizing way in which to
encourage milk drinking.

*Cold milk may be flavored in same way; blend well in
electric mixer; omit butter.*

Anisette Liqueur   TIME: 30 minutes
Age 2 months

1 oz. whole anise seed   *1 pt. pure-grain alcohol*
2 drops anise seed oil   *4 ozs. sugar*
1 pt. good brandy

Place whole anise seed in mortar; bruise seed well with pestle.
Blend anise seed oil with sugar; add brandy and alcohol; blend
well. Pour into wide-mouthed jar; add bruised anise seed;
seal jar tightly. Place in cool, dark place for 2 months; shake
occasionally. Filter liqueur through filter paper; recork liqueur.
Serve, as desired, at room temperature. Yield: 1 quart.

CARAWAY SEED, *Carum carvi*

Ground in ½ to 1 ounce containers at groceries and markets; also from herb dealers.
Whole in ½ to 1 ounce containers at groceries and markets;
also in bulk from herb dealers.
See also Caraway.

Caraway seed is the dried fruit of the caraway herb. Although
the herb is widely grown in various parts of the United States,
our largest supply of the seed still comes from Holland and
the Tyrol.

The tiny, curved brown seed with pale yellow edges is not
more than ¼ inch long and looks like a miniature crescent
moon. It has a sharp aroma and a most agreeable odor and
taste when crushed and chewed.

Using: Caraway seed is perhaps best known to us for its
use in breads, especially rye. Some of our manufacturers include caraway in their formula of pickling spices and in pork
sausage seasoning. In the former, it is used whole; but the
sausage manufacturers use ground caraway seed.

In European cookery caraway seed has many interesting
uses which we are increasingly learning to enjoy. The German,
Dutch, Hungarian, Russian, Swedish, and Yugoslav homemakers flavor cakes, cheeses, meats, soups, and vegetables with
this delicious, tiny seed. One of the best kümmel liqueurs is
made in Holland from the native caraway seed.

Some of our colonial grandmothers chewed caraway seed
to sweeten the breath and chase away the ennui of long winter

twilights. But we have learned that this aromatic seed lends interest and enticing flavor to many foods. Caraway Cheese Wedges served piping hot, become an exciting experience and an hors d'oeuvre which is the envy of a host of friends. See also chapter on Herb Butters.

APPETIZERS: See Caraway Cheese Wedges; also in cheese.

BREADS: *Flavor basic dough* or a *prepared mix* with 1 teaspoon whole seed.

Sprinkle *favorite biscuit dough* with caraway and coarse salt before baking.

BUTTER: Crush seed before using. See Herb Butters.

CAKES: Spice Cake. Sprinkle top lightly with seed before baking.

CHEESES: *Cottage, cream.* Mix ½ to 1 teaspoon seed with ¼ pound cheese. Use as canapé or in sandwiches.

COOKIES: See Caraway Cookies.

FRUITS: *Apples, baked.* Sprinkle fruit lightly with sugar and whole seed.

MEATS: *Beef stew.* To each pound of beef use 1 teaspoon seed tied in cheesecloth and placed in stew before cooking; remove bag before serving.

Pork roast. Sprinkle roast with 1 teaspoon seed before placing in oven.

Mutton stew. Same as for beef stew.

PIE: *Sprinkle crust of pie with seed* before baking.

POULTRY: *Goose, roasted.* Place 1 teaspoon seed in bottom of roasting pan.

SOUPS: *Cabbage, potato, cream of.* Flavor with ¼ teaspoon seed while cooking.

VEGETABLES: *Cabbage, potatoes, turnips, creamed* or *scalloped;* also *plain buttered.* Sprinkle lightly with seed before serving.

Sauerkraut. Use ¼ teaspoon seed to each pound of sauerkraut. Cook with the vegetable.

VINEGAR: See chapter on Herb Vinegars.

For 4 servings use approximately:

¼ teaspoon to ½ teaspoon ground seed.

½ teaspoon to 1 or 2 tablespoons whole seed, as suggested in specific recipes.

Caraway Cheese Wedges   TIME: 45 minutes

1½ slices lean bacon,
   chopped
½ medium onion, minced
¾ cup shredded Swiss cheese
3 eggs, well beaten
3 tbs. sour cream

½ tsp. salt
⅛ tsp. black pepper
¼ tsp. caraway seed
½ tsp. caraway seed, extra,
   or ground caraway
1 Flaky Piecrust

Place chopped bacon in frying pan over medium flame. Brown lightly; do not allow to become crisp; add minced onions. Brown 3 minutes very lightly. Remove from fire. Cool. Add cheese, eggs, sour cream, salt, pepper, and ¼ teaspoon caraway seed; mix well.

Line 8-inch pie plate with piecrust. Pour in caraway-cheese mixture; sprinkle lightly with caraway seed or ground caraway. Bake in preheated moderate oven (350° F.) 30 minutes. Remove from oven. Cut pie into thin wedges. Serve piping hot as hors d'oeuvre. Yield: 2 dozen wedges.

Caraway Cookies   TIME: 30 minutes

½ cup butter
½ cup sugar
1 egg, beaten
2 cups enriched flour

2 tsp. baking powder
½ tsp. salt
¼ cup milk
1½ tsp. caraway seed

Cream butter and sugar until smooth in large mixing bowl; add beaten egg; mix well.

Sift flour, baking powder, and salt. Gradually add flour to butter-and-sugar mixture; add milk. Mix dough gently; add caraway seed. Mix gently until seeds are evenly distributed. Roll out ½ inch thick on lightly floured board. Cut into desired shapes; place on greased baking sheet. Bake in preheated hot oven (400° F.) 6 minutes. Yield: 36 to 40 cookies. Before baking cookies may be brushed with milk and sprinkled with extra caraway seed if desired. *Two tablespoons poppy seed may be used instead of caraway seed.*

CARDAMOM SEED, *Elletaria cardamomum maton*

Ground in ½ to 1½ ounce containers at groceries and markets, also from herb dealers.

Whole in ½ to 1 ounce containers at groceries and markets; also in bulk from herb dealers.

Cardamom seed is the fruit or dried seed of a perennial herb which belongs to the ginger, *Zinziberaceae,* family.

The herb is native to India and is cultivated there, especially in the western part, and on the island of Ceylon. To some extent it is also commercially grown in Central America and Mexico.

The seed is irregular, somewhat angular, and not more than ³⁄₃₂ inch long and less than ¹⁄₁₆ inch thick. It may vary in color from a light to a dark reddish brown and is usually bleached to a creamy white before being marketed. The texture is extremely hard. The seed has an unusually pleasant, pungent aroma and is highly aromatic to the taste.

Using: The Scandinavians, especially the Danes, use either the whole or ground cardamom seed to flavor spiced cakes, sweet pastries, breads, and cookies. The East Indians prepare a candy flavored with the seed; and whole cardamom seed are found in some of the New York City cocktail lounges, for chewing one of the seeds will sweeten the breath.

A crushed cardamom seed flavor in grape jelly is most unusual and slightly mysterious. Both the ground and the whole seed are wonderful additions to fruit salads. See also Curry Powder chapter and Herb and Tree-blossom Honeys.

BREAD AND ROLLS: *Buns, coffeecake, Danish pastry, sweet breads.* Use from ¼ to 1 teaspoon ground cardamom, according to individual taste.

COOKIES: *Plain sugar.* Flavor with ground cardamom only, or sprinkle a few seed over each cooky before baking.

FRUITS: *Apples, baked.* Sprinkle with ground cardamom instead of cinnamon.

GELATINE: *Coffee.* Flavor with ½ teaspoon ground cardamom.

HONEY: *Clover-blossom, orange-flower.* Blend in ½ teaspoon ground cardamom with ½ pint honey.

JELLIES: *Grape.* See also chapter on Herb Jellies.

SALADS: *Fruits,* especially *grapefruit* and *oranges.* See recipe for Cardamom Fruit Salad.

SOUPS: *Pea, green.* Flavor purée of green pea soup with ¼ teaspoon ground cardamom.

WINES: *Spiced hot wines.* Blend ¼ teaspoon cardamom with other sweet spices before serving.

For 4 servings use approximately:

¼ to 1 teaspoon ground seed.
½ to 2 teaspoons whole seed.

Cardamom Fruit Salad with Cardamom Sauce

TIME: 30 minutes

1 large banana   *½ tsp. cardamom seed, whole*
1 large grapefruit   *1 large orange*
1 large apple   *Juice of 1 lemon*

Peel and cut banana in half crosswise, then slice lengthwise; peel and section the grapefruit; peel and slice orange and apple crosswise, forming rings; remove center seed and pulp. Pour lemon juice over banana and apple slices to prevent them turning brown. Place all prepared fruit in covered dish; sprinkle lightly with cardamom seed. Chill fruit in refrigerator while sauce is being prepared.

Cardamom Sauce

½ cup water   *6 large mint leaves*
½ cup clover honey   *¼ tsp. salt*
¼ tsp. ground cardamom   *½ cup black muscat wine or*
Lettuce leaves   *heavy port wine*

Blend water, honey, and cardamom in small saucepan; place mixture over low flame. Simmer 5 minutes, stirring constantly; add salt; add mint leaves. Simmer 2 minutes. Remove from flame. Allow sauce to cool at room temperature.

When ready to serve, add wine and 2 tablespoons liquid from chilled fruits to make 1½ cups sauce; stir well. Arrange chilled fruit rings and slices over crisp lettuce leaves placed on salad plates. Pour Cardamom Sauce over salad. Serves 4 generously.

Peter's Swedish Gloegg

TIME: 45 minutes

1 bottle heavy port wine   *12 whole cloves*
1 bottle claret wine   *½ lb. blanched almonds*
1 tbs. dried orange peel   *½ lb. raisins*
1 cinnamon stick, 4 ins.   *½ lb. lump sugar*
10 whole cardamom seed   *1 pt. brandy*

Pour the port wine and claret into large, heavy saucepan.

Crush slightly the orange peel, cinnamon stick, cardamom seed, and cloves; tie loosely in small square of cheesecloth. Add seasoning to blended wines in saucepan; bring to boil over low flame. Simmer gently 15 minutes.

Meanwhile blanch almonds by plunging into boiling water; allow to stand 5 minutes; plunge in cold water to rub off skins; dry almonds in slow oven 5 minutes. Add blanched almonds and raisins to hot wines. Simmer gently 15 minutes. Remove saucepan from flame; place wire grill over top; spread sugar on grill; gradually pour brandy over sugar. Light sugar with match; brandy will blaze up and melt all sugar. Remove grill; extinguish blazing brandy by covering saucepan. Serve piping hot with few almonds and raisins in each glass. After first serving remove bag of spices. Yield: 2 quarts.

Swedish Cardamom Coffee Braid   TIME: Variable

1 pt. milk	*7½ cups sifted flour*
1 cake yeast	*1 tbs. butter, extra*
1 cup sugar	*1 egg yolk, beaten*
¼ cup butter	*½ tsp. cold water*
1½ tsp. salt	*½ cup cinnamon sugar*
20 cardamom seed, pounded	
fine	

Scald milk in top section double boiler placed over lower section half filled with boiling water. Remove from flame. Pour off ½ cup of the milk. Allow it to cool to lukewarm. Soften yeast cake by crumbling it and adding to lukewarm milk. To the remaining hot milk add sugar, butter, salt, and cardamom seed. Allow to cool, then blend in the softened yeast.

Sift flour in large, shallow mixing bowl; gradually stir in the liquid; mix well, preparing a firm dough. Knead dough on lightly floured board 15 minutes, or until light and dough springs back when pressed with fingers. Arrange dough in large greased bowl; grease top of dough with butter; cover with towel. Allow to stand in warm place 2 hours, or until dough is double in bulk.

Dough may be divided if desired. Use one half for coffee braid, other half for fancy rolls.

For braid: Cut half dough into 3 pieces of uniform size; roll between palms of hands until even and smooth, then braid.

Arrange in greased pan; cover. Stand in warm place 1 hour, or until dough has doubled in bulk. Brush with egg yolk beaten with ½ tablespoon cold water. Sprinkle with cinnamon-sugar made by blending ½ cup sugar with 1 teaspoon ground cinnamon. Bake in moderate oven (350° F.) 45 minutes.

For fancy rolls: Break off small pieces of dough; roll between palms of hands; shape into crescents, knots, or curls. Follow recipe as for braid. Add chopped nuts to top if desired. Bake in moderate oven (350° F.) 20 to 25 minutes, or until golden brown.

CELERY SEED, *Apium graveolens*

Ground in 1¼ ounce containers at groceries and markets; also in bulk from herb dealers.

Whole in ½ to 1½ ounce containers at groceries and markets; also in bulk from herb dealers.

See also Celery.

Celery seed are the dried fruits of the celery plant, a biennial cultivated in France, Great Britain, Holland, India, and the United States. The best-quality seed is said to be that which is imported from France.

The color of the tiny mericarps is light brown with 5 little ridges that are a paler brown. Each seed is less than ⅟₁₆ inch long and when viewed through a microscope its ridges seem very prominent.

Using: Celery seed may be used in all the ways in which fresh celery is used. The seed add the sweetly aromatic flavor of the fresh herb plus a slight, natural bitterness of the seed covering when placed in pastries or used to flavor pot roasts, salad dressings, salads, sauces, soups, stews, and sandwich spreads. These tiny seed are always an important ingredient in prepared pickling spices; when ground the celery seed powder is made into celery salt and is added to many of the curry blends. Fish stews, scrambled eggs, stew tomatoes, fish, and shellfish salads are all improved by the use of celery seed. See also chapters on Herb Dressings and Herb Salts.

APPETIZERS: *Canapés, cheese, fish, shellfish.* Sprinkle lightly with celery seed just before serving.

BREAD AND ROLLS: *Biscuits, salty bread.* One teaspoon celery seed may be added to dough mixture instead of caraway seed; also sprinkle dough lightly with seed before baking.

COCKTAILS: *Tomato-juice, mixed-vegetable juice.* Add ⅛ teaspoon seed to each serving.

EGGS: *Scrambled.* Add 1 teaspoon seed to 4 eggs before cooking.

FISH: *Chowders, stews.* Add ½ teaspoon before cooking.

MEATS: *Loaf, stews, stuffings.* Add ½ teaspoon seed to other ingredients.

Pot Roast: Veal. See recipe Spicy Roast of Veal.

PASTRY: See recipe for Celery Seed Sticks.

PICKLES: *Sweet.* Add 1 teaspoon seed to each quart pickles. See Favorite Recipes.

SALAD DRESSINGS: See Herb Salad Dressings.

SALADS: *Aspic.* Add 1 teaspoon seed when preparing gelatine.

Fish, potato, vegetables, especially *cabbage.* Add 1 teaspoon seed to dressing.

Fruits. Add ¼ teaspoon seed to favorite dressing and serve.

SANDWICH SPREADS: *Cream cheese, minced ham, peanut butter.* Use ½ teaspoon seed in mixture for 6 sandwiches.

VEGETABLES: *Tomatoes, stewed.* Add ½ teaspoon seed to tomatoes before cooking.

For 4 servings use approximately:

⅛ to ½ teaspoon ground seed.
¼ to 1 teaspoon whole seed as flavoring.
1 teaspoon to ½ cup whole seed in pickles.

Savory Celery Seed Sticks   TIME: 30 minutes

1½ cups flour	*½ tsp. celery seed*
½ tsp. celery salt	*½ cup grated cheddar cheese*
½ cup butter	*3 tbs. cold water, about*
2 tbs. butter, extra	*1 tsp. celery seed, extra*

Blend flour and celery salt on mixing board. Cut in butter with tips of fingers or pastry blender; add celery seed and grated cheese; mix gently but well; add sufficient water to hold mixture together. When smooth, gently pat or roll into a piece from ¼ to ½ inch thick. Cut pastry into finger strips; arrange on cooky sheet.

Melt 2 tablespoons butter over low flame; quickly stir in celery seed. Remove from heat. While still warm, brush seed mixture over strips of pastry. Bake in preheated hot oven (450° F.) 15 minutes. Sprinkle with extra grated cheese if desired. Serve piping hot. Approximate yield: 24 sticks.

Spicy Roast of Veal   TIME: 2½ to 3 hours

5 lbs. veal rump	*2 medium-sized onions,*
4 tbs. bacon fat or oil	* minced*
3 tbs. flour	*1 tbs. minced fresh parsley*
1 tbs. dry mustard	*½ cup red wine vinegar*
1½ tsp. salt	*12 small potatoes*
¼ tsp. white pepper	*12 small carrots*
½ tsp. ground marjoram	*ᵀresh parsley sprigs, extra*
2 tsp. celery seed	

Purchase veal in one piece. Spread 1 tablespoon bacon fat or oil over meat.

Blend well flour, mustard, salt, pepper, and marjoram on mixing board. Roll veal in seasoned flour.

Melt other 3 tablespoons bacon fat in heavy roasting pan over high flame; add seasoned veal; brown quickly on all sides. Remove from flame. Add celery seed, onions, parsley, and wine vinegar. Roast in preheated slow oven (300° F.) 2 hours. Add carrots and potatoes. Roast ½ hour longer, or until meat thermometer registers 170° to 180° F. and vegetables are done.

If more liquid is desired, baste occasionally with prepared Herb Baste or hot water. Serve piping hot with pan juices. Garnish with parsley sprigs. Serves 6 to 8 generously.

CORIANDER SEED, *Coriandum sativum*

Ground in ½ to 1 ounce containers at groceries and markets; also from herb dealers.

Whole in 1¼ ounce containers at groceries and markets; also in bulk from herb dealers.

Coriander seed is the dried fruit of a delicate, lacy-looking annual herb called coriander. It is native to Europe and Asia, and is cultivated in all the European Mediterranean countries. Coriander plantations are found all along the coast of northern Africa as well as in Asia Minor, England, Holland, India,

South America, and to a limited degree in the United States. Kentucky supplies most of the American coriander seed.

It is the dried seed which has the delightfully aromatic aroma and taste. The minute, little yellowish-brown globes vary in size from ⅛ to ¼ inch in diameter, and under a microscope show 4 straight primary ridges and 5 less wavy secondary ridges. When the seed is crushed or ground, its warm flavor is like a mixture of lemon peel and sage.

Using: The ground coriander seed is used extensively for flavoring cookies, candies, and some soups. Danish pastries and gingerbreads practically always contain ground coriander. Certain liqueurs and gins are flavored with coriander. The early Romans used ground coriander to flavor *polenta,* a cornmeal mixture often served with sausages, and some Italian families today use it. Many blended spices, condiments, and curries contain coriander. Both the ground and, sometimes, the whole seed are used in the manufacture of sausages and frankfurters. Stuffings for wild game and poultry may be seasoned with coriander and sage.

A whole coriander seed freshly crushed in a demitasse gives coffee a new and exciting taste. And how many of us as youngsters took pennies to the confectionery shop to buy gaily-colored "candy marbles"? Then, as the last vestige of the candy ball disappeared, there was a sweetly delicious coriander seed left on the tongue ready to be bitten into with relish and carefully chewed to tasty bits with great glee. The English merely sugar-coat the seeds and call them "comfits," or Scotch candy. See also Anise Seed, Fennel Seed, recipe Curry Blend English Style, and recipe Spice Blend *Italiana.*

BREAD AND ROLLS: *Biscuits, buns. Sweet* biscuits and buns may be flavored with ¼ teaspoon ground coriander.

CAKES AND COOKIES: *Gingerbread* and *cookies.* ¼ teaspoon ground coriander blends well with other spices. See also Serbian Holiday Diamonds.

CHEESES: *Cheddar, cream.* As sweet canapé, flavor ¼ pound cheese with ¼ teaspoon ground coriander.

COFFEE: *Demitasse.* Crush 1 coriander seed in bottom of each cup.

FRUITS: *Apples, pears, baked, sauce, stewed.* Use ¼ teaspoon ground coriander; flavor before cooking.

MEATS: *Ham, pork roast.* Rub surface of ham and pork lightly with ground coriander and sage before roasting.

PICKLES: *Mixed, sweet.* Add ½ teaspoon coriander seed for
each ½ pint pickles.

PUDDINGS: *Rice, tapioca.* Sprinkle with ground coriander
instead of cinnamon.

SALAD: *Mixed-green.* Use ½ teaspoon coriander seed; toss
with ingredients.

SOUPS: *Beef, mutton.* Add ⅛ teaspoon ground coriander
before cooking.

Pea, cream of. Sprinkle each portion with ground coriander just before serving.

For 4 servings use approximately:

⅛ to ¼ teaspoon ground seed.
¼ to 1 teaspoon whole seed.

Serbian Holiday Diamonds   TIME: 1 hour
Allow to stand overnight
As prepared in Belgrade, Yugoslavia.

2 cups sugar	*2 tsp. ground cinnamon*
4 eggs, well beaten	*1 tsp. ground cloves*
½ lb. blanched almonds	*½ cup citron, chopped*
3 cups flour (about)	*2 tbs. melted butter*
¼ tsp. ground coriander	

Blend sugar and eggs in large mixing bowl; stir until smooth
and creamy, or about 30 minutes.

Blanch almonds by covering with boiling water for 5 minutes then plunging into cold water; skins rub off easily. Mince
almonds with sharp knife; add almonds to sugar-and-egg mixture; gradually stir in coriander, cinnamon, cloves, and citron;
mix well; gradually stir in sufficient flour to make soft dough,
which will be firm enough to roll as one rolls piecrust. Place
dough on lightly floured board; roll out ¾ inch thick; cut into
diamond shapes; arrange on board; cover with towel. Allow
to stand overnight at room temperature.

The next day arrange diamonds in shallow bread pan; brush
tops with melted butter. Bake in preheated moderate oven
(350° F.) 25 minutes. While still lukewarm, spread diamonds
with frosting made by blending 1 cup confectioners' sugar with
¼ teaspoon almond extract and 2 tablespoons milk. Yield:
12 to 14 diamonds.

CUMIN SEED or COMINO, *Cuminum cyminum*

Ground in ½ to 1 ounce containers at groceries and markets; also from herb dealers.

Whole in 1½ ounce containers at groceries and markets; also from herb dealers.

Wild in Egypt, Hindustan, and Syria.

Cumin seed is the dried fruit of the small annual herb cumin, which belongs to the parsley, *Umbelliferae,* family. The cumin seed is often simply called *comino* in many European countries and throughout Mexico.

This delicate and fragile little plant is native to Egypt, western Asia, and the Mediterranean countries. It is grown extensively in Sicily and on the small island of Malta south of Sicily in the Mediterranean Sea; also all along the west coast of Africa, in Arabia, China, India, Iran, and Palestine.

The minute seed is a yellowish brown and is from ⅛ to ¼ inch long. It is oval, somewhat pointed like the caraway seed, and under the microscope its 9 hairy ridges are clearly visible. Its strong, warm, slightly bitter taste is much like the caraway and its aroma equally aromatic.

Using: Breads, soups, sausages, cheeses, and many meat and rice dishes are flavored with cumin. In India the seed is used as a condiment; and the ground seed is a necessary ingredient in curry powder, chili powder, blended Hindu spices, pickles, and chutneys. In Holland there is a special Edam cheese which is always flavored with cumin seed. When mixed with a soft cheddar, cottage, or cream cheese, the result is delicious.

Cumin by itself has a rather strong flavor and should be used sparingly at first. In prepared seasonings and pickling spices the warm flavor of cumin adds greatly to the tastiness of the blended product. The whole seeds are used to a great extent in oriental cookery to flavor fish, game, meats, poultry, sauces, spiced vinegars, stews, and vegetables. Because of cumin's resemblance to caraway in both looks and flavor it is often used instead of caraway in Germany. In Mexico, practically all the national dishes, such as Chili Con Carne and Hot Tamales, are seasoned with comino. See also Caraway Seed.

APPETIZERS: *Cheddar, cottage, cream cheeses.* Blend in ½ teaspoon cumin seed with each ¼ pound cheese. Use as canapé spread or sandwich filling.

BREAD: *Rye, salty.* Substitute cumin seed for caraway seed, using but half the amount suggested for caraway in familiar recipes.

COOKIES: *Plain sugar.* Sprinkle top with cumin seed before baking.

CHEESES: *Cheddar, cottage, cream, Edam.* Sprinkle few cumin seed over top of each serving.

EGGS: *Deviled.* Blend in ⅛ teaspoon ground cumin in other ingredients; mix with hard-boiled yolks.

MEATS: *Meat loaf,* Mexican dishes, such as Chili Con Carne and Hot Tamales.

PIES: *Fruit.* Add ¼ teaspoon ground cumin to fruit pies with other spices.

VEGETABLES: *Cabbage, rice, sauerkraut.* Add ½ teaspoon cumin seed to water in which vegetable is cooked. Seed adheres to vegetable and is eaten with it.

For 4 servings use approximately:

⅛ to ½ teaspoon ground cumin.
½ to 2 teaspoons whole seed.

DILL SEED, *Anethum graveolens*

Ground in ½ to 1 ounce containers at groceries and mar-kets; also from herb dealers.
Whole in ½ to 2 ounce containers at groceries and markets; also in bulk from herb dealers.
See also Dill Herb.

Dill seed is the dried fruit of the dill herb, an annual, which belongs to the parsley, *Umbelliferae,* family.

Perhaps many of us think of pickles at the mere mention of dill. But these minute, warmly aromatic seed of the dill have been used as a condiment all over the world for countless centuries. Sold in the market places in India, the natives chew the tiny, light-brown oval seed as a sweetmeat as our colonial ancestors did also.

It takes more than 11,000 separate mericarps to make even an ounce of seed. These infinitesimal pieces of fruit are less than ⅓ inch long and scarcely ⅛ inch wide. Many of them are often smaller and may measure only 1/16 inch in width.

The microscope discloses the seed as concave on the inner surface and convex and ridged on the dorsal surface.

The seed has a wonderfully warm, aromatic scent and tastes somewhat sharp, as does caraway. It has many flavoring uses in cookery and is one of the most satisfactory of all the spices, for *it will add new flavor to most foods from an appetizer to an apple pie.*

Using: The whole seed will give an aromatic taste to certain strong vegetables, such as cabbage and turnips, and it will make many an everyday soup far more tasty than you can possibly imagine until you have tried it out. Dill seed is also a delectable addition to many vegetable salads, especially potato, cabbage, and cucumber. Broiled or boiled fish or a lamb stew with dill seed is a flavor to be remembered for its unusual deliciousness.

The ground seed also may be used instead of the whole in pickling and in cooking the more strongly scented vegetables such as turnips and cabbage. Some cooks prefer the ground seed when using it in cooking fish and mollusks, or when preparing herb butters and sauces. But *interchanging the whole seed and the ground is largely a matter of personal taste and preference,* for both of them are equally delightful. The manufacturers of sausages and bologna prefer the ground dill to the whole seed largely because it blends more easily. See also chapters on Herb Butters and Herb Vinegars.

APPETIZERS: *Cheese, cottage, cream; fish cocktails.* Lightly sprinkle each serving with dill seed to taste.

BUTTER: See chapter on Herb Butters.

CHEESES: *Cheddar, cottage, cream.* Blend 1 teaspoon crushed seed with ¼ pound cheese. Use as canapé and sandwich spread.

FISH: *Halibut, salmon, all fat fish, boiled.* Use ½ teaspoon ground dill in water in which fish is boiled.

MEAT: *Lamb chops, broiled.* Lightly sprinkle chops with whole seed before broiling.

Lamb stew. Add ½ teaspoon seed to 3 pounds meat before cooking.

PIE: *Apple.* Lightly sprinkle seed over fruit before baking.

POULTRY: *Chicken, creamed.* Add ½ teaspoon seed to cream sauce.

SALADS: *Avocado, cabbage, cucumber, potato* with French Dressing. Add ¼ teaspoon seed to dressing before serving.

SOUPS: *Navy bean, beet, tomato, cream of.* Flavor sparingly with ground or whole seed just before serving.

VEGETABLES: *Beets, cabbage, cauliflower, sauerkraut, string beans, turnips.* Add 1 to 2 teaspoons seed to vegetable while cooking; seed adheres to vegetable and is eaten with it.

For 4 servings use approximately:

⅛ to ½ teaspoon ground seed.
¼ to 2 teaspoons whole seed.

Bernese Oberland Dill Potato Soup   TIME: 1¼ hours

This soup of the Bernese Oberland is served every Saturday night in that quaint and attractive little Swiss village of Lauterbrunnen, situated in the heart of the Oberland at the foot of the majestic Jungfrau in the Wengern Alp. *Wahrschaffe Berner Kartoffel Suppe* is as much a tradition there as baked beans and brown bread are in Boston.

1 tbs. butter
3 tsp. flour
1 medium-sized onion,
    minced
4 large potatoes, cubed
2 tsp. minced parsley
1 leek, minced
6 cups water

½ tsp. dill seed or
1 tsp. dried dill, crushed, or
1 small sprig fresh dill
1 stalk celery, minced
1 tsp. salt
⅛ tsp. white pepper
Paprika

Melt butter in large, heavy saucepan over medium flame; add onion; brown lightly 3 minutes; stir constantly; add flour; stir constantly; brown 5 minutes, or until rich brown color. Add all other ingredients except paprika; cover. Simmer gently 45 minutes, or until potatoes are very soft. Remove dill sprig if used. Lower flame. Beat mixture with egg beater until it is a creamy purée. Serve piping hot in preheated soup plates with Emmenthaler (or other Swiss) cheese and glasses of muscat wine. Serves 4.

Ham Dill Seed Spread   TIME: 15 minutes

½ cup minced cooked ham
6 tbs. peanut butter

1 tsp. whole dill seed
⅛ tsp. paprika

Blend ham with peanut butter and dill seed; add paprika; mix well. Use as canapé or sandwich spread. Yield: ⅔ cup.

Any preferred seed may be substituted for dill seed, such as *celery seed, lovage seed, mustard seed,* and *poppy seed.* Prepare spread as suggested in recipe.

FENNEL SEED, *Foeniculum vulgare,* var. *dulce*

> Ground in ½ ounce containers at groceries and markets; also from herb dealers.
> Whole in ½ ounce to 1½ ounce containers at groceries and markets; also in bulk from herb dealers.
> See also Fennel or Sweet Fennel.

Fennel seed is the nearly ripe, dried fruit of the annual or perennial herb called fennel or sweet fennel: the *Foeniculum vulgare,* var. *dulce.*

The whole fennel seed is a light chartreuse color, but a light brown when ground. Not more than ¼ inch long, the oblong seed looks something like the caraway. It has 5 tiny ridges along its oval side but is less curved than the caraway. Many fennel seed have a short piece of stem attached to them.

Though commercially cultivated in California and many of our eastern and southern states, the majority of fennel seed used in America is imported from France, Germany, India, and Russia. The seed is also widely cultivated in Italy, Japan, Rumania, and Syria.

Fennel seed has a sweet, agreeable, aromatic taste like the fresh leaves of the fennel herb; and the flavor resembles licorice or anise. Our Puritan ancestors were so fond of nibbling this tasty seed in church that it was given the nickname of "Meetin' Seed."

Using: Today the seed is increasingly popular because of the appetizing quality which it imparts to sweet pickles, pastries, fish, and meats. The Italians cover their crusty bread and rolls with fennel seed, and use fennel seed in cakes and cookies. The resulting combination of the flavors of the baked flour and the seed is unusually good. The Italian cooks also use either ground or whole fennel seed when roasting pork, and the warm flavor of the fennel proves an aromatic seasoning of rare deliciousness.

> BREAD AND ROLLS: Sprinkle tops with seed before baking; use generously.

CAKES AND COOKIES: See recipe for Anise Squares. Prepare Fennel Seed Squares in same way, using fennel seed instead of anise seed.

CHEESE: *Bel Paese* (mild, delicate Italian cheese). Serve cheese with light sprinkling of seed.

EGGS: *Omelet, jelly.* Garnish with seed just before serving.

FISH: *Cod, halibut, all lean fish, boiled.* Add ¼ teaspoon seed to water in which fish is boiled.

FRUITS: *Apple, baked; pie.* Sprinkle fruit with seed before baking.

MEATS: *Beef, braised* or *stewed.* Add ½ teaspoon seed to liquid before cooking.

Lamb, mutton, pork, roasted. Rub meat with ½ to 1 teaspoon ground fennel seed before putting in oven.

SALADS: *Fish, mixed-green, shellfish.* Blend ½ teaspoon seed with dressing.

SHELLFISH: *Hard-shell crab, shrimps.* Add 12 or more seed to water in which shellfish is boiled.

VEGETABLES: *Lentils, sauerkraut.* Add ½ teaspoon seed to vegetable while cooking.

For 4 servings use approximately:

½ to 1 teaspoon ground fennel seed.
¼ teaspoon to 2 tablespoons whole seed.

JUNIPER BERRIES, *Juniperus communis*

Whole at some drugstores; also in bulk at herb dealers.

Wild late in the autumn, on dry, sterile hills from Canada south to New Jersey, west to Nebraska, and in the Rocky Mountains south to New Mexico; also in Central America, northern Asia, and Europe.

Juniper berries are the dried ripe fruit of a small evergreen bush or tree, the COMMON JUNIPER, which grows wild in a large part of the Northern Hemisphere.

The round berry-like fruit usually ripens in October. Each dark purple fruit contains 3 bony seeds embedded in a brownish pulp. When dried, these seeds grow much darker and are almost perfect little globes about ⅛ inch in diameter. The taste of the dried seed is slightly bittersweet, and the aroma is fragrant and spicy.

Using: Juniper berries are used in certain blends of whole kitchen spices which are prepared for use in pickling meats and game, especially beef and venison. The Laplanders make an herb tea of the juniper berries. In Sweden a conserve is prepared and served with cold meats. In German cookery the juniper berry is sometimes used to give a different flavor to sauerkraut instead of caraway. Usually 4 or 5 berries will suffice.

Perhaps the uses best known to many of us are those connected with the manufacture of gins, juniper-berry liqueurs, and bitters. But the whole berry may also be used sparingly when a slightly bitter, pungently spiced sauce is served with beef and game. When the juniper berries are not available, angelica seed are sometimes used as a substitute. The berries, added to the liquid in which grouse and wild duck are partially cooked, take away the strong, gamy taste to which some of us object.

Some cooks before roasting game, such as wild duck and grouse, prefer to parboil it in a good beef stock to which lemon, bay leaves, and juniper berries have been added. The liquid is then strained and saved for use in preparing a pan gravy from the roast. Giblets and burgundy or port wine are added, if desired, and the final results are temptingly different. The berries add a piquant flavor to meat and game stews also. See recipe for Savory Wild Duck.

GAME: *Wild duck, pheasant, quail, roasted.* Add 4 berries to liquid in which game is parboiled before roasting; or add berries to liquid in bottom of roasting pan.

MEATS: *Braised* or *pot roast of beef* or *lamb.* Four or 5 berries in the pot will cut any excessive grease and add an intriguing flavor to the meat.

POULTRY: *Duck, goose.* Add 4 to 6 berries to juice in roasting pan. Remove berries before making gravy.

SAUCES: *Spiced sauces* served *with beef* and *game.* Season sauce with 3 or 4 berries. Remove berries before serving.

SOUPS AND STEWS: *Lamb* and *poultry broth, beef stew.* Add 2 or 3 berries to ingredients. Remove berries before serving.

VINEGARS: Add 4 to 8 berries to *vinegars used for marinating* and *pickling beef* and *venison.*

WINES: *Add* 4 to 8 berries *to wine in which beef, game,* and *venison are marinated.* See also Juniper-berry Baste and Marinade.

For 4 servings use approximately:

4 to 6 berries. Always use sparingly.

Savory Wild Duck   TIME: 1 hour

2 canvasback ducks	1 small onion, sliced
or 1 duck (5 lbs.)	⅛ tsp. mace
2 cups beef stock, hot	6 peppercorns
Boiling water	1½ cups burgundy or claret
1½ tsp. salt	4 tbs. butter
1 bay leaf	6 egg yolks, beaten
¼ tsp. marjoram	¼ tsp. celery salt
¼ tsp. rosemary	⅛ tsp. white pepper
¼ tsp. thyme	Buttered toast
6 juniper berries	

Carefully singe and wipe outside of duck; draw and wipe inside; cut into serving pieces. (As a rule only the breast of canvasback is eaten.) Arrange duck pieces in heavy pan; cover with boiling beef stock; add water if necessary; add salt. Tie loosely in cheesecloth the bay leaf, marjoram, rosemary, thyme, juniper berries, onion, mace, and peppercorns; add to sauce; add 1 cup burgundy. Bring to boil over medium flame; lower flame; cover. Simmer gently 40 minutes, or until tender. Remove duck pieces to preheated hot platter; keep hot over steam. Remove spice bag.

Quickly cream butter with ½ cup burgundy and beaten egg yolks in mixing bowl; add mixture to stock in which duck was cooked. Taste; add ¼ teaspoon celery salt or more to taste; add white pepper. Heat sauce thoroughly. Pour piping hot sauce over duck. Serve duck with sauce over ½ slice buttered toast placed on preheated hot plates. Serves 4.

LOVAGE SEED, *Levisticum officinale*

Ground in ¼ ounce containers and in bulk from some herb dealers.

Whole in 1¼ ounce containers at fancy groceries and markets; also in bulk from herb dealers.

See also Lovage.

Lovage seed is the dried fruit of the lovage plant. The seed grow in pairs and look very much like the caraway seed. They are slightly curved and ribbed on the outer side and quite flat and smooth on the inner.

In northwestern Italy the lovage seed is sometimes used instead of fennel and anise seed because of its rather sweet and extremely pleasant taste. The Greeks and Romans chewed the aromatic seed and believed it aided digestion.

When the plant was brought to New England our early colonists also learned to chew the seed. Confectionery and cordials were flavored with it.

Using: Lovage seed may be used instead of celery seed when a slightly sweeter effect is desired. When spiced cookies are flavored with the seed, the taste is deliciously different and lifts the cookies into a class quite above the ordinary.

Stewed beef, mutton, and game, meat pies and braised or roasted pork are delicately flavored and definitely more appetizing when lovage seed have been added to the liquid or a few seed have been scattered over a roast before placing it in the oven. See also Celery Seed.

CAKES AND COOKIES: Sprinkle over top as garnish or include as ingredient, as for Caraway Cookies.

GAME: *Hare, rabbit, venison, stew.* Tie ½ teaspoon seed in cheesecloth bag; place in stew while cooking. Remove before serving.

MEAT PIES: *Beef, lamb, mutton, veal.* Use ¼ teaspoon seed to each pound of meat. *Include in all other meat and poultry pies* in which sweet vegetables are also used.

MEATS: *Beef, lamb, mutton, stew.* Tie ½ teaspoon seed in cheesecloth bag; place in stew while cooking. Remove before serving.

Pork, braised or *roasted.* Sprinkle meat with 1 teaspoon seed instead of sage or other herbs.

SALADS: *Fruit, mixed.* Blend ½ teaspoon whole seed with 1 cup favorite sweet salad dressing.

For 4 servings use approximately:

⅛ to ¼ teaspoon ground seed.
½ to 2 teaspoons whole seed.

Lovage Cordial   TIME: 30 minutes; Age 2 months

1 oz. lovage seed   *4 ozs. sugar*
1 pt. brandy

Use only freshly harvested seed and the best quality brandy. Crush seed lightly in a mortar with pestle, or tie in clean muslin cloth and crush with wooden mallet; add crushed seed to brandy; add sugar; stir well; seal tightly. Place in cool, dark place 2 months; shake occasionally. Filter cordial through filter paper; recork. Serve at room temperature, as desired. Yield: 1 pint.

MUSTARD SEED, *Brassica sinapis*

Whole in 1½ ounce containers at groceries and markets; also in bulk from drugstores and herb dealers.
See also Dry Mustard and Mustard Plant.

The seed of the various kinds of *Brassica* differ only slightly in size. In color they range from the pale yellow of the WHITE MUSTARD SEED, *Sinapis alba,* to the dark reddish brown of the BLACK MUSTARD SEED, *Brassica nigra.*

The tiny seed of the *white* variety is from ³⁄₆₄ to ³⁄₃₂ inch in diameter; and some patient soul counted more than 5,000 of these tiny little globes in a single ounce. The seed is round and clean, with tiny pit marks showing on the surface when it is seen through a microscope. There is no aroma whatsoever to the whole seed. However, when it is crushed and the resulting powder or flour mixed with water, its taste is at once pungent, sharp, and piercing. When one smells the pure, newly blended paste, the result is often so irritating that tears come to the eyes.

The *black* mustard seed is of the same appearance as the white but is considerably smaller. It takes more than 12,000 of these tiny seeds to make an ounce. The flour from this crushed seed is more pungent than that of the white.

California and Montana produce good crops of mustard seed but not enough to supply our demand. The finest grade of seed still comes from England and Holland.

Using: Other than being crushed into flour for use in prepared mustards and condiments, the whole seed are useful in pickling and preserving. Sometimes they are used in preserving meats and in the manufacture of sausage. The tiny seed make a most attractive and unusual garnish for vegetable salads and add real flavor to boiled cabbage and sauerkraut when used instead of dill or caraway seed. Many of the popular pickle recipes call for mustard seed, especially those for sweet mustard pickles. They are also one of the important ingredients used in pickling white onions. See also Caraway Seed, Condiments, and Dill Seed.

PICKLES: *Cucumber, onion, tomato.* Amounts vary with recipe. See Tiny Pickled Onions.

SALADS: *Mixed-green vegetables.* Blend in ½ to 1 teaspoon seed with vegetables. See recipe Herb Seed Coleslaw.

VEGETABLES: *Beets, boiled.* Sprinkle hot beets lightly with a few seed just before serving.

Cabbage, sauerkraut. Use 1 teaspoon seed; boil with the vegetable.

For 4 servings use approximately:

⅛ to 1 teaspoon seed, according to pungency preferred.

Herb Seed Coleslaw   TIME: 20 minutes; Chill 15 minutes

3 cups shredded cabbage   *1 tsp. mustard seed*
¼ tsp. salt   *1 tsp. celery seed*
½ tsp. onion salt   *6 tbs. olive oil*
½ tsp. celery salt   *2 tbs. white wine vinegar*
¼ tsp. white pepper   *½ green pepper, chopped*
1 tbs. sugar   *½ sweet red pepper, chopped*

Blend all seasonings, beginning with ½ teaspoon salt, in large bowl. When well blended, add cabbage, green pepper, and sweet red pepper; mix well with fork. Cover bowl. Place in refrigerator to chill 15 minutes. Garnish with fresh herb, such as chervil, parsley, or water cress just before serving. Serves 4 to 6.

Tiny Pickled Onions   TIME: 2 hours; Marinate 24 hours

8 pts. tiny white onions   *3 tbs. white peppercorns*
2 pts. distilled vinegar   *3 tbs. whole allspice*
¼ cup sugar   *1 sweet red pepper*
3 tbs. white mustard seed

BRINE:

1 cup salt   *3 pts. boiling water*

Select tiny, firm onions. Peel carefully. Set aside. Wash red pepper; cut in half, remove seeds; chop or cut pepper into very small, thin strips about an inch long. Place onions and pepper in heavy kettle.

Blend salt and boiling hot water to make brine; pour boiling brine over onions and pepper. Allow to stand 24 hours at room temperature. Drain; pour fresh cold water over onions and red pepper. Allow to stand 1 hour. Drain well.

Pour vinegar into saucepan placed over medium flame; add sugar, mustard seed, peppercorns, and allspice. Boil mixture 1 minute, stirring well.

Pack onions and few pepper strips in hot, sterilized jars. Cover onions with boiling liquid; seal jar carefully. Allow to cool at room temperature. Store in cool, dark place 2 weeks before using. Approximate yield: 6 pints.

Use as *condiment, hors d'oeuvre, and in Gibson* (gin) *cocktails.*

NASTURTIUM SEED. See NASTURTIUM

POPPY SEED, *Papaver rhoeas*

Ground in ½ or 1 ounce containers at groceries and markets; also from herb dealers.

Whole in ½ ounce to 1½ ounce containers at groceries and markets; also from herb dealers.

Poppy seed is the dried seed of an annual plant which belongs to the poppy, *Papaveraceae,* family, of which there are more than 200 species.

Though the poppies are native to Asia, the plant is widely cultivated in Austria, Canada, England, France, Germany, Holland, Hungary, India, Poland, Turkey, and the United States. *The beautiful blue commercial seed has no narcotic properties.* (Opium is obtained from the shell of the seed pod of the opium poppy *Papaver somniferum*).

The seed grown in India is usually white and is just as good as the blue seed, but since the trade prefers the blue seed, the white is sometimes colored artificially. Actually the seed is not blue but rather slate-colored. It appears round, but when examined under a microscope it is really kidney-shaped and the surface is covered with a network of tiny ridges. It is less than $\frac{3}{64}$ inch in size, and there are about 52,000 seed in a single ounce.

Using: The whole seed are used in fancy cakes and pastries; and many foods are made more delicious by the addition of the nutty, oily flavor of these tiny little globes of goodness. Eggs, salads, vegetables, and even piecrusts have an unusual taste appeal when flavored with the rich tastiness of the fragrant seed. Slavic homemakers use ground poppy seed in spiced breads and cakes. They often make a wonderful cake filling with poppy seed, milk, nuts, sugar, and citron. Hungarian strudel nearly always have a generous amount of poppy seed in the filling. An interesting jam may be made by blending strained honey and poppy seed. See also Anise Seed, Caraway Seed, Herb Butters, and Herb Honeys.

CAKES AND COOKIES: *Plain, vanilla.* Heat 1 to 2 tablespoons seed in pan over a low flame for 2 minutes. Top cakes and cookies with warm seed before baking.

CANAPÉS: *Cream cheese, potato chips,* et cetera. Dab canapé with mayonnaise; sprinkle lightly with seed. Serve at once.

FILLING FOR CAKES: *Plain cake, layer.* See recipe for Poppy-seed Filling.

JAM: *Honey.* Add 1 tablespoon seed to 1 pint strained honey; blend well. Use as desired on breads and coffee-cakes.

SALADS: *Fruits, canned* or *raw.* Sprinkle lightly with seed before serving.

SAUCES: See recipe, Poppy-seed Herb Sauces.

VEGETABLES: *All sweet* vegetables, such as *peas, potatoes, turnips,* et cetera. Sprinkle with seed just before serving.

For 4 servings use approximately:

1 tablespoon seed for flavoring.
½ to 1 cup seed for cake fillings.

Poppy-seed Crust   TIME: 20 minutes

2 cups graham cracker   *3 tbs. poppy seeds*
*   crumbs*   *½ cup sugar*
½ cup butter

Crush graham cracker crumbs on mixing board. Cream butter with large spoon in mixing bowl until soft; add sugar and poppy seeds; beat vigorously until mixture is smooth. Add crumbs gradually until all is well blended. Gently but firmly pat mixture onto bottom and sides of a 9-inch piepan. Bake in preheated slow oven (300° F.) 10 minutes, or until a golden brown. Allow to cool at room temperature before filling with fruit or custard. Yield: *1 piecrust* for a 9-inch pan.

Poppy-seed Danish Ring   TIME: Variable

¾ cup scalded milk   *6 tbs. melted butter*
½ tsp. salt   *1 egg*
½ cup sugar   *Poppy Seed Filling*
1 cake compressed yeast,   *6 tbs. butter, extra*
*   crumbled*   *1 beaten egg, extra*
3½ cups enriched flour   *4 tbs. milk, extra*

Pour scalded milk into large mixing bowl; add salt and 1 tablespoon sugar. Allow milk to cool until lukewarm, then add yeast; mix well. Sift in 1½ cups flour; blend well; cover. Let rise in warm place 1 hour, or until light.

Add balance of sugar, melted butter (not hot), and egg; beat vigorously. Gradually sift in enough of remaining flour to make a smooth, firm dough, at the same time keeping it as soft as possible. Turn dough onto floured board; knead 5 to 10 minutes, or until dough is smooth and satiny. Place dough in greased bowl; brush top with melted butter; cover with towel. Let rise in warm place 3 hours, or until very light and double in bulk.

Again turn out on lightly floured board; punch down and knead dough lightly. Place in covered container. Chill in refrigerator 1 hour.

Roll chilled dough into rectangle ½ inch thick on lightly floured board; scatter bits of softened butter evenly over ⅔ of dough surface. Fold unbuttered portion over ⅓ of buttered dough, then fold remainder on top, making 3 layers. Roll out again until 1 inch thick; place on cooky sheet; cover with waxed paper. Chill in refrigerator ½ hour.

Roll out chilled dough and fold in thirds again; repeat. Let stand at room temperature ½ hour. Roll into a square ¼ inch thick. Dough is ready for filling. Spread generously with *Poppy-seed Filling;* roll up like a jelly roll; moisten ends slightly; overlap them and press together to form a ring.

Place ring on greased baking sheet. With sharp knife or scissors cut slanting gashes 2 inches apart almost to the center of ring. Turn slices partly on their sides to form petals. Cover ring with towel. Let rise in warm place 1 hour, or until double in bulk. Brush ring lightly with 1 beaten egg yolk mixed with 4 tablespoons milk. Bake in preheated moderately hot oven (375° F.) 25 to 30 minutes. Remove from oven; cool few moments. While still warm, frost with simple icing made of powdered sugar blended with a little milk to make spreadable consistency.

Sprinkle with 1 cup mixed candied chopped fruits, cherries, citron, and nuts, if desired.

Poppy-seed Filling for Danish Ring

⅓ cup seedless raisins	*⅔ cup milk*
3 tbs. chopped candied orange peel	*1 cup whole poppy seed*
	½ cup sugar
3 tbs. chopped candied citron	*⅓ cup honey*
6 seeded dates	*1½ tbs. butter*

Put fruits through meat grinder. Blend fruits well. Set aside.

Scald milk in small, heavy saucepan; add poppy seed. Bring to boil over medium flame, stirring constantly. Cook gently 3 minutes; add sugar, honey, and butter, stirring constantly. Bring to boil. Cook gently 2 minutes more. Remove from flame. Allow to stand until lukewarm. Stir in mixed candied fruits. Allow to cool. Fill Danish Ring as shown in recipe.

Poppy-seed Cake Slavic Style   TIME: 1½ hours

4 eggs	*1 cup ground poppy seed*
2 tbs. flour	*½ tsp. cinnamon*
2 tbs. sweet cream	*⅛ tsp. salt*
1½ tsp. grated lemon rind	*6 tbs. sugar*
¼ tsp. ground cloves	*1 cup whipped cream*

Break eggs and separate; place yolks in large mixing bowl, whites in a smaller bowl. Beat egg yolks until lemon colored; gradually stir in flour and cream; blend well; stir in lemon rind, cloves, and cinnamon. Beat egg whites with salt until frothy; gradually beat in sugar. Fold whites into egg-yolk mixture; mix gently; lightly fold in poppy seed. When well blended, pour into greased 7-inch tube cake pan. Bake in preheated low oven (300° F.) 45 to 50 minutes. Invert cake pan. Allow to cool thoroughly at room temperature. Slice and serve with whipped cream. Serves 6 to 8.

Dutch Poppy-seed Noodles TIME: 20 minutes

8 ozs. broad noodles
1 tbs. butter
½ cup slivered blanched
*   almonds*
1 tsp. lemon juice

3 tbs. whole poppy seed
¼ tsp. salt
⅛ tsp. cayenne pepper
2 tsp. minced parsley

Cook noodles 10 minutes, or until tender but not soft, in rapidly boiling salted water in large kettle.

While noodles are cooking, prepare sauce. Melt butter in small pan over low flame; add poppy seeds and almonds; toast lightly, stirring constantly; add lemon juice, salt, and cayenne.

Drain noodles well; place in preheated hot serving dish. Pour poppy-seed sauce over noodles. Garnish with minced parsley. Serve piping hot. Serves 6.

SESAME SEED, *Sesamum orientale*

Whole in 1 to 1½ ounce containers at groceries and markets; also in bulk from herb dealers.

Sesame seed is the dried fruit of a beautiful tropical annual herb which belongs to the species known as *Pedaliaceae.* Though native to Asia, the herb is also widely cultivated in many parts of Asia for the delicious, nutty richness of the seed, which resembles the warm flavor of toasted almonds.

Sesame seed is often called the BENE SEED, and in India it is commonly known as TIL. Both in China and India the sesame seed is cultivated on an enormous scale, since it is one of the staple foods; and in China the seed is as valuable for food as the soy bean.

The unhulled seed vary in color from grayish white to black, and there is a fancy grade of unhulled Turkish seed which is a beautiful orange color. When hulled, these infinitesimal, oval seed, with a tiny point at one end, are smooth, slippery, and creamy white in color. The size varies from $\frac{3}{32}$ to about ⅛ inch in length, and more than 12,000 are found in a single ounce.

Using: In many of the oriental countries the macerated seed are made into a paste and spread on bread as butter. Many tons of seed are utilized every year in the manufacture of the rich Jewish candy, *Halvah.* The hulled seed is used more than the unhulled, and the rich nutlike flavor improves the taste of bread, rolls, and cookies. When the sesame seed are toasted in butter and spread over cheese, potatoes, or noodles, the effect is exceedingly delectable. In fact, these tiny seed may be used in all the ways in which almonds and other nuts are used. See also chapter on Herb Butters.

APPETIZERS: *Canapés, soft cheeses, fish.* Sprinkle lightly with whole seed.

BREAD AND ROLLS: *Biscuits, bread, crumpets, scones.* Sprinkle generously with seed before baking.

CAKES AND COOKIES: Use seed instead of other nuts.

CHEESES: *Cheddar, cottage, cream.* Blend 1 teaspoon toasted seed with ¼ pound cheese. Use as canapé or sandwich spread.

GARNISH: For *fish, meat,* and *poultry casserole topping* instead of bread crumbs. Sprinkle generously before placing casserole in oven.

SALADS: *Fruits.* Garnish with 1 to 2 teaspoons seed. *Vegetable, potato.* Sprinkle generously with seed just before serving.

SAUCES: Use instead of other nuts *in all sweet sauces.*

SOUPS: *Cream.* Sprinkle lightly with seed as garnish just before serving.

VEGETABLES: *Potatoes, rice.* Garnish with toasted seed just before serving.

For 4 servings use approximately:

1 teaspoon to 2 tablespoons seed, as suggested.

Mexican Pablano with Sesame Seed   TIME: 1 hour

1 broiling chicken, 4 lbs.	*1 stalk celery, diced*
2 tbs. bacon fat	*2 tsp. salt*
1 large onion, diced	*3 cups water*

Have chicken cleaned and cut into serving pieces. Melt bacon fat in heavy skillet over medium flame; brown chicken quickly in hot fat by turning each piece; add onion, celery, salt, and water; cover; lower flame. Simmer gently 30 minutes.

MEANWHILE PREPARE MOLE SAUCE WITH SESAME SEED

Mole powder is a blended Mexican condiment sold in 3 ounce tins at fancy groceries and herb dealers.

Pablano is said to be the idea of the nuns of Puebla. There are many different kinds of chili peppers usually in the ingredients. This recipe has been somewhat modified to make it less pungent to the taste.

4 ozs. butter	*2 tsp. sugar*
1 medium onion, minced	*3 cups chicken broth*
1 cup mole powder	*1 sq. sweet chocolate*
1 can tomato paste	*½ tsp. salt*
2 tbs. toasted ground bread crumbs	*4 tbs. sesame seed*

Melt butter in large, heavy skillet over medium flame; add minced onion. Sauté 5 minutes, stirring constantly until dark. Add tomato paste, bread crumbs, and chicken broth; stir well; add chocolate, sugar, and salt; stir well; cover; lower flame. Simmer gently 20 minutes.

Add chicken mixture from first skillet; cover. Simmer gently over low flame 15 minutes; if sauce becomes too thick, add small amount broth or hot water. Serve piping hot. Sprinkle each serving generously with sesame seed. Serves 4 to 6.

Before reheating, place over boiling water to prevent scorching.

CHAPTER FOUR

Herb Bastes

and Marinades;

Blends and Bouquets

Herb blends, bouquets, and *bouquets garni* become the individual formulas of personal tastes and preferences. There are as many possibilities of combinations as there are individuals to create them. And when the fundamentals of the true flavors of each herb become known through taste and use, the amount of experimenting which can be done is infinite.

The exact formulas of many of the commercial blends are guarded trade secrets. And the many delicious flavors of the great variety of the different herb combinations on the market are the results of the numerous experiments made in the laboratories of individual grinders and manufacturers.

The pungent herbs, such as leek, garlic, sage, rosemary, winter savory, and onion, are used carefully and most sparingly when blended with other herbs. Among some of the herbs strong enough to have accents even when blended with chervil, chive, parsley, and summer savory are the sweet basil, dill, sweet marjoram, peppermint, spearmint, tarragon, and thyme.

We have become accustomed to associating certain basic herbs and spices with particular foods. For example, when pork is mentioned, sage immediately comes to mind. However, when a pork roast is rubbed with a combination of dill, lemon juice, sweet marjoram, and a few caraway seed before cooking, a new taste thrill is created.

Veal is delicious with thyme, we all know; and when a combination of thyme and summer savory, or thyme and chervil is used, the result is exceedingly appetizing and different.

The same is true of all the other essential foods, such as cheese, eggs, fish, beef, lamb, poultry, soups, and stews. One or two herbs or spices only may be used as flavoring; but very often a more complicated combination of them adds to the food's palatability when the combination is used with discretion and judgment.

The several combinations suggested here include those which are particularly delicious with the essential foods. These are given as an example of the way in which other combinations may be created by all who enjoy discovering more delicious ways in which to flavor foods.

Usually when any combination of either dried or fresh herbs is finely powdered or chopped, it is best to allow the herb particles to remain in the food and the herbs eaten with it. This is the true French use of *aux fines herbes*. For example, as in the instructions given for using the various aux fines herbes blends shown in this chapter.

The combination of herbs called the herb bouquet, which consists of leaves and sprigs of several fresh herbs tied together, is the bouquet garni of the French cuisine. One may also prepare an herb bouquet with crushed dried herbs carefully tied in a small cheesecloth bag. This is very easily removed before serving the food.

Aux Fines Herbes Blend #1

Use ½ teaspoon of blend to flavor *ragouts, soups,* and *stews.* For *beef* and *pork roasts,* and *beef* or *veal steaks,* sprinkle lightly with herb mixture before cooking.

1 tbs. pulverized thyme	*1 tbs. pulverized dried parsley*
1 tbs. pulverized summer savory	*1 tbs. powdered sage*
	1 tbs. grated lemon rind
1 tbs. pulverized sweet marjoram	*1 tbs. celery seed*
	6 bay leaves, crushed

Blend all ingredients in mixing bowl by stirring vigorously with fork and spoon. Pack in wide-mouthed 2 ounce bottles. Net weight of herb mixture in each bottle will be approximately 1½ ounces. Yield: 4 bottles.

Aux Fines Herbes Blend #2

Use ¼ to ½ teaspoon blended powder to flavor *meat sauces, soups,* and *vegetable casseroles.*

1 oz. dried parsley
1 oz. dried winter savory
1 oz. dried sweet marjoram
1 oz. dried lemon thyme

1 oz. dried sweet basil
½ oz. dried lemon peel,
   powdered

Blend all ingredients in mixing bowl. Strain through extra-fine sieve. Mix thoroughly again. Pack in tightly covered bottles. Yield: 5½ ounces.

Aux Fines Herbes Blend #3

Use ¼ to ½ teaspoon herb powder to season boiled *carrots, cauliflower, peas, string beans,* and *other sweet vegetables.*

1 oz. dried mint
1 oz. dried sage

⅛ oz. celery seed
⅛ oz. white pepper

Crush and blend mint, sage, celery seed, and pepper in mortar. Rub through very fine sieve. Pack in tightly covered container. Yield: 2¼ ounces.

Fresh aux Fines Herbes Blend #1   TIME: 10 minutes

Use to flavor *meat* and *vegetable soups;* also *stews.*
As garnish for *fish, roasts,* and *steaks,* sprinkle lightly with aux fines herbes just before serving.

1 tsp. chopped chervil
1 tsp. chopped chives

2 tbs. chopped parsley
1 tsp. chopped tarragon

Select fresh young leaves. Wash thoroughly under cold running water; dry on absorbent paper. Mince herbs by chopping with sharp knife. Serves 4.

Fresh aux Fines Herbes Blend #2: 1 tablespoon chopped chives, 1 teaspoon chopped chervil, 3 teaspoons chopped parsley, ½ teaspoon chopped tarragon.

Fresh aux Fines Herbes Blend #3: 1 teaspoon chopped thyme, ½ teaspoon chopped tarragon, ½ teaspoon chopped sweet marjoram, 2 teaspoons chopped parsley.

Fresh aux Fines Herbes Blend #4: 1 teaspoon chopped thyme, ½ teaspoon chopped sweet basil, 1 teaspoon chopped summer savory, 2 teaspoons chopped parsley.

Fresh Bouquet Garni #1

Use in *meat* and *vegetable soups;* also *stews.*

1 sprig parsley
1 sprig summer savory
1 sprig chervil

2 stalks celery with tops
1 small sprig basil
½ doz. chive leaves

Select fresh young herbs. Wash thoroughly under cold running water. Tie sprigs securely with white thread. Place bouquet in liquid at beginning so flavor permeates the food. Remove bouquet before serving.

Fresh Bouquet Garni #2: 1 sprig parsley, 1 leek, 1 celery stalk with leaves.

Fresh Bouquet Garni #3: 1 small sprig sweet marjoram, 1 celery stalk with leaves, 6 chive leaves.

Fresh Bouquet Garni #4: 1 sprig each summer savory, thyme, and parsley.

Fresh Bouquet Garni #5: 2 sprigs parsley, 1 sprig thyme.

Fresh Bouquet Garni #6: 1 sprig chervil, 6 chive leaves, 2 sprigs parsley.

Fresh Bouquet Garni #7: 1 sprig parsley, 2 scallions, 1 sprig basil.

Herb Baste and Marinade

1 pt. red wine vinegar
1 tsp. cloves, crushed
2 tsp. salt
⅛ tsp. cayenne pepper
6 tsp. sugar

1 large onion, grated
Grated rind of 1 lemon
½ cup olive oil
½ tsp. dried orégano

Blend cloves, salt, cayenne pepper, sugar, and orégano in large mixing bowl. Gradually pour in sufficient wine vinegar to make a thick paste; add grated lemon rind; blend well. Gradually pour in olive oil, stirring vigorously. Add grated onion and balance of wine vinegar; blend well. Pour marinade in quart jar; seal tightly. Allow to stand at room temperature overnight. Store in refrigerator and use as needed. Keeps indefinitely. Approximate yield: 1½ pints.

To tenderize and flavor beef pot roast: Pour ¾ cup over meat and allow to stand at room temperature overnight. Cook as usual, basting occasionally with marinade.

See also Spicy Golden Marinade (for fish).

Herb Baste with Wine

TIME: 15 minutes
Marinate overnight

1 cup claret wine
2 tbs. red wine vinegar
½ cup olive oil
1 small onion, minced
1 clove garlic, halved
⅛ tsp. dried rosemary

½ tsp. salt
½ tsp. celery salt
⅛ tsp. black pepper
⅛ tsp. cayenne pepper
⅛ tsp. dried thyme
⅛ tsp. dried marjoram

Blend all ingredients, beginning with minced onion in widemouthed jar; mix vigorously. Pour claret, vinegar, and olive oil over mixture; stir well; cover tightly. Allow to marinate at room temperature overnight. Remove garlic. Yield: 1½ cups.

Use to baste or brush *over chicken, chops,* or *steaks* during broiling.

Juniper-berry Baste and Marinade

½ cup red wine vinegar
3 cups burgundy wine
12 black peppercorns
1 large onion, sliced
1 clove garlic, halved
½ tsp. celery salt

5 juniper berries
1½ tsp. salt
⅛ tsp. mace
4 whole cloves
¼ tsp. thyme
1 bay leaf, crushed

Baste and marinade may be prepared by blending all ingredients in large mixing bowl. Pour mixture into quart jar. Allow to stand at room temperature overnight. Store in refrigerator for a day before using. Yield: 3½ cups—sufficient for 8 pounds.

Marinade may immediately be poured over beef and game to be marinated without blending in separate bowl.

Use to flavor and tenderize beef; also *wild game, such as caribou, elk, pheasant, reindeer, venison, wild boar,* and *wild duck.* Pour marinade over game or meat; allow to stand from 1 to 3 days, depending upon degree of marinade flavor desired. Strain. Use marinade as baste while roasting.

Minted Wine Baste   TIME: 20 minutes

¼ cup freshly chopped mint   *½ cup claret or burgundy*
½ cup consommé or beef   *wine*
broth

Place consommé and claret wine in heavy saucepan over medium flame; add freshly chopped mint leaves. Simmer gently 15 minutes. Yield: 1 cup.
Use as baste while *roasting chicken, lamb,* or *veal.*

Special Soup-seasoning Bouquet

1 tsp. dried parsley leaves and   *½ tsp. dried savory leaves*
stems   *and flowers*
1 tsp. dried thyme leaves and   *2 tsp. celery leaves and stems*
stems   *½ tsp. crushed sage leaves*
1 tsp. dried marjoram leaves   *and flowers*
and stems   *½ tsp. crushed bay leaves*

Blend herbs in mixing bowl by stirring vigorously with spoon.
Prepare 2-inch squares of cheesecloth or thin muslin. Place 1 teaspoon of blended herb mixture in cloth; tie securely. Use 1 bag *as seasoning for all soups* serving 6. Yield: 6 bags.

Triple Herb Combinations

Use to *flavor* and *garnish cheese, fish, omelets, salads, soups, stews,* and *vegetables.*

1. Blend 1 teaspoon dried basil with ½ teaspoon dried marjoram and ½ teaspoon freshly chopped chives.
2. Blend ½ teaspoon dried borage with ¼ teaspoon burnet and ½ teaspoon chopped chives.
3. Blend 1 teaspoon dried burnet with 1 teaspoon dried thyme and 2 teaspoons freshly minced parsley.
4. Blend 1 tablespoon minced celery with 1 teaspoon freshly minced burnet and 1 teaspoon freshly minced parsley.
5. Blend 1 teaspoon dried chervil with ½ teaspoon dried parsley and ½ teaspoon chopped chives.
6. Blend 1 tablespoon freshly minced lovage with 1 teaspoon freshly minced parsley and ¼ teaspoon dried orégano.
7. Blend 1 teaspoon freshly minced sweet marjoram with 1 teaspoon freshly minced parsley and ½ teaspoon dried rosemary.

8. Blend ½ teaspoon dried sweet marjoram with ½ teaspoon dried summer savory and 1 teaspoon chopped chives.
9. Blend ½ teaspoon dried mint with ¼ teaspoon burnet and ½ teaspoon freshly minced parsley.
10. Blend ½ teaspoon dried rosemary with 1 teaspoon freshly minced parsley and 2 teaspoons minced celery.

Freshen dried herbs by allowing to stand in lemon juice for 5 minutes before blending.

Twin Herb Combinations

Use to *flavor* and *garnish meats, salads, soups,* and *stews.*

1. Blend 1 teaspoon dried basil with ½ teaspoon chopped chives.
2. Blend 2 teaspoons freshly minced·dill with ½ teaspoon minced garlic.
3. Blend ½ teaspoon dried marjoram with 1 teaspoon freshly minced chervil.
4. Blend 1 teaspoon dried to 3 teaspoons freshly minced parsley with ½ teaspoon chopped chives.
5. Blend 1 teaspoon dried or 2 teaspoons freshly minced summer savory with ½ teaspoon chopped chives.
6. Blend ½ teaspoon dried tarragon with ¼ teaspoon dried marjoram.
7. Blend ½ teaspoon dried or 1 teaspoon freshly minced tarragon with 1 teaspoon chopped chives.
8. Blend ½ teaspoon dried thyme with ¼ teaspoon dried marjoram.
9. Blend ½ teaspoon dried thyme with ½ teaspoon dried orégano.
10. Blend 2 teaspoons freshly minced dill with ½ teaspoon minced garlic.

CHAPTER FIVE

Herb,

Condiment,

and Spice Butters

One of the most interesting and satisfactory ways in which to first use and become acquainted with herb and spice flavors is to combine them with fresh, unsalted butter. The butter fat readily absorbs the delicate, aromatic flavors and makes a delicious-tasting garnish for broiled fish and meats, poultry, roasts, and boiled or poached eggs.

Some cooks and homemakers will use margarine or rendered chicken fat or salt butter instead of sweet. However, I find that the sweet butter is more delicate and may be used more generally. It makes an excellent canapé spread to serve with either tea or cocktails, and an unusual sandwich filling.

The fresh herbs may be minced fine with a sharp knife, or crushed and ground in a mortar, then carefully and thoroughly blended with the softened creamed butter. By adding a teaspoonful of lemon juice, the herb flavor is accentuated. A little salt to taste is included, and the delicacy is ready to serve after it has stood at room temperature for an hour or two. After the herb flavors have permeated the butter, it may be kept for several days in the refrigerator in small, tightly covered jars.

The usual proportions when using freshly minced herbs is 1 tablespoon of the herb to each ¼ pound butter and 1 teaspoon lemon juice. When dried herbs are used, it is best to freshen them by allowing them to stand in lemon juice before mixing with the softened butter.

When the herb butter is being prepared with an herb powder or spice, it is best to use less seasoning rather than too much, for more may be gradually added as the butter is being blended. For example, a most delicious *Garlic* or *Mustard Butter* may be prepared by blending ½ teaspoon of the herb or spice powder with ¼ pound butter, while a *Paprika Butter* is usually sufficiently flavored when but ¼ teaspoon of the spice is used. On the other hand, 1½ tablespoons of prepared mustard is not too much to use when preparing a Mustard Butter with that condiment.

Certain condiments are most delicious in Herb Butter, especially when the butters are used to prepare canapés.

A few drops of green coloring added to a mint or parsley butter makes it most attractive. Also some homemakers like a drop or two of tabasco or Worcestershire sauce in butter made from some of the more pungent herbs, such as chives, onions, and garlic.

Here, too, as in other uses, herbs may be blended, and a combination herb butter will result. Thyme and summer savory, or water cress and chives, or summer savory and tarragon. The list can be endless, and one of particularly personal individual tastes and preferences. The recipes and lists of herbs and spices included here are guides into a wonderland of delicate new flavors.

Herbs, Condiments, and Spices Especially Good in BUTTERS

(For specific suggestions, please see under each herb or spice; also Herb Butters.)

Basil, sweet	Garlic	Parsley, fresh
Capers	Garlic powder	Parsley salt
Caraway seed	Garlic salt	Poppy seed
Celery seed	Horseradish	Rosemary
Chili sauce	Mints	Rose petals
Chives	Mustard, dry	Sage
Chutney	Mustard, prepared	Savory, summer
Cress, land	Onion	Sesame seed
Curry powder	Onion powder	Shallot
Dill, fresh	Onion salt	Tarragon
Dill, ground seed	Orégano	Thyme
Dill, whole seed	Paprika	Water cress

Basic Recipe for Herb, Condiment,   TIME: 20 minutes
or Spice Butter

¼ cup sweet butter   *1 tbs. freshly minced herb*
1 tsp. lemon juice   *or ½ tsp. dried herb or*
Salt to taste   *powder*

Allow butter to stand at room temperature to soften. Cream butter with spoon in mixing bowl; gradually add salt and lemon juice. Blend in freshly minced herb or dried herb or powder. Set aside at room temperature for 1 or 2 hours, so herbs may permeate butter. Store in small, tightly covered jars in refrigerator until ready to use. Serves 4.

Caper Butter: Use 2 teaspoons chopped capers instead of minced herb. Follow recipe.

Chili-sauce Butter: Use 1½ tablespoons chili sauce with each ¼ cup sweet butter. Follow recipe.

Chive Butter: Use 1 tablespoon minced chives with each ¼ cup sweet butter. Follow recipe.

Curry-powder Butter: Use ¼ to ½ teaspoon curry powder to taste with each ¼ cup sweet butter. Follow recipe.

Dill Butter: Use 1 tablespoon minced fresh dill with each ¼ cup sweet butter. Follow recipe.

Basic Recipe for Herb-flavored Clear Butter TIME: 20 minutes

4 ozs. sweet butter   *Fresh herb leaves and sprigs*

Select young, tender tips of the particular herb desired. Wash thoroughly; dry on absorbent paper.

Allow butter to stand at room temperature to soften slightly, so it may absorb the herb flavor more readily.

Arrange thin layer of herbs in bottom of jar or dish which may be tightly covered; place butter over herbs; cover butter with a thin top layer of herbs; cover jar tightly. Allow to stand at room temperature 1 hour. Store in refrigerator overnight. When ready to use, remove herbs.

Use herb-flavored butter as desired in cooking, also as canapé spread at teatime. Sprinkle with salt if desired.

Basil or Sweet Basil-flavored Butter: Use tender young leaves. Follow recipe.

Dill-flavored Butter: Use tender young dill sprigs. Follow recipe.

Mint-flavored Butter: Use tender sprigs of peppermint or spearmint. Follow recipe.

Rose Petal-flavored Butter: Use heavily scented petals of red roses. Follow recipe. Spread butter on canapé bread diamonds; *garnish each with a fresh rose petal.* Serve at teatime.

Combination Herb Butter   TIME: 30 minutes

¼ cup butter   *2 tsp. minced summer savory*
1 tsp. lemon juice   *1 tsp. minced tarragon*

Allow butter to stand at room temperature to soften. Cream butter with spoon until soft and fluffy in mixing bowl; gradually add lemon juice (and salt to taste if necessary). Blend in freshly minced herbs. Set aside at room temperature for 1 or 2 hours, so herb flavors may permeate butter. Store in small, tightly covered jars in refrigerator until ready to use. Serves 4. Other suggested combinations:

Burnet, thyme, and parsley: Use 1 teaspoon each herb freshly minced. Follow recipe.

Chives and water cress: Use 2 teaspoons cress, 1 teaspoon chives. Follow recipe.

Chives, chervil, and parsley: Use 1 teaspoon each herb freshly minced. Follow recipe.

Dill and garlic: Use 2 teaspoons minced dill, 1 small clove garlic, mashed. Follow recipe.

Dill-seed Herb Butter   TIME: 15 minutes
                                              Marinate 2 hours

¼ lb. butter   *1 tsp. lemon juice*
½ tsp. salt   *2 tsp. minced fresh parsley*
⅛ tsp. white pepper   *⅛ tsp. cayenne pepper*
2 tsp. ground dill seed

Cream butter with spoon in mixing bowl; gradually add salt, pepper, dill seed, parsley, and cayenne pepper. When very smooth, gradually add lemon juice; blend well. Set aside at room temperature for 1 hour, so herbs may permeate butter. Place in refrigerator to chill 1 hour before using. Serves 4.

Place slice of Dill Seed Herb Butter over *baked* or *broiled fish* or *steak* just before serving.

Caraway-seed Herb Butter: Use 1 teaspoon *ground* caraway or 1½ teaspoons *whole* caraway seed instead of dill seed. Follow recipe.

Celery-seed Herb Butter: Use 1½ teaspoons *ground* celery seed or 2 teaspoons *whole* celery seed instead of dill seed. Follow recipe.

Poppy-seed Herb Butter: Use 1 teaspoon *ground* poppy seed or 2 teaspoons *whole* poppy seed instead of dill seed. Follow recipe.

Horseradish Butter TIME: 30 minutes
Freezing: 30 minutes

1 small horseradish root *1 tsp. lemon juice*
(about 6") *¼ tsp. salt*
8 ozs. butter *⅛ tsp. white pepper*
1 tsp. vinegar

Allow butter to stand at room temperature until soft.

Wash and scrape horseradish root; grate into deep bowl. Blend grated root with butter; add vinegar, lemon juice, salt, and pepper; blend very thoroughly. Rub mixture through very fine sieve. Spread mixture on large flat plate. Place in refrigerator for 30 minutes. When serving, cut into small cubes. Yield: Approximately 1 pint.

Serve as desired *with steamed* or *broiled fish, broiled chops, steaks,* and *roasts.*

Mustard Butter TIME: 15 minutes

⅓ cup butter *½ tsp. minced parsley*
1 tsp. Dijon-style mustard
or 1½ tsp. other pre-
pared mustard

Cream butter in small mixing bowl; blend in prepared mustard; add minced parsley. Chill 10 minutes in refrigerator. Serves 4.

Use with *fish* and *meat sandwich spreads;* also on toast served with *egg dishes,* such as *Eggs Benedict.*

CHAPTER SIX

Herb and
Tree-Blossom Honeys

Herb honeys and herb jellies are among the rarest and most delicious of foods. Most of the herb honeys on the market are those which come from the various apiaries throughout the world. Some honeys may be the delicately flavored ones of the exotic blossoms of tropical shrubs and trees, and others are the nectars of the blossoms of the myriad wild flowers of the fields and mountains.

There are honeys to suit every taste and to pamper every whim of the palate. Practically all of them are the pure nectar of the blossoms whose names are used for identification. For example, Avocado Honey from California is the nectar of the blossoms of the avocado tree. Black Locust Honey from Italy is the pure, sweet liquid of the locust blossoms; and Blue Curls Honey from California is the blossom nectar from any shrub of the genus *Trichostema,* which belongs to the mint family. *Trichostema lanceolatum* is one of the species of blue curls which grows abundantly in California.

The list of herb honeys which follows includes those which may readily be purchased at groceries, markets, and health-food stores, or from any number of the many herb farms and herb dealers throughout the country.

There are also a number of the garden herbs which may be infused or heated with a clover honey to impart a different flavor. But it seems almost an affront to the generosity of nature to wish to improve any of the natural honey flavors. However, there is no set rule against it and there are those who enjoy the excitement and thrill of experimenting with new and exotic flavors.

A sweetly aromatic seed and certain of the sweet spices are sources of added flavorings for the pure clover-blossom and orange-blossom honeys. A list of suggestions is given later in the chapter for those who enjoy blending and discovering new flavors and tastes.

There are two methods of imparting an extra herb flavor to a clover honey; one is to warm the honey slightly and the other is the English method of boiling. I prefer the first. Bruise fresh herb leaves very slightly; place a layer of the leaves in a small saucepan; pour clover honey over the herbs. Warm over low flame 2 minutes. Pour into jar; seal tightly. Allow to stand in warm room for 1 week. Warm only enough so that the herbs may be strained from the honey.

The English are fond of flavoring honeys with herbs, flower petals, or dried rosebuds. An herb infusion made with distilled water is carefully strained, then boiled with the honey until the mixture becomes a thick syrup. It is used to sweeten beverages. Since boiling seems to take away something of the original natural flavor of the honeys, I suggest merely warming them.

Herb Leaves and Spices Which May Be Used to Flavor Clover-blossom and Orange-blossom NATURAL HONEYS *(See also Herb Blossom Honeys.)*

Allspice	Ginger, ground
Anise seed, ground	Horehound
Balm or Lemon Balm	Marjoram or Sweet Marjoram
Basil or Purple Basil	Mints, Apple
Basil or Sweet Basil	Mints, Orange
Bergamot or Red Bergamot	Mints, Peppermint
Borage	Mints, Spearmint
Cardamom seed, ground	Poppy seed, whole
Cinnamon, ground	Rose hips
Cinnamon sticks	Rose petals
Cloves, ground	Sage
Cloves, whole	Savory or Winter Savory
Coriander seed, ground	Sesame seed, crushed
Fennel, fresh	Thyme
Fennel seed, ground	

Cardamom-flavored Honey   TIME: 20 minutes

1 pt. pure clover honey   *1 tsp. ground cardamom*
   or 1 pt. orange-blossom
   honey

Purchase best-quality clover- or orange-blossom honey. Allow
to stand in warm room, so blending process will be easier.
Pour honey into small bowl; stir in cardamom; blend well;
cover. Allow to stand in warm room 2 days before using.
Honey will absorb the warm, sweet flavor of the cardamom.
Use as desired.

Poppy-seed Clover Honey   TIME: 20 minutes

1 pt. pure clover honey   *1 tbs. whole poppy seed*
   or 1 pt. orange-blossom
   honey

Purchase best-quality clover- or orange-blossom honey. Allow
to stand in warm room, so blending process will be easier.
Pour honey into small bowl; add poppy seed; blend well; cover.
Allow to stand in warm room 2 days before using. Honey will
absorb the delicate flavor of the poppy seed. Use as desired.

Herb and Tree-blossom HONEYS

Sold in ½ pound, 1 pound, and larger size jars, cans, and
parchment containers at fancy groceries, markets, herb
dealers, health-food stores, and some herb farms.

Alfalfa Honey: From *California* and *Texas*. The nectar of the
alfalfa, *Medicago sativa,* blossoms.
Apple-blossom Honey: From *Washington State*. The nectar of
the apple blossoms of the genus *Malus.*
Avocado Honey: From *California*. The nectar of the avocado
blossoms of the genus *Persea persea.*
Bean or **Lima-bean Honey:** From *California* and *New Jersey.*
The nectar of the lima bean, *Phaseolus lunatus,* blossoms.
Berry-blossom and Basswood Honey: From *Wisconsin.* The
blended nectar of the blossoms of the wild black raspberry,
Rubus occidentalis; the wild red raspberry, *Rubus strigosus;*
and of the basswood blossoms. The basswood is any tree of
the genus *Tilia.*

Blackberry Honey: From *Washington State.* The nectar of the blackberry, *Rubus nigrobaccus,* blossoms.

Black-locust Honey: From *Italy.* The nectar of the black locust, *Robinia pseudacacia,* blossoms.

Blossomtime Honey: From *New Jersey.* A blend of the nectars of the blossoms from several of the wild flowers of the state.

Blueberry Honey: From *Maine.* The nectar of the blueberry blossoms. Any berry of the genus *Vaccinium.*

Blue Curls Honey: From *California.* The nectar of the blue curls blossoms. Any plant of the genus *Trichostema* of the mint family.

Blue Vine Honey: From *Missouri.* The nectar of the blossoms of the blue vines or climbing milkweeds, identified as *Gonolobus gondcarpos* and *Gonolobus laevis.*

Buckwheat or **Wild Buckwheat Honey:** From *California.* The nectar of the blossoms of a polygonaceous plant, *Eriogonum fasciculatum,* somewhat like the buckwheat.

Buckwheat Honey: From *New York* and *Pennsylvania.* The nectar of the buckwheat blossoms. A polygonaceous plant of the genus *Fagopyrum.*

Cabbage Honey: From *Washington State.* The nectar of the blossoms of the cabbage, *Brassica oleracea,* plant.

Candied Honey: From *Australia.* The nectar of the blossoms of the white gum tree. A species of the eucalyptus called *Eucalyptus viminalis.*

Candied Honey Blended: From *Australia.* A blend of the nectar of the blossoms of the white and yellow boxwood, *Schaefferia frutescens,* or any tree of the *Buxus* family; and of the blossoms of the red gum tree, a *Eucalyptus rostrata.*

Chamonix Honey: From *France* and *Switzerland.* The nectar of the lavender, *Lavandula vera,* blossoms.

Cherry or **Wild-cherry Honey:** From *California.* The nectar of the wild-cherry, *Prunus serotina,* blossoms.

Chinese Tallow Honey: From *Texas.* The nectar of the blossoms of the Chinese tallow tree. A euphorbiaceous tree, *Sapium sebiferum,* now cultivated in the southern part of the United States.

Citrus Honey: From *Texas.* A blend of the nectars of the orange, *Citrus aurantium;* lemon, *Citrus medica limon;* and grapefruit, *Citrus decumana,* blossoms.

Clover Honey: From *California, Colorado, Iowa, New York, Vermont, Washington State,* and other states in the northern

part of the United States. The nectar of the clover blossoms
of any species of the *Fabaceae* family.

Clover and Milkweed Honey: From *Michigan*. The blended
nectar of the sweet clover, *Melilotus,* blossoms; and the
blossoms of the milkweed, which is any plant of the genus
Asclepias.

Cotton Honey: From *California*. The nectar of the blossoms
of the white basswood tree. Any tree of the genus *Tilia.*

Creamed Honey: From *Canada*. The nectar of the blossoms of
the white basswood tree. Any tree of the genus *Tilia.*

Dandelion Honey: From *Colorado*. The nectar of the dandelion, *Taraxacum taraxacum,* blossoms.

Desert Honey: From *Arizona*. The blended nectar of the
blossoms of the cactus plant, any plant of the genus *Cac-
taceae,* and of other desert flowers.

Eucalyptus Honey: From *California*. The nectar of the blossoms of the eucalyptus trees. Any myrtaceous tree of the
genus *Eucalyptus.*

Fireweed Honey: From *Washington State*. The nectar of the
blossoms of the fireweeds which spring up in the charred
woods after they have been swept by forest fires. This honey
appears in markets only at rare intervals.

Gallberry Honey: From *Georgia*. The nectar of the blossoms
of the gallberry or inkberry, *Kibara macrophylla,* which
grows in the swamplands of Georgia and along the Florida
coast.

Goldenrod Honey: From *New York*. The nectar of the goldenrod blossoms. An asteraceous plant of the genus *Solidago.*

Greek Honey: See Hymettus Honey.

Guajillo-Catsclaw Honey: From *Texas*. The nectar of the
blossoms of a mimosaceous shrub of the genus *Zygia
unguis-cati.*

Heartsease Honey: From *Illinois*. The nectar of the blossoms
of the weed *Polygonum persicaria,* found growing in Illinois
and along the banks of the Mississippi River. Heartsease
is also called *Smartweed, Polygonum hydropiper.*

Heather Honey or **Adelshoeve:** From *Holland*. The nectar of
the heather, *Calluna vulgaris,* blossoms.

Horehound Honey: From *Texas*. The nectar of the horehound,
Marrubium vulgare, blossoms.

Horsemint Honey: From *Texas*. The nectar of the blossoms
of the wild horsemint shrub, *Monarda punctata.*

Hymettus Honey: From *Greece*. The nectar of the blossoms of the wild thyme, *Thymus serpyllum,* which grows on the slopes of the mountain of Hymettus near Athens.

Hyssop Honey: From herb farms in various states. The nectar of the hyssop, *Hyssopus officinalis,* blossoms.

Irish Honey: From *Eire.* The blended nectar of the wild flowers of Ireland or Eire.

Japanese Honey: From *Japan.* The blended nectar of the blossoms of the horsechestnut tree, *Aesculus hippocastanum;* the milkweed, any plant of the genus *Asclepias* which belongs to the *Asclepiadaceae* family; and the Chinese milk vetch, a fabaceous plant of the genus *Vicia,* which belongs to the immense *Fabaceae* family.

Jarrah Liquid Honey: From *Australia.* The nectar of the blossoms of the Australian eucalyptus tree.

Karri Liquid Honey: From *Australia.* The nectar of the blossoms of the *Eucalyptus marginata.*

Lavender Honey: From le Provence, and from Chamonix, *France.* The nectar of the lavender, *Lavandula vera,* blossoms. See also Chamonix Honey.

Lespedeza Bicolor Honey: From *South Carolina.* The nectar of the blossoms of the giant gum tree native to western Australia but now cultivated in South Carolina, where it is known as the *Eucalyptus diversicolor.*

Lima-bean Honey: From *New Jersey.* See Bean or Lima-bean Honey.

Locust Honey: From *Italy.* See Black-locust Honey.

Locust Honey: From *Washington State.* The nectar of the blossoms of the honey locust tree, the *Gleditsia triacanthos.*

Loosestrife or **Purple Loosestrife Honey:** From *New York.* The nectar of the blossoms of any of the primulaceous plants of the genus *Lysimachia vulgaris.*

Lupine or **Purple Lupine Honey:** From *Colorado.* The nectar of the blossoms of a plant of the genus *Lupinus.*

Mangrove Honey: From *Florida.* The nectar of the blossoms of any tropical plant of the genus *Rhizophora.*

Manzanita Honey: From *Oregon.* The nectar of the blossoms of any shrub of the genus *Arctostaphylos.*

Marigold Honey: From *New Jersey.* The nectar of the marigold, *Calendula officinalis,* blossoms.

Mesquite Honey: From *California.* The nectar of the blossoms of any mimosaccous tree or shrub of the genus *Prosopis glandulosa. All honeys may be used as sweetening instead of sugar.*

Milkweed and Clover Honey: From *Michigan.* See Clover and Milkweed Honey.

Mint Honey: From *Washington State.* See Peppermint Honey.

Mountain-flowers Honey: From *California.* The blended nectar of the blossoms of sage, *Salvia officinalis;* buckwheat, a polygonaceous plant of the genus *Fagopyrum;* alfalfa, *Medicago sativa;* and orange blossoms, *Citrus aurantium.*

Mountain Honey: From *Mexico.* The blended nectar of the blossoms of the wild flowers indigenous to Mexico.

Mountain Lilac Honey: From *California.* The nectar of the blossoms of the wild lilac which grows abundantly on the slopes of the Sierra Nevadas. Wild lilac is a shrub which belongs to the *Ceanothus* family, a kind of thistle of which there are fourteen varieties.

Onion Honey: From *California.* The nectar of the blossoms of the onion plant, *Allium cepa.*

Orange-blossom Honey: From *California.* All orange-blossom honeys are the nectars of the orange, *Citrus aurantium,* blossoms.

Orange-blossom Honey with the Blossoms: From *California.*

Orange Creamy Honey: From *California.*

Orange Honey: From *California* and *Texas.*

Palm Honey: From *Florida.* The nectar of the blossoms of the palmetto tree of the genus *Trinax.*

Pax Honey: From Mt. St. Benedict Monastery. See also Trinidad Honey.

Peppermint Honey: From *Washington State.* The nectar of the peppermint, *Mentha piperita,* blossoms.

Poison-oak Honey: From *Oregon.* Also called *Sumac Honey.* The nectar of the blossoms of any tree or shrub of the genus *Rhus.*

Purple Loosestrife Honey: From *New York.* See Loosestrife Honey.

Purple Lupine Honey: From *Colorado.* See Lupine Honey.

Raspberry or **Wild Raspberry Honey:** From *Michigan.* The blended nectar of the blossoms of the wild black raspberry, *Rubus occidentalis,* and the wild red raspberry, *Rubus strigosus.* See also Berry Blossom and Basswood Honey.

Sage Honey: From *California.* The nectar of the sage, *Salvia officinalis,* blossoms.

Sourwood Honey: From *South Carolina.* The nectar of the blossoms of the sorrel tree, a small ericaceous tree of the genus *Oxydendrum.*

Spearmint Honey: From *Indiana.* The nectar of the spearmint, *Mentha spicata,* blossoms.

Sumac Honey: From *Oregon.* See also Poison-oak Honey.

Thistle or **Star Thistle Honey:** From *California.* The blended nectar of the blossoms of the purple thistle, *Centaurea calcitrapa;* and the yellow thistle, *Centaurea solstitialis.*

Thyme Honey: From *Greece.* See Hymettus Honey.

Thyme or **Wild Thyme Honey:** From *Maryland* and *New York.* The nectar of the wild thyme, *Thymus serpyllum,* blossoms.

Trappist Honey: From the Trappist Monastery of Our Lady of the Prairies in St. Norbert, Manitoba, *Canada.* The blended nectar of the blossoms of the basswood tree, any tree of the genus *Tilia,* and of wild flowers indigenous to eastern Canada.

Trinidad Honey: From Mt. St. Benedict Monastery in *Trinidad.* This honey is also known as *Pax Honey.* The Pax monks still hold the secret of the exact blend of blossom nectars contained in this honey.

Tulip-tree Honey: From *Maryland.* The nectar of the blossoms of the tulip tree, *Liriodendron tulipifera.*

Tupelo Honey: From *Florida* and *Georgia.* The nectar of the blossoms of the tupelo tree, *Nyssa multiflora.*

Uvalde Honey: From *Texas.* The nectar of the blossoms of a mimosaceous shrub of the genus *Zygia unguis-cati.* See also Guajilla-Catsclaw Honey.

Vetch Honey: From *Oregon.* The nectar of the blossoms of any fabaceous plant of the genus *Vicia.*

White-gum Honey, Candied: From *Australia* The nectar of the blossoms of the white gum tree, a species of eucalyptus known as *Eucalyptus viminalis.*

Wild Buckwheat Honey: From *California.* The nectar of the wild buckwheat, *Eriogonum fasciculatum,* blossoms.

Wild-flower, Horsemint Honey: From *Texas.* See Horsemint Honey.

Wild-raspberry Honey: From *Michigan.* The blended nectars of the blossoms of the wild black raspberry, *Rubus occidentalis;* and the wild red raspberry, *Rubus strigosus.*

Wild-thyme Honey: From *Maryland* and *New York.* The nectar of the wild thyme, *Thymus serpyllum,* blossoms. See also Hymettus Honey.

CHAPTER SEVEN

Herb and

Spice Jellies

A whole volume easily could be devoted to herb and spice jellies. The basic suggestions given here are intended simply as guides or stimuli to your own unlimited imagination.

Use any preferred fruit-juice base made with or without commercial pectin. If you have the perfect recipe for the perfect jelly, you may flavor that particular fruit base with as many different herbs and spices as you care and dare to experiment with.

There are many homemakers who prefer to save time by using a commercial pectin. If you are one of these, the herb or spice of your choice may be added to the fruit when it is first boiled. If, however, the fruit base is cooked without commercial pectin, the herb or spice may be added to the clear fruit juice at the time it is ready for the final boiling to the jelly stage.

Even a purchased prepared jelly may be made into an herb jelly by simply blending it with the freshly minced leaves. See recipe for Mint Currant Jelly à la Minute.

No doubt our grandmothers would frown on such procedure, but it does save time and provides an unusual and delicious change.

Petals of flowers are so easy to use as exotic flavorings for fruit jellies. Simply place a petal in the bottom of the jelly glass; fill it with the cooked juice; float another petal on top;

cover with paraffin and then seal tightly. When the jelly is used, it will have the faintly delicate taste of the petal. Rose petals, mint leaves, lemon verbena, and rose geranium are but a few of the sweet-scented herbs which will add not only to the flavor of the jellies but to their attractive appearance. Why not experiment with the petals of lavender or rosemary, or with a leaf of the perfumed lemon balm?

Apple Jelly Base for HERB JELLIES   TIME: Variable

3 lbs. tart   *Warm water*
or sour apples   *Sugar*

Select firm, tart or sour apples only. Wash and slice. Do not remove skins or cores. Place apples in extra-heavy saucepan over high flame; barely cover apples with warm water. Cook rapidly 15 minutes, or until apples are soft. Strain cooked apples through jelly bag; do not squeeze if clear jelly is desired. *This should yield 5 cups of juice.*

Measure clear juice; pour into extra-heavy saucepan; measure ¾ of the amount of sugar. (For 5 cups of juice, 3¾ cups sugar.) Bring juice to rapid rolling boil over high flame; gradually add sugar, stirring constantly. Boil rapidly until 2 drops hang on side of cold spoon, or until sugar thermometer registers 222° F. Skim if necessary; pour juice quickly into hot, sterilized glasses; cover with melted paraffin immediately. Yield: 6 glasses, ½ pint size.

Angelica Apple Jelly: Suspend small bunch of washed angelica in saucepan in which measured apple juice is brought to boil. Allow to boil 2 minutes. Remove herb. Finish as for Apple Jelly Base.

Apple Mint Apple Jelly: Suspend small bunch washed apple mint in saucepan in which measured apple juice is brought to boil; allow to boil 3 minutes. Remove herb. Finish as for Apple Jelly Base.

Basil Apple Jelly: Suspend small bunch washed sweet basil in saucepan in which measured apple juice is brought to boil. Allow to boil 2 minutes. Remove herb. Finish as for Apple Jelly Base.

Costmary Petal Apple Jelly: Prepare Apple Jelly Base. Place 1 leaf costmary in bottom of each jelly glass; pour in hot juice; cover with melted paraffin; seal.

Curly-mint Apple Jelly: Suspend small bunch washed curly mint in saucepan in which measured apple juice is brought to boil. Allow to boil 3 minutes. Remove herb. Finish as for Apple Jelly Base. When ready to pour into glasses, add desired amount green coloring; pour into hot glasses; cover with melted paraffin; seal.

Lavender-petal Apple Jelly: Prepare Apple Jelly Base. Place tiny petals lavender blossom in bottom of jelly glass; pour hot juice over; cover with melted paraffin; seal.

Lemon-verbena Apple Jelly: Prepare Apple Jelly Base. Place 1 small leaf lemon verbena in bottom of jelly glass; pour in hot juice; float 1 small leaf lemon verbena on top; cover with melted paraffin; seal.

Orange-mint Apple Jelly: Suspend small bunch washed orange mint in saucepan in which measured apple juice is brought to boil. Boil 3 minutes. Remove herb. Finish as for Apple Jelly Base. When ready to pour into glasses, add desired amount orange coloring; pour into hot glasses; cover with melted paraffin; seal.

Peppermint Apple Jelly: Suspend small bunch washed peppermint in saucepan in which measured juice is brought to boil. Allow to boil 3 minutes. Remove herb. Finish as for Apple Jelly Base. When ready to pour, add desired green coloring; pour jelly; cover with melted paraffin; seal.

Rose-geranium Apple Jelly: Prepare Apple Jelly Base. Place 1 small rose-geranium leaf in bottom of glass; pour hot juice over; float rose-geranium leaf on top; cover with melted paraffin; seal.

Rose-petal Apple Jelly: Prepare Apple Jelly Base. Place 1 rose petal in bottom of jelly glass; pour hot juice over; float rose petal on top; cover with melted paraffin; seal.

Spearmint Apple Jelly: Suspend small bunch washed spearmint in saucepan in which measured juice is brought to boil. Allow to boil 3 minutes. Remove herb. Finish as for Apple Jelly Base. When ready to pour, add desired amount green coloring; pour jelly; cover with melted paraffin; seal.

Cardamon Seed Grape Jelly   TIME: Variable

Prepare as for Clove Cinnamon Grape Jelly. Use 6 crushed cardamon seed as flavoring instead of cloves and cinnamon. Especially delicious.

Clove Cinnamon Grape Jelly   TIME: Variable

3 lbs. ripe Concord grapes   1 tsp. whole cloves
½ cup cider vinegar   ½ bottle fruit pectin
1 4-in. stick cinnamon   7 cups sugar

Select fully ripe but firm Concord grapes. Wash carefully; remove grapes from stems. Crush grapes in extra-heavy saucepan; add vinegar, stick cinnamon, and cloves. Bring to boil over high flame; cover; lower flame. Simmer grapes 10 to 15 minutes, or until tender.

Turn into jelly bag; press out juice; measure. (Three pounds grapes usually makes 4 cups juice.) Mix 4 cups juice with 7 cups sugar in large saucepan placed over high heat. Bring to boil. Immediately add fruit pectin, stirring constantly. Bring to full rolling boil. Allow to boil 30 seconds (½ minute). Remove from heat at once. Skim; pour into hot, sterilized jelly glasses; cover with melted paraffin immediately. Yield: 6 glasses.

Use any preferred fruit instead of Concord grapes.

Clove Cinnamon Apple Jelly: Use 3 pounds tart apples. Follow recipe.

Clove Cinnamon Crabapple Jelly: Use 3 pounds tart crabapples. Follow recipe.

Clove Cinnamon Currant Jelly: Use 3 pounds half-ripe currants. Follow recipe.

Clove Cinnamon Quince Jelly: Use 3 pounds tart quinces. Follow recipe.

Grenada Mace Apple Jelly   TIME: Variable

5 lbs. tart apples   1 pkg. powdered pectin
3 cups hot water   (3 ozs.)
½ oz. stick cinnamon   1 tsp. red liquid coloring
1 tsp. whole cloves   7 cups sugar
2 tsp. blades of mace or
    1 tsp. ground mace

Tie spices in thin muslin bag. Wash apples; remove stems. Cut unpeeled and uncored apples into small pieces; place in heavy saucepan; add hot water; add spice bag. Bring to boiling point over medium flame; turn down flame; cover. Simmer 20 minutes, or until apples are soft. Remove spice bag. Turn mixture into jelly bag; let drip, then gently squeeze out juice. (Good tart apples should produce 6 cups juice.)

Pour juice in large, heavy saucepan placed over high heat; gradually stir in pectin and coloring; continue stirring constantly until liquid boils; gradually add sugar, stirring constantly. Bring to heavy rolling boil; continue boiling for ½ minute. Remove from heat. Skim off any foam. Quickly pour liquid into hot, sterilized jelly glasses; cover with melted paraffin immediately. Cool at room temperature, then cover glasses. Yield: 12 glasses, ⅓ pint size.

Marjoram Herb Jelly   TIME: 1 hour

1 cup marjoram infusion   *½ cup liquid pectin*
3 cups sugar   *2 to 3 drops orange or*
Juice of 2 lemons (⅓ cup)   *red coloring*

If possible, use fresh marjoram to prepare infusion, as for strong herb tea; otherwise, pour 1 cup boiling water over 2 tablespoons dried marjoram. Cover. Allow to stand 20 minutes. Strain through very fine cheesecloth. Add sufficient water to make 1 full cup infusion.

Strain lemon juice through very fine cheesecloth. Pour marjoram infusion and lemon juice into heavy saucepan over high flame; add sugar; stir well. Bring mixture to boil. Add pectin, stirring vigorously; add coloring; continue stirring until liquid is at full rolling boil. Boil hard ½ minute only. Remove from flame; skim. Pour hot liquid into 5 ounce hot, sterilized jelly glasses (or into small 2½ ounce glasses); cover with melted paraffin immediately. Cool at room temperature. Cover and label. Yield: 2 small jars; or 4 5 ounce glasses.

Basil Herb Jelly: Prepare basil infusion. Follow recipe.

Fennel Herb Jelly: Prepare fennel infusion. Follow recipe. Use green coloring instead of orange or red.

Rosemary Herb Jelly: Prepare rosemary infusion. Follow recipe.

Sage Herb Jelly: Prepare sage infusion. Follow recipe.

Sorrel Herb Jelly: Prepare sorrel infusion. Follow recipe.

Summer Savory Herb Jelly: Prepare summer savory infusion. Follow recipe. Use green coloring instead of orange or red.

Thyme Herb Jelly: Prepare thyme infusion. Follow recipe. Use green coloring instead of orange or red.

Mint Apple Jelly   TIME: Variable

5 cups apple juice   *3 tbs. prepared mint juice*

PREPARE MINT JUICE DAY IN ADVANCE:

4 cups chopped fresh mint   1 cup water
1 cup sugar

Select crisp mint leaves. Wash under cold running water; dry on absorbent paper. With sharp knife chop fine. Arrange chopped mint in wide-mouthed jar. Dissolve sugar in water; pour over mint; cover tightly. Allow to stand overnight. Place mixture in heavy saucepan over medium flame. Bring to boiling point. Strain.

   Prepare Apple Jelly Base. When jellying point is reached, add 3 tablespoons mint juice and desired amount green coloring. Pour into hot sterilized glasses; cover with melted paraffin; seal. Yield: 6 glasses, ½ pint size.

Mint Lemon Verbena Jelly: Prepare as for Mint Apple Jelly. When ready to pour, place leaf in bottom of jelly glass; pour juice over; float lemon verbena leaf on top; cover with melted paraffin; seal.

Mint Lavender Petal Jelly: Prepare as for Mint Apple Jelly. When ready to pour, place lavender blossom in bottom of jelly glass; pour juice over; cover with melted paraffin; seal.

Mint Rose Geranium Jelly: Prepare as for Mint Apple Jelly. When ready to pour, place rose geranium leaf in bottom of glass; pour hot juice over; float rose geranium leaf on top; cover with melted paraffin; seal.

Mint Rose-petal Jelly: Prepare as for Mint Apple Jelly. When ready to pour, place rose leaf in bottom of glass; pour hot juice over; float rose petal on top; cover with melted paraffin; seal.

Mint Currant Jelly à la Minute   TIME: 15 minutes
                                              Chill 24 hours

2 tsp. freshly chopped mint   ½ tsp. grated orange rind
1 glass currant jelly

Place jelly in small bowl; add mint and orange rind; stir gently but thoroughly until well blended. Replace jelly in glass; cover. Allow to stand 24 hours in refrigerator. Use as desired.

Other preferred fruit jellies, such as *apple, crabapple, grape,* and *quince,* may be flavored in same way.

Herb-flavored JELLIES

Sold in 2 ounce, 4 ounce, and larger glasses at fancy groceries and markets; also at herb farms and studios.

Angelica Herb Jelly: Serve with *egg dishes, salads,* and *desserts.*

Basil Herb Jelly: Serve with *desserts, fish, game, poultry,* and *roasts.*

Caraway-thyme Herb Jelly: Serve with *chops, roast beef,* and *steaks.*

Costmary Herb Jelly: Serve with *chicken, roast beef, wild duck.*

Fennel Herb Jelly: Serve with *cheese dishes, creamed vegetables,* and *fish.*

Lavender Herb Jelly: Serve with *salads* and *desserts.*

Marjoram or **Sweet Marjoram Herb Jelly:** Serve with *all meats, chicken, game, turkey, shellfish,* and *venison.*

Mints: Apple-, Curly-, Orange-, and **Spearmint-herb Jelly:** Serve with *beef, chicken, eggs, desserts, lamb, mutton, pork,* and *veal.*

Rose-geranium Herb Jelly: Serve with *chicken, desserts, salads, pork, turkey,* and *veal.*

Rosemary Herb Jelly: Serve with *eggs, lamb, pork, poultry,* and *veal.*

Rose-petal Jelly: Serve with *desserts, salads, poultry,* and *veal.*

Sage Herb Jelly: Serve with *duck, goose, pork,* and *poultry.*

Savory, or **Summer Savory Herb Jelly:** Serve with *fish, game, meats, poultry,* and *venison.*

Sorrel Herb Jelly: Serve with *goose, lamb, pork, poultry,* and *veal.*

Tarragon Herb Jelly: Serve with *fish, meats, salads, poultry,* and *shellfish.*

Thyme, or **Lemon Thyme Herb Jelly:** Serve with *cheese dishes, eggs, fish, game, meats, poultry,* and *shellfish.*

Verbena or **Lemon Verbena Herb Jelly:** Serve with *desserts, salads, eggs, fish, game, poultry,* and *all meats.*

CHAPTER EIGHT

Herb Powder;
Herb and Spice Salts

There is an ever-increasing number of herb powders and herb and spice salts being prepared, packaged, and sold for the convenience of homemakers everywhere. The powder is usually packed in tiny ½ ounce bottles, and the herb and spice salts in bottles which contain from 1 to 2½ ounces.

These products may be purchased at all groceries, markets, food departments, and also from herb dealers. A list of the various herbs now available in powder and salt form is given later in this chapter. It also includes herb extracts, *mono sodium glutamate*, or MSG, and spice salts.

An *herb powder* such as chive powder, parsley powder, garlic powder, and so on down through the list, is the pure, ground product of the dehydrated herb. Parsley powder, for example, is the finely ground dehydrated parsley leaf, and garlic powder is the finely ground dehydrated clove of the garlic.

Therefore all pure herb powders have the same natural flavors as those of the fresh herbs. However, since the herb loses some flavor in the drying process, it is only to be expected that the powder imparts a slightly milder flavor than does the fresh herb. This has its advantages, nevertheless, when one wishes to achieve a particular effect. Some cooks prefer to use garlic powder or garlic salt instead of the fresh herb, simply because it is less pungent and imparts a milder flavor than the freshly minced garlic clove. There are times, too, when one needs to hurry, and it is very convenient just to reach for an herb powder or herb salt without taking the time to freshen the dried herbs or mince the fresh ones.

Salt, or *sodium chloride,* is that marvelous white substance found all over the world, either in water or in rock formation. Salt has been used by mankind and animals since the beginning of time. Proverbs and sayings galore fill the pages of books in praise of salt, but perhaps the greatest of all phrases associated with salt is the one in Matthew V: 13, which reads: "Ye are the salt of the earth." This immortal phrase uttered in appreciation of a great loyalty has come to mean praise and admiration of the highest quality.

The salt which we use to bring out the individual flavors in all our foods has been refined and purified of all chemicals which might interfere with the natural flavors. About 1 per cent of carbonate of magnesia is added to table salt to prevent it from caking in damp weather. The iodized salt is *sodium chloride* to which *sodium* or *potassium iodide* has been added. The proportion in this type salt is usually one part iodide to 5,000 parts salt.

An *herb salt* is a blend of the ground dehydrated herb or herb powder and pure, regular, free-running table salt. One uses an herb salt when a milder seasoning is desired than that which the herb powder imparts. When an herb salt is added to any favorite recipe, the amount of regular salt should naturally be reduced by one half the amount called for.

One of the newest forms of herb and spice flavoring is a liquid extract: *Sperb,* the product of a chemist. This extract is prepared in the same way as the more familiar almond and vanilla extracts. The essential oils of the herbs and spices, such as cinnamon, garlic, tarragon, et cetera, are combined with alcohol and water to form a concentrated seasoning. This may be added to foods at the last moment before serving. Since the extract is highly concentrated, the originator and manufacturer suggests that it be added drop by drop until the exact and desired degree of flavor is secured.

The extracts will keep over an extended period of time if carefully and tightly covered after each using. Naturally there is a certain amount of normal evaporation in any product with an alcohol base. The average amount of seasoning extract to use in recipes serving 4 is from 5 to 10 drops; but here also personal tastes may vary to a great degree.

Using: Both herb powders and herb salts may be used in all the foods in which one might use a particular dried or fresh herb. In addition to using the herb powders and salts as flavoring for foods while they are being cooked, these dehydrated forms make attractive and tasty garnishes. Try dusting potato chips with celery or parsley salt before heating and serving; or season a fish or shellfish salad with a light sprinkling of a favorite herb powder or salt. A half teaspoon of herb powder blended with ¼ pound of a soft, creamy cheese makes a delicious canapé or sandwich spread. See also the uses of each particular herb or spice.

The following list includes those herb powders and salts, liquid extracts, and spice salts which are on the market at the time of this volume's going to press. All other spices in ground and powdered form are included in the spice sections. Undoubtedly, as the use of powdered herbs and salts increases, the variety will also increase.

Herb- and Spice-flavored Powders and Salts (*In ½ ounce to 2 ounce bottles, or larger, at groceries and markets; also from herb dealers.*)

Celery salt	Hickory-smoked salt
Charcoal-flavored salt	Mono Sodium Glutamate,
Chive powder	or MSG
Chive salt	Onion powder
Curry salt	Onion salt
Garlic powder	Parsley salt
Garlic salt	

MSG is a powder prepared from vegetable derivatives; "not a condiment, not an ordinary seasoning."

Tips on Using Mono Sodium Glutamate, MSG

MSG may be used in conjunction with all herbs and spices. It adds no additional aroma but brings out true flavors in foods. MSG is also sold under the trade names of *Ac'cent* (Pure MSG) and *Enhance* (MSG with 3 herbs added). For specific suggestion on uses of MSG, see Sauces and Stuffings.

APPETIZERS: *Prepared Spreads.* Blend in ¼ to ½ teaspoon MSG with each cup of spread.

CHEESES: *Cooked.* Allow ⅛ to ¼ teaspoon MSG for each ¼ pound or 1 cup grated cheese.
Melted. Blend in ⅛ to ¼ teaspoon MSG with other ingredients as soon as cheese is hot.

FISH: *Boiled, steamed.* Add ¼ teaspoon MSG to water in which 2 pounds fish is cooked.

GRAVIES: *Leftover* and *pan gravy.* Add ¾ teaspoon MSG to gravy while heating.

LEFTOVERS: *Meats, poultry, vegetables.* Sprinkle lightly with MSG during reheating process.

MEATS: *Hamburgers, loaves.* Blend in ½ teaspoon MSG for each pound of meat.

POULTRY: *Chicken, turkey, creamed.* Add ½ to ¾ teaspoon MSG to 2 cups sauce during preparation.

SAUCES: All *brown* and *creamed.* Add ½ to ¾ teaspoon MSG to 2 cups sauce during preparation.

SOUPS: *Bouillons, chowders, consommé, purées.* Add few crystals MSG to each portion at time of serving.

STEWS: *Meat, poultry.* Add ½ teaspoon MSG to each 2 pounds while preparing.

VEGETABLES: *All sweet vegetables,* such as *asparagus, carrot,* and *celery.* Add ¼ teaspoon MSG to water in which vegetables are boiled.

Sperb Liquid Herb and Spice Extracts (*In 1 ounce to 2 ounce bottles; also in sets of 4 to 6 varied flavors, at fancy groceries and markets.*)

Allspice	Garlic	Rosemary
Anise	Marjoram	Tarragon
Cinnamon	Mint	Thyme
Clove	Nutmeg	

Pot Roast with Herb Salts and Blended Spices

TIME: Variable

4 lbs. beef, bottom round
1 large onion, sliced
2 tbs. bacon fat or margarine
½ tsp. celery salt
½ tsp. garlic or onion salt

2 tsp. poultry seasoning
2 bay leaves
¼ tsp. black pepper
1 to 2 cups hot water

Purchase bottom or eye-round beef cut in uniform piece.

Blend celery salt, garlic or onion salt, poultry seasoning, and pepper. Rub seasoning well into all sides of meat.

Melt fat in deep pan over high flame; brown meat on all sides; add onion, bay leaves, and 1 cup hot water. (Place rack under meat to prevent scorching.) Cover; lower flame. Cook evenly and gently 3 hours, or until tender, adding small amount hot water if necessary. Serve with pan gravy and Mustard Dumplings. Serves 8.

To save time, meat may be cooked in pressure cooker.

Oven-braised Spareribs with Herb Salts   TIME: 1½ hours

1 sheet spareribs (3 lbs.)
½ tsp. onion salt
½ tsp. celery salt
¼ tsp. garlic salt
¼ tsp. parsley salt
¼ tsp. white pepper
½ tsp. ground sage

¼ tsp. ground marjoram
1 cup water
8 small white onions, peeled
8 new or small potatoes, peeled
8 small carrots, peeled

Select lean, meaty spareribs. Place in shallow baking pan.

Blend all seasonings in cup by stirring vigorously with spoon. Rub seasoning on top side of spareribs; turn; rub seasoning over other side. Brown in preheated hot oven (425° F.) 10 minutes; pour water carefully into bottom of baking pan; reduce oven heat to 350° F.; cover baking pan; bake 30 minutes.

Arrange onions and potatoes around spareribs; cover; bake 20 minutes; add carrots; cover; bake 10 minutes. Remove cover; carefully turn vegetables; baste with pan gravy. Bake uncovered 20 more minutes, or until vegetables are tender and spareribs are *well done*. Serve piping hot with liquid pan gravy. Serves 4.

Tomato Juice with Herb Salts   TIME: 15 minutes
Chill 15 minutes

1 qt. tomato juice
¼ tsp. onion salt

¼ tsp. celery salt
1 tbs. prepared mustard

Blend herb salts with prepared mustard. Add seasoning to tomato juice. Chill in refrigerator 15 minutes. Serve ice cold as cocktail. *Other preferred vegetable juices* may be seasoned in same manner.

CHAPTER NINE

Herb, Condiment, and Spice Salad Dressings

Herbs, Condiments, and Spices Especially Good in SALAD DRESSINGS and MAYONNAISE (*For specific suggestions, please see pages devoted to each herb or spice. See also list of Herbs and Spices especially good with Salads and Salad Dressings.*)

Bay leaf	Cress, land	Mints
Borage	Curry powder	Mustard, dry
Capers	Curry salt	Mustard, prepared
Caraway seed	Dill, fresh	Onion
Catsup	Dill, ground seed	Onion powder
Celery	Dill, whole seed	Onion salt
Celery salt	Garlic	Paprika
Celery seed	Garlic powder	Parsley salt
Chili powder	Garlic salt	Shallot
Chili salt	Horseradish, dry	Tarragon
Chives, fresh	Horseradish, prepared	Thyme
Chive powder	Lovage, fresh	Water cress
Chive salt	Lovage seed	

Basic Herb French Dressing   TIME: 10 minutes

1 cup olive oil
¼ cup red wine vinegar
½ tsp. sugar
1 tsp. salt

⅛ tsp. white pepper
¼ tsp. paprika
½ tsp. dry mustard
1 clove garlic, halved

Blend all dry ingredients; place in wide-mouthed jar; pour olive oil and vinegar over all; stir vigorously; add garlic. Allow to stand at room temperature 1 to 2 hours. Remove garlic. Shake thoroughly before using. Yield: Approximately 1⅓ cups.

Herb French Dressings with Condiments

CATSUP FRENCH DRESSING: Add 1 tablespoon catsup to Basic Herb French Dressing. Stir well before serving.

CHILI SAUCE FRENCH DRESSING: Add 1½ tablespoons chili sauce to Basic Herb French Dressing. Stir well before serving.

CHUTNEY FRENCH DRESSING: Add 2 tablespoons chutney to Basic Herb French Dressing. Stir well before serving.

Herb French Dressings with Fresh Minced Herbs (*If dried herbs are used, blend in ½ teaspoon of the selected herb and other ingredients when preparing recipe. Allow to stand 15 minutes before serving.*)

BORAGE FRENCH DRESSING: Add 1 teaspoon minced borage to Basic Herb French Dressing. Stir in just before serving.

BURNET FRENCH DRESSING: Add 1 teaspoon minced burnet to Basic Herb French Dressing. Stir in just before serving.

CAPERS FRENCH DRESSING: Add 2 teaspoons chopped capers to Basic Herb French Dressing. Stir in just before serving.

CHERVIL FRENCH DRESSING: Add 2 teaspoons minced chervil to Basic Herb French Dressing. Stir in just before serving.

CHIVES FRENCH DRESSING: Add 2 teaspoons minced chives to Basic Herb French Dressing. Stir in just before serving.

CRESS (LAND) FRENCH DRESSING: Add 2 teaspoons minced land cress to Basic Herb French Dressing. Stir in just before serving.

FENNEL FRENCH DRESSING: Add 2 teaspoons minced fennel to Basic Herb French Dressing. Stir in just before serving.

LOVAGE FRENCH DRESSING: Add 2 teaspoons minced lovage to Basic Herb French Dressing. Stir in just before serving.

PARSLEY FRENCH DRESSING: Add 2 teaspoons minced parsley to Basic Herb French Dressing. Stir in just before serving.

SCALLION FRENCH DRESSING: Add 1 teaspoon minced scallions to Basic Herb French Dressing. Stir in just before serving.

WATER-CRESS FRENCH DRESSING: Add 2 teaspoons minced water cress to Basic Herb French Dressing. Stir in just before serving.

See also French Dressing with Tarragon Vinegar in recipe for Sorrel and Herbs Salad.

Herb French Dressings with Aromatic Seeds

CELERY-SEED FRENCH DRESSING: Add ½ teaspoon celery seed to Basic Herb French Dressing just before serving. Stir well.

DILL-SEED FRENCH DRESSING: Add ¼ teaspoon dill seed to Basic Herb French Dressing just before serving. Stir well.

LOVAGE-SEED FRENCH DRESSING: Add ¼ teaspoon lovage seed to Basic Herb French Dressing just before serving. Stir well.

Herb French Dressings with Spices

CHILI-POWDER FRENCH DRESSING: Omit dry mustard for Basic Herb French Dressing. Stir in chili powder instead.

CURRY-SALT FRENCH DRESSING: Omit dry mustard and ½ teaspoon regular salt from Basic Herb French Dressing. Stir in ½ teaspoon curry salt instead.

Condiment-herb Mayonnaise   TIME: 20 minutes

1 cup mayonnaise   *1 tsp. chives, minced*
¾ cup chili sauce   *1 tsp. fresh chervil, minced*
⅛ tsp. curry powder   *1 tsp. fresh parsley, minced*
⅛ tsp. paprika   *2 tsp. tarragon vinegar*
1 tsp. fresh tarragon, minced

Blend well chili sauce, curry powder, paprika, herbs, and vinegar in wide-mouthed jar. Gradually stir in mayonnaise; mix gently until herbs, mayonnaise, and condiment are thoroughly blended. Cover. Allow to stand at room temperature several hours so herb flavors may permeate dressing. Chill in refrigerator, as preferred, shortly before serving. Yield: Approximately 1 pint.

If fresh herbs are not available, use ⅛ teaspoon dried tarragon and ¼ teaspoon other dried herbs.

Curry-and-garlic Mayonnaise TIME: 10 minutes
Marinate 2 hours

½ pt. mayonnaise *½ tsp. garlic salt*
1 tsp. curry powder

Blend curry powder and garlic salt. Place mayonnaise in mixing bowl; gradually stir in blended powder. Allow to stand 2 hours before using. Yield: ½ pint.
Excellent with *sea-food cocktails* and *salads*.

Dry Mustard Mayonnaise TIME: 5 minutes

1 pint mayonnaise *2 tbs. distilled vinegar*
2 tsp. dry mustard

Blend well mustard and vinegar in mixing bowl; when smooth, add mayonnaise, stirring well until blended. Set aside and use as desired with *baked, boiled,* or *broiled fish*. Yield: 1 pint.

Chili Powder Mayonnaise may be prepared in same way. Use only 1 teaspoon powder unless more pungent flavor is desired.

Herb Health Salad Dressing TIME: 10 minutes

1 tsp. celery seed *1 cup fresh yogurt*
1 clove garlic, minced *¼ cup French Dressing*

Blend celery seed and minced garlic in mixing bowl.
Stir vigorously the fresh yogurt and French Dressing in separate bowl. Add to celery-seed mixture; blend well.
Serve immediately as *dressing for coleslaw, cucumbers, mixed-green,* or *potato salad*. Serves 4 generously.
Yogurt is a cultured milk food of custard consistency. In America it is made from pure, fresh, whole, pasteurized, homogenized cows' milk with added lactic cultures.

Herb Wine Salad Dressing TIME: 15 minutes
Marinate 15 minutes

½ cup sauterne wine *½ tsp. dry mustard*
½ cup olive oil *½ tsp. onion salt*
¼ cup white wine vinegar *¼ tsp. celery salt*
¼ tsp. salt *1 tsp. grated onion*
1 tsp. sugar *⅛ tsp. white pepper*

Mix and blend salt, sugar, mustard, onion salt, celery salt, onion, and pepper in wide-mouthed jar. Gradually stir in wine, olive oil, and vinegar; blend by stirring well. Set aside to marinate 15 minutes before using. Yield: 1¼ cups.

Shake well before pouring over any preferred *hearty salads* containing *hard-boiled eggs, fish, minced ham, potatoes,* or *cooked vegetables.*

Horseradish Herb Dressing

TIME: 10 minutes
Chill 15 minutes

*1 tbs. freshly grated horse-
   radish*
¾ cup sour cream
2 tsp. tarragon vinegar
2 tsp. chopped chives

2 tsp. sugar
½ tsp. salt
⅛ tsp. paprika
1 tsp. minced fresh dill

Blend well grated horseradish, sour cream, and vinegar in mixing bowl; when smooth, add chives, sugar, salt, paprika, and dill. Mix. Taste. If more salt is preferred, add very little before retasting. Cover bowl. Place mixture in refrigerator; chill well 15 minutes or longer. Serves 4.

Serve over *tossed-green salad, sliced tomatoes, combination vegetable,* or *cucumbers.*

If freshly grated horseradish root is not available, use prepared ground horseradish condiment and only 1 teaspoon vinegar. *If fresh dill is not available,* substitute chopped parsley.

Piquant Spice Salad Dressing

TIME: 10 minutes
Marinate 2 hours

1 tsp. dry mustard
½ tsp. mustard seed
½ tsp. celery seed
½ tsp. paprika
⅛ tsp. turmeric

3 tbs. cider vinegar
1 tbs. tarragon vinegar
1 cup olive oil
2 cloves garlic, halved
1 tsp. salt

Blend first 5 spices in wide-mouthed jar; pour in vinegars. then olive oil, stirring constantly; add garlic and salt; stir again. Cover tightly. Allow to stand 1 hour at room temperature. Chill 1 hour in refrigerator. Remove garlic before serving. Yield: 1½ cups.

Use with all salads which are usually served with French Dressing.

Savory Mustard Salad Dressing   TIME: 15 minutes

¾ tsp. dry mustard   *2 egg yolks, beaten*
2 tbs. flour   *½ cup wine vinegar*
1 tsp. salt   *1¼ cups milk, scalded*
1 tbs. sugar   *2 tbs. butter, melted*
⅛ tsp. paprika

Blend well mustard, flour, salt, sugar, and paprika in top section double boiler; add egg yolks; mix until smooth. Gradually
stir in scalded milk. Place over lower section double boiler
half filled with boiling water. Cook mixture 5 minutes, or until
thickened, stirring constantly. Remove from flame; blend in
vinegar and melted butter. Pour into glass jar. Allow to cool
at room temperature. Chill only slightly. *Use* as desired *with
fish* and *meat.* Yield: 1½ cups.
   Dressing may be thinned with cream before using if preferred.

Shallot Mint Dressing   TIME: 15 minutes
                                          Chill 15 minutes

1½ tsp. minced shallots   *¼ cup cider vinegar*
1½ tbs. chopped fresh mint   *1 tsp. salt*
1 cup olive oil   *⅛ tsp. white pepper*

Peel and mince shallots; chop mint. Pour oil and vinegar into
pint jar; add salt and pepper; stir well; add shallots and mint;
stir well. Cover tightly. Chill in refrigerator 15 minutes. Stir
vigorously before using. Serves 4 generously.
   Serve with *avocado pear,* or *orange-and-grapefruit salad.*

Spicy Salad Dressing with Yogurt   TIME: 10 minutes

1 pt. fresh yogurt   *4 tsp. lemon juice*
½ tsp. salt   *½ tsp. onion juice, optional*
2 tbs. strained honey   *⅛ tsp. paprika*
¾ tsp. curry powder

Use strictly fresh yogurt. Blend well salt, honey, curry powder,
lemon juice, onion juice, if used, and paprika in mixing bowl.
Gradually stir in yogurt until thoroughly blended. Serves 4
generously.
   Use with *fruit, shellfish,* or *water-cress salad.* Mixture *may
be eaten* separately *as a dessert.*

CHAPTER TEN

Herb and

Spice Sauces

and Stuffings

Herbs and Spices Especially Good In SAUCES And STUFFINGS

Basil, sweet
Bay leaf
Capers
Caraway seed
Celery
Celery salt
Celery seed
Chervil
Chili powder
Chive salt
Chives, fresh
Cinnamon
Cloves
Curry powder
Curry salt
Dill, fresh

Dill, ground seed
Dill, whole seed
Fennel
Garlic
Garlic powder
Garlic salt
Marjoram
Mints
Mole powder
Mono Sodium
   Glutamate, or
   MSG
Mustard, dry
Mustard, prepared
Nutmeg, ground
Onion

Onion powder
Onion salt
Orégano
Paprika
Parsley, fresh
Parsley salt
Peppers
Rosemary
Saffron
Sage
Savory
Scallions
Shallot
Tarragon
Thyme
Water cress

Please see condiments; specific recipes for sauces and stuffings; also pages devoted to each herb or spice.

Sauces

Basic White Sauce Thin   TIME: 30 minutes

1 tbs. butter   *1 cup milk*
1 tbs. flour   *¼ tsp. salt*
⅛ tsp. pepper

Melt butter in top section double boiler placed over lower
section half filled with boiling water. Stir in flour; gradually
add milk, salt, and pepper. Cook 5 minutes, or until smooth
and well done; stir occasionally. Yield: 1 cup thin sauce.

Medium Thick White Sauce: Use 2 tablespoons butter and 2
tablespoons flour. Follow recipe.

Mustard White Sauce, Hot: Add ½ to ¾ teaspoon dry mustard to basic ingredients; omit pepper. Follow recipe.

Mustard White Sauce, Tangy Mild: Add 1 teaspoon prepared
mustard to basic ingredients. Follow recipe.

Paprika Sauce, Mild: Add ¾ teaspoon paprika to basic ingredients. Follow recipe.

Paprika Sauce Piquante: Add 1 teaspoon paprika to basic
ingredients. Follow recipe.

Mono Sodium Glutamate, MSG, or Ac'cent, may be added
to all sauces. Use ⅟₁₆ to ¼ teaspoon, according to individual
tastes. Add MSG to other ingredients while cooking. See also
Tips on Using Mono Sodium Glutamate, MSG.

Black Muscat Spice Sauce   TIME: 15 minutes

1 cup boiling water   *⅛ tsp. ground nutmeg*
Rind of ½ lemon   *2 tbs. butter*
½ cup sugar   *2 tbs. lemon juice*
2 tbs. cornstarch   *¾ cup American black mus-*
⅛ tsp. salt   *cat wine*
¼ tsp. ground cinnamon

Pour boiling water into top section double boiler placed over
lower section half filled with boiling water; add lemon rind.
Cook 3 minutes.

Meanwhile blend sugar, cornstarch, cinnamon, and nutmeg;
gradually add to boiling water, stirring constantly 8 minutes,

or until sauce is thick and smooth. Remove lemon rind. Gradually stir in butter, lemon juice, and wine; continue stirring gently until very hot. Yield: 1½ cups.

Serve piping hot over *steamed puddings* and *custards*.

If black muscat is not available, substitute good heavy port wine. See also Cardamom Sauce.

Blended Herb Sauce   TIME: 15 minutes

½ tsp. minced fresh parsley
½ tsp. minced chervil
½ tsp. minced fennel
4 tsp. minced celery
½ tsp. minced fresh thyme
½ tsp. sweet marjoram, minced

¼ tsp. powdered sage or ½ tsp. minced fresh sage
2 ozs. butter
1 shallot, minced
White wine or cider vinegar
Salt and pepper to taste
2 tbs. olive oil

Melt butter in small saucepan over medium flame; add shallot. Sauté gently 3 minutes. Add all herbs and seasonings except salt and pepper; cover with preferred vinegar. Allow sauce to simmer 10 minutes, then add salt and pepper to taste. Blend in olive oil; stir well. Yield: Approximately 1 cup.

Serve hot over *boiled beef, roast veal, chicken,* or *fish.*

Creamy Horseradish Sauce   TIME: 15 minutes

½ cup heavy cream
3 tbs. grated horseradish root
½ tsp. salt

⅛ tsp. cayenne pepper
1 tbs. distilled or white wine vinegar

Pour cream into mixing bowl; whip until stiff. Blend freshly grated horseradish root, vinegar, salt, and cayenne pepper in large cup. Beat this mixture gradually into the whipped cream. When smooth, place in refrigerator to chill for 10 minutes. Serves 4.

Serve with *fish, shellfish, roast beef, baked ham,* or with *meat loaves* and *all foods with which a cold, tangy sauce is desired.*

Celery Golden Sauce   TIME: 1 hour

1 bunch celery
1 qt. milk
½ tsp. salt
⅛ tsp. white pepper

4 egg yolks, well beaten
¼ pint cream
⅛ tsp. cayenne pepper
Chopped chervil or parsley

Wash celery thoroughly under cold running water; cut into small pieces. Pour milk into heavy saucepan over medium flame; add celery, salt, and pepper. Simmer gently 45 minutes. Rub mixture through very fine sieve.

Beat egg yolks and cream until smooth; add cayenne pepper. Add to celery mixture. Heat slowly 5 minutes over very low flame, stirring constantly, until sauce thickens. Garnish with chopped chervil, parsley, or favorite green herb. Serves 6 to 8.

Serve piping hot *over baked* or *boiled fish.*

Fennel Sauce   TIME: 25 minutes

1 small bunch Florence fennel	*3 ozs. butter*
½ tsp. salt	*1 cup boiling water, extra*
1 cup water	*⅛ tsp. cayenne pepper*
1 tbs. flour	

Purchase young fresh Florence fennel. Wash thoroughly under cold running water; cut fennel into small pieces.

Pour 1 cup water into saucepan placed over medium flame; add salt; when boiling rapidly, add fennel. Boil 3 minutes. Remove from flame. Drain. Chop fennel fine. Set aside.

Place flour in heavy saucepan over low flame; stir constantly for 3 minutes, or until golden brown. Remove from flame; add butter; stir and blend well until very smooth; gradually stir in 1 cup boiling water. Replace saucepan over medium flame. Boil 10 minutes, stirring constantly. Add chopped fennel. Heat thoroughly 3 minutes. Serves 4 to 6.

Serve piping hot *over baked, broiled,* or *steamed fish.*

Ginger Cream Sauce   TIME: 20 minutes

2 tbs. butter	*¼ tsp. ground ginger*
1 cup rich milk	*¼ tsp. salt*
2 tbs. flour	*⅛ tsp. white pepper*

Melt butter in heavy saucepan over medium flame or in top section double boiler placed in lower section half filled with boiling water; gradually add flour; stir until smooth; add ginger, salt, and pepper. Gradually pour in cold milk, stirring constantly, until sauce is very smooth and thickens. Cook 5 to 10 minutes. Taste; if stronger flavor of ginger is preferred, use ¼ teaspoon more. Serves 4.

Serve piping hot *over boiled chicken, fish,* or *shellfish.*

Other herb or spice sauces may be prepared in same manner. Substitute the preferred dried or fresh herb as flavoring in place of the ground ginger and follow recipe. The amounts as given will make a medium-thick sauce. If a thinner sauce is preferred, use but 1 tablespoon flour.

Ginger Hard Sauce
TIME: 15 minutes

⅓ cup butter
2 cups powdered sugar

¾ tsp. ground ginger
¼ cup corn syrup

Cream butter well in mixing bowl. Blend sugar and ginger; gradually add half amount to butter; add syrup; stir well; gradually add balance of seasoned sugar; beat thoroughly. Chill before serving *over mixed bread* and *fruit puddings.* Yield: 1½ cups.

Herb-flavored Curry Sauce
TIME: 30 minutes

2 ozs. butter
1 carrot, sliced
2 onions, sliced
2 stalks celery, chopped
½ tsp. salt
⅛ tsp. white pepper

1 tsp. curry powder
⅛ tsp. ground mace
1 tsp. dried thyme
1 bay leaf
2 cups chicken broth or water
1 tbs. flour

Melt butter in heavy saucepan over medium flame; add carrot, onions, celery, salt, and pepper. Sauté 15 minutes, or until vegetables are soft. Add curry powder, mace, thyme, bay leaf, and broth or water; stir well. Allow to come to boiling point.

Dissolve flour in small quantity cold water or cooled liquid from saucepan; add to liquid in saucepan; stir constantly 5 minutes, or until sauce is of desired consistency. Strain sauce through coarse sieve. Reheat sauce.

Serve piping hot *with chicken, eggs, fish, meat loaf, shellfish,* or *vegetables.* Serves 4 to 6.

Herb Mayonnaise Heated Sauce
TIME: 20 minutes

½ cup mayonnaise
6 tbs. rich milk
2 tbs. minced parsley
2 tbs. minced green pepper

2 tbs. minced scallions
1 tbs. minced pimiento
2 hard-boiled eggs, chopped
2 tbs. water cress, minced

Blend mayonnaise and milk in top section double boiler placed over lower section half filled with boiling water. Heat 3 minutes, or until lukewarm. Gently stir in all herbs except water cress; add chopped eggs. Heat sauce thoroughly for 5 minutes, then add minced water cress; stir gently. Serves 4 generously.

Serve immediately over steaming hot vegetables, such as *asparagus, broccoli, celery, carrots, peas,* and *string beans.*

Herb Sauce Piquante   TIME: 45 minutes

¼ lb. butter	*3 whole allspice*
1 small carrot, minced	*1 blade mace or ⅛ tsp. mace*
4 shallots, minced	*⅛ cup vinegar*
1 sprig parsley, minced	*½ tsp. sugar*
½ bay leaf, crushed	*1 cup chicken broth*
3 whole cloves	*⅛ tsp. cayenne pepper*
6 peppercorns	*¼ tsp. salt*
2 slices bacon, minced	*1 Bouquet Garni*

Melt butter in deep saucepan over medium flame; add carrot, shallot, parsley, bay leaf, cloves, peppercorns, bacon, allspice, and mace. Simmer gently 10 minutes, or until bacon is golden brown; stir occasionally. Gradually blend in vinegar, sugar, chicken broth, cayenne, and salt, stirring constantly; add Bouquet Garni; cover. Simmer gently 20 minutes. Remove Bouquet Garni. Skim off all excess fat. Serves 4 to 6.

Serve unstrained, piping hot, over *roast lamb* and *veal. If clear sauce is preferred,* strain through very fine sieve before serving.

Herb Wine Sauce   TIME: 20 minutes

2 tbs. capers	*¼ cup Rhine wine*
1 cup mayonnaise	*1 tbs. minced parsley*
10 stuffed olives, chopped	*1 tbs. grated onion*
¼ tsp. salt	*⅛ tsp. white pepper*

Blend mayonnaise, capers, olives, salt, wine, parsley, grated onion, and pepper in top section double boiler placed over lower section half filled with boiling water. Stirring gently, heat thoroughly for 10 minutes.

Serve piping hot over *baked* or *steamed fish,* such as *halibut, salmon,* and *whitefish.* Yield: 1½ cups.

Horseradish Herb Jelly Sauce   TIME: 10 minutes
                                          Chill 15 minutes

4 tbs. horseradish   *2 tbs. rosemary jelly or 2 tbs.*
¾ cup heavy cream   *tart currant jelly*
½ tsp. salt   *1 tsp. sugar*

Whip heavy cream until stiff in small mixing bowl; add horseradish, salt, rosemary jelly, and sugar. Mix well. Chill 15
minutes in refrigerator.
    Serve with *baked, broiled,* or *roast ham* or *pork.* Yield: 1
cup.

Horseradish Mustard Sauce, Mild   TIME: 30 minutes

4 tbs. freshly grated horse-   *¼ tsp. white pepper*
*   radish*   *4 tbs. cream*
1 tsp. sugar   *Distilled or white wine vine-*
¾ tsp. salt   *   gar*
2 tsp. dry mustard

Blend sugar, salt, mustard, and white pepper in large bowl;
add horseradish; stir well; moisten with very little vinegar (not
more than 2 teaspoonfuls); blend well; stir in enough cream
to make smooth sauce; blend well again. Chill in refrigerator
15 minutes. Serves 4 to 6.
    Serve with *cold roasts.* If desired, this sauce may be heated
and served with *hot meats,* such as *steaks* and *roasts.*

Mint Sauce, Boiled   TIME: 15 minutes

3 tbs. dried mint leaves   *3 tbs. distilled vinegar*
¼ cup water   *2 tbs. sugar*

Pour water into small saucepan over high flame; add vinegar
and sugar; stir well. Bring to boil. Add dried mint leaves. Remove saucepan to back of stove where it will keep hot; cover
tightly. Steep leaves 12 minutes. Serves 4.
    Serve piping hot over *roast lamb, lamb chops,* or *hash.*

Mint Sauce #1   TIME: 1¼ hours

¼ cup minced fresh mint   *½ cup cider vinegar*
*   leaves*   *1 tbs. powdered sugar*

Select fresh leaves only. Wash thoroughly; remove from stems; mince with sharp knife; place minced leaves in small saucepan.

Dissolve sugar in vinegar; pour over mint leaves. Stand in warm place (near flame or oven). Allow to infuse 1 hour, then allow to cool. Yield: ¾ cup.

Serve cold with *roast lamb* or *veal*.

Two teaspoons dried mint leaves may be used instead of fresh; if so, freshen leaves by allowing them to stand in lemon juice about 5 minutes before blending.

Mint Sauce #2   TIME: 20 minutes

¼ cup minced fresh mint leaves	*½ cup sugar*
	¼ cup water
½ cup lemon or lime juice	*⅛ tsp. salt*

Blend lemon or lime juice, sugar, water, and salt in small saucepan. Heat over low flame 5 minutes. Add mint leaves; stir well. Allow to stand near heat 15 minutes. Yield: ¾ cup.

Serve hot with *fish, lamb* or *veal*.

Two teaspoons dried mint leaves may be used instead of fresh; if they are, freshen leaves by allowing them to stand in lemon juice about 5 minutes before blending.

Mint Sauce #3   TIME: 15 minutes

¼ cup minced fresh mint or spearmint	*1 cup cider vinegar*
	⅛ tsp. salt
2 tbs. powdered sugar	

Select fresh leaves only. Wash thoroughly; dry with absorbent paper. Mince herb with sharp knife.

Pour vinegar into heavy saucepan; add sugar and salt. Dissolve and heat thoroughly over low flame; when hot, add mint leaves. Yield: 1 cup.

Serve piping hot over *roast lamb* or *veal*. If cold mint sauce is preferred, blend all ingredients and allow to stand at room temperature for 1 hour, then serve.

Two teaspoons dried mint leaves may be used instead of fresh; if they are, freshen leaves by allowing them to stand in lemon juice about 5 minutes before blending.

Mustard Sauce Épicé   TIME: 15 minutes
Mustard Sauce Hot to the Taste

1 tbs. dry mustard	*⅔ cup evaporated milk or*
2 tbs. butter	*light cream*
¾ tsp. salt	*1 egg yolk, beaten*
2 tsp. cornstarch	*1 tbs. cider vinegar*
1½ tsp. sugar	

Melt butter over medium flame in top section double boiler placed over lower section half filled with boiling water.

Blend mustard, salt, cornstarch, and sugar in small bowl by stirring vigorously; gradually add to melted butter; stirring constantly, gradually pour in evaporated milk. Boil gently 6 to 8 minutes, stirring occasionally. When smooth, gradually stir in egg yolk; blend well; add vinegar; stir again. Boil gently 2 minutes, or until sauce is of desired consistency. Yield: ⅔ cup. Sauce thickens when standing. To thin, add small quantity evaporated milk and reheat. Serve piping hot over *fish, hamburgers, hash,* or *frankfurters.*

Mustard Sauce Piquant   TIME: 20 minutes

2 tbs. butter	*1¼ tsp. dry mustard*
1 tbs. flour	*2 tbs. diced sweet pickle*
1 cup milk	*1 hard-boiled egg, minced*
½ tsp. salt	*⅛ tsp. paprika*
⅛ tsp. pepper	*½ tsp. Worcestershire sauce*

Melt butter in heavy saucepan over medium flame. Remove from heat. Gradually add flour, stirring constantly until smooth. Gradually add milk, stirring until very smooth. Return to heat. Cook slowly, stirring constantly, about 5 minutes, or until sauce thickens slightly. Add all seasonings and remaining ingredients, stirring gently and carefully. Cook 3 minutes more, or until sauce is thoroughly heated and of desired thickness. Yield: 1½ cups.

Serve piping hot over *boiled* or *broiled fish.*

Parsley Sauce Poulette   TIME: 20 minutes

3 tbs. butter	*¼ cup milk*
3 tbs. enriched flour	*⅛ tsp. paprika*
1½ cups chicken broth	*⅛ tsp. salt*
⅓ cup chopped parsley	

Melt butter over medium flame; in top section double boiler placed over lower section half filled with boiling water. Gradually stir in flour; when smooth, add chicken broth; blend thoroughly by stirring constantly. Boil gently 6 minutes. Add parsley, milk, paprika, and salt; stir gently until piping hot. Serves 4 generously.

Serve immediately over *broiled* or *fried fish, hash,* or *roast game,* and *poultry.*

Many *other green herbs* may be used to flavor sauce instead of parsley.

Celery Sauce Poulette: Use ⅓ cup chopped celery. Follow recipe.

Chervil Sauce Poulette: Use ⅓ cup chopped chervil. Follow recipe.

Chive Sauce Poulette: Use 1 tablespoon minced chives. Follow recipe.

Dill Sauce Poulette: Use 2 teaspoons chopped dill. Follow recipe.

Fennel Sauce Poulette: Use ⅓ cup chopped fennel. Follow recipe.

Leek Sauce Poulette: Use 2 teaspoons minced leek. Follow recipe.

Water-cress Sauce Poulette: Use ⅓ cup chopped water cress. Follow recipe.

Poppy-seed Herb Sauce #1   TIME: 10 minutes

2 tsp. poppy seed   *⅛ tsp. marjoram*
¼ cup butter   *⅛ tsp. paprika*
1 tbs. lemon juice

Melt butter in small saucepan over medium flame; gradually stir in poppy seed, lemon juice, marjoram, and paprika. Yield: Sufficient for 1 pound vegetables.

Serve piping hot over vegetables, such as *asparagus, beets, onions, carrots, cauliflower,* and *peas.*

Poppy-seed Herb Sauce #2   TIME: 10 minutes

2 tsp. poppy seed   *⅛ tsp. salt*
¼ cup butter   *⅛ tsp. cayenne pepper*
Juice of ½ lemon

Melt butter in small saucepan over low flame; add poppy seed, lemon juice, salt, and cayenne; blend well. Yield: Sufficient for 1 pound vegetables.

Serve piping hot over *asparagus, broccoli, cabbage, cauliflower, peas, string beans* or any preferred *sweet vegetable.*

Shallot Wine Sauce   TIME: 30 minutes

1 tbs. minced shallots   *4 white peppercorns, crushed*
1 cup dry white wine   *3 egg yolks*
1 tbs. tarragon vinegar   *¼ cup soft butter*
2 sprigs parsley, minced   *2 tbs. tomato paste*
1 sprig fresh tarragon, minced   *½ cup rich cream*

Heat wine, vinegar, shallots, parsley, tarragon, and peppercorns in small saucepan over high flame. Boil gently 20 minutes, or until liquid is reduced to half the quantity. Remove from heat. Cool few minutes. Strain through fine sieve. Pour strained liquid into top section double boiler placed over lower section half filled with boiling water. One at a time gradually beat in each egg yolk alternately with one-third amount of butter, then stir in tomato paste and cream; blend well. Yield: 1 cup.

Serve piping hot over *baked, boiled,* or *broiled fish, poultry,* or *roast veal.*

Spicy Sweet Sauce   TIME: 20 minutes

1 cup sugar   *1 tbs. flour*
⅛ tsp. cinnamon   *1 cup boiling water*
⅛ tsp. allspice   *2 tbs. butter*
⅛ tsp. nutmeg   *1 tsp. vanilla extract*
⅛ tsp. mace

Blend well all dry ingredients in top section double boiler placed over lower section half filled with boiling water; gradually stir in boiling water; add butter; blend well. Cook gently 8 to 10 minutes, or until sauce thickens; add vanilla. Serves 4.

Serve *hot* or *cold* over *custards* and *puddings.* If served cold, allow sauce to cool before adding vanilla.

Stuffings

Blended Herb Stuffing   TIME: 30 minutes

2 tsp. dried sage
1 tsp. dried summer savory
2 tsp. freshly chopped celery
    leaves
1 tsp. dried thyme
½ tsp. salt
¼ tsp. white pepper

1 egg, well beaten
1 small onion, minced
    (optional)
6 cups soft bread crumbs
½ cup sliced mushrooms
2 tsp. chopped parsley
3 tbs. butter, melted

Melt butter in small skillet over low flame. Sauté onion 5 minutes but do not brown.

Blend all other ingredients thoroughly in large mixing bowl. Add sautéed onion if used; mix well. If moister stuffing is preferred, add small quantity milk after all ingredients are well mixed. Sufficient to stuff 7-pound *capon* or 6-pound *boned veal shoulder*.

Blended Sage Stuffing   TIME: 20 minutes

7 cups cubed stale bread
1 medium onion, minced
2 tbs. butter
½ tbs. poultry seasoning
1 tsp. salt
1 tsp. ground sage

½ tsp. celery salt
½ tsp. garlic salt
½ tsp. pepper
1 cup melted butter
½ cup boiling water

Melt butter in heavy skillet over medium flame; add minced onion. Sauté 3 minutes, or until onion is light brown.

Blend poultry seasoning, salt, sage, celery salt, garlic salt, and pepper in cup.

Place bread in large mixing bowl; add blended seasonings; mix by tossing lightly; add onion; combine butter and water; add gradually to bread; mix lightly. Yield: Sufficient for 10- to 12-pound *turkey*.

If moister stuffing is desired, add ¼ cup more water.

Blended Sage Chestnut Stuffing: Boil 1 pound chestnuts 20 minutes, or until soft; peel; chop; fold into stuffing.

Blended Sage Oyster Stuffing: Purchase 1 pint oysters in liquor; drain. Heat oysters 3 minutes in 2 tablespoons butter placed in heavy saucepan. Chop; fold oysters into stuffing.

Poultry Seasoning Pistachio Stuffing   TIME: 20 minutes

6 slices stale bread
½ cup milk
¼ lb. boiled ham, minced
1 poultry liver, boiled and
*   chopped fine*
1 stalk celery, minced

½ tsp. poultry seasoning
1 cup shelled pistachio nuts
⅛ tsp. thyme
4 tsp. salt
¼ tsp. pepper
1 small onion, minced

Soften and mix bread with milk in large mixing bowl; gradually add all other ingredients. Stir gently but well as each is added to the mixture.

Stuff lightly into roasting *chicken* or *duck*. Sufficient for a 4- to 5-pound chicken or duck. Double or triple recipe for large turkey. A delectable stuffing for *lamb shoulder* and *breast of veal.*

Sage Walnut Stuffing   TIME: 30 minutes

¼ lb. butter, melted
1 small onion, minced
2 stalks celery, chopped
3½ cups dry bread crumbs
1 tsp. powdered sage

1 cup toasted walnuts,
*   chopped*
¾ tsp. salt
⅛ tsp. white pepper

Melt butter in deep saucepan over low flame; add onion and celery. Sauté gently 5 minutes, or until onion is light brown. Remove from flame; blend in well bread crumbs, sage, walnuts, salt, and pepper. Serves 6.

Use as stuffing for *fish, poultry,* or *meats,* especially *black sea bass, bluefish, sea trout, goose, turkey, veal,* and *pork.*

CHAPTER ELEVEN

Herb Teas and

Spiced Beverages

Many of us have used various herbs as additional flavoring to either hot or cold Chinese tea. One may also place a sprig of spearmint, apple mint, or lemon thyme in a sparkling glass of iced tea. However, many delicious and refreshing drinks can be prepared by using the herb leaves, flowers, or seed, without combining them with the teas of the Orientals.

The flavors of these herb teas, like those of the Chinese and East Indian flower teas, are unusually delicate and can be very easily tainted by metal. So the same care should be taken in preparing them as one takes when brewing regular tea. The utensil used for the infusion or decoction should be earthenware, china, porcelain, granite, or enamel, but *not* metal.

Too long steeping also can wreck the flavor of delicate herbs, therefore it is best to steep the leaves a shorter time and use more of the herb if a very strong infusion is desired. When I prepare an herb tea with dried leaves, I place 1 teaspoon of the leaves in a strainer and pour the boiling water through them, then repeat the same process for each cup. The resulting flavor is a most delicate and subtle one. However, bergamot and bee balm require about 10 minutes' boiling to bring out the full flavor. The same is true of the aromatic seed. They, too, must be crushed and boiled at least 10 minutes to secure a good, tasty tea.

The average amount of dried leaves to use in the preparation is 1 teaspoon of herb for each cup and 1 for the teapot. With fresh herbs, the proportion should be 3 teaspoons of the herb for each cup. The fresh leaves should be bruised gently by crushing them lightly in a clean cloth before infusing. When making an aromatic seed tea, use 1 tablespoon seed to each pint of water and crush the seed well before boiling.

The procedure for preparing herb teas is quite simple and the results delicious, soothing, and very refreshing.

To Prepare Herb Teas from Dried or Fresh Leaves

Rinse porcelain teapot with boiling water.
Dry teapot thoroughly.
Place dried or freshly crushed herb leaves in teapot. (If preferred, tie herb leaves in thin bags, as many commercial teas are packaged.)
Pour boiling water over herb leaves or bags.
Allow to steep 3 to 5 minutes only.
Remove leaves.
If stronger infusion is desired, use more leaves at beginning of preparation.

To Prepare Aromatic Seed Herb Teas

Bruise seed slightly with pestle to bring out oil.
Pour boiling water into enamel pan placed over high flame.
Add bruised seed.
Simmer gently 5 to 10 minutes.
Strain quickly.
Serve piping hot.

To Prepare Iced Herb Teas

Place crushed herb in earthenware pitcher.
Pour boiling hot water over herb.
Allow to steep 5 minutes.
Remove leaves; cover pitcher.
Place pitcher in refrigerator to cool.

A list of the leaves, flowers, and aromatic seed which are especially good in herb teas follows. One can derive a great deal of pleasure from concocting blends, and several such are suggested in the list.

Leaves, Flowers, and Aromatic Seed Especially Good in HERB TEAS

ANGELICA: Dried or fresh leaves; infused; served hot.

ANISE: Dried or fresh leaves; infused; served hot or iced.

ANISE SEED: Seed crushed; infused; served hot. The Swiss and Dutch flavor hot milk with anise seed and drink it before retiring. Its pleasant, aromatic flavor relaxes jangled nerves and induces a restful sleep.

BALM OR LEMON BALM: Dried or fresh leaves; infused; served hot or iced; *also blended with mints.*

BERGAMOT OR WILD BERGAMOT: Dried or fresh leaves; infused; served hot.

BORAGE: Dried or fresh leaves; infused; served hot or iced.

BURNET: Dried or fresh leaves; infused; served hot.

CAMOMILE: Dried flowers; infused; served hot.

CARAWAY SEED: Seed crushed; infused; served hot.

CATNIP: Dried or fresh leaves; infused; served hot as a stimulating tonic.

COSTMARY: Dried or fresh leaves; infused; *also blended with mints;* served hot.

DILL SEED: Seed crushed; infused; served hot.

FENNEL SEED: Seed crushed; infused; served hot.

HOREHOUND: Dried or fresh leaves; infused; served hot as "bitters."

HYSSOP: Dried or fresh leaves; infused; served hot. A great favorite in France and England.

LAVENDER: Dried or fresh leaves and flower buds; infused; *also blended with mints and rosemary;* served hot or iced.

LOVAGE: Dried or fresh leaves; infused; served hot as a restful, relaxing drink.

MARJORAM, SWEET: Fresh leaves; infused; *also blended with mints;* served hot or iced.

MINTS: *Apple, orange, peppermint, spearmint.* Dried or fresh leaves; infused; *also blended with sweet marjoram and lemon verbena;* served hot or iced.

PARSLEY: Dried or fresh leaves; infused; served as tonic.

PARSLEY SEED: Seed crushed; infused; served hot.

ROSE GERANIUM: Dried or fresh leaves; infused; *also blended with mints;* served hot or iced.

ROSEMARY: Dried or fresh leaves and flowering tops; also young sprigs; infused; *also blended with lavender flowers;* served hot or iced.

ROSE PETALS: Dried or fresh petals; infused; *also blended with mints;* served hot or iced.

SAFFRON: Dried or fresh stigmas crushed slightly; infused; served hot as spring tonic.

SAGE, GARDEN AND PINEAPPLE: Dried or fresh leaves; infused; *also blended with mints and lemon thyme;* served hot or iced.

THYME, GARDEN AND LEMON: Dried or fresh leaves; infused; *also blended with sage;* served hot.

VERBENA, LEMON: Dried or fresh leaves; infused; *also blended with mints;* served hot or iced.

WOODRUFF: Dried or fresh leaves; infused; served hot as stimulating tea.

Anise Seed Herb Tea   TIME: 10 minutes

1 tbs. anise seed   *1 pt. boiling water*

Use whole anise seed. Bruise slightly with pestle to bring out oil and flavor. Pour boiling water into enamel pan over high flame. Add bruised seed. Simmer gently 5 to 10 minutes. Strain. Serve piping hot. Serves 2.

Will relax jangled nerves and induce sleep.

Caraway-seed Herb Tea: Use caraway seed instead of anise. Follow recipe.

Fennel-seed Herb Tea: Use fennel seed instead of anise. Follow recipe.

Dried Leaves and Flowers Herb Tea   TIME: 10 minutes

5 tsp. selected dried herb   *4 cups boiling water*
*   for tea*   *Honey or sugar*

Rinse porcelain teapot with boiling water; dry teapot thoroughly. Place 5 teaspoons dried leaves in teapot; pour boiling water over leaves. *Allow to steep 3 to 5 minutes only.* Remove leaves. If stronger flavor is desired, use more herb when preparing infusion. Serve steaming hot in preheated hot cups; sweeten with honey or sugar to taste. Serves 4.

All herb teas made with leaves and flowers may be prepared in same way except bergamot and bee balm, which should be boiled or simmered 10 minutes to bring out real flavor.

Spiced Tea Punch   TIME: 15 minutes
                                                      Freeze 2 hours

3 cups brewed tea   *¼ tsp. ground allspice*
1½ cups orange juice   *¼ tsp. ground cinnamon*
1½ cups cranberry juice   *¼ tsp. ground nutmeg*
Sugar to taste   *Mint sprigs*

Blend tea, orange juice and cranberry juice; add sugar to taste;
stir in spices. Freeze liquid to mush in refrigerator. Spoon into
tall glasses. Garnish with mint sprig. Serve at once. Serves 4.

Spiced Wine Cup   TIME: 20 minutes

1 pt. cranberry-juice cocktail   *10 whole cloves*
½ cup sugar   *1 bottle burgundy wine*
3 strips lemon peel   *Nutmeg*
1 2-in. stick cinnamon

Pour cranberry juice into heavy saucepan over medium flame;
add sugar, lemon peel, cinnamon, and cloves. Bring to a boil.
Simmer gently 10 minutes. Remove from flame. Strain through
fine sieve. Add burgundy wine. Heat only to simmering; do
not allow mixture to boil. Serve piping hot in punch glasses
or mugs. Sprinkle each serving with nutmeg to taste. Serves 6.

Spicy Mulled Wine   TIME: 20 minutes

½ cup sugar   *12 whole cloves*
1½ cups boiling water   *1 4-in. stick cinnamon*
Rind of ½ lemon   *1 bottle burgundy wine*
Nutmeg   *or claret wine*

Dissolve ½ cup sugar in 1½ cups boiling water in heavy
saucepan over medium flame; add lemon rind, cloves, and stick
cinnamon. Boil 15 minutes. Strain into top section double
boiler placed over lower section half filled with boiling water
over high flame. Add burgundy wine. Heat 8 minutes, or until
piping hot but not boiling. Serve in glasses or mugs. Sprinkle
nutmeg lightly over each serving. Serves 6.

CHAPTER TWELVE

Herb and

Spice Vinegars

One of the most delightful and satisfactory uses of herbs and spices is in the preparing of various vinegars. With careful watching and tasting, as the vinegars are seasoned, one may easily develop into an exceptionally clever blender.

Fresh or *dried leaves, flowering tops, flower petals, aromatic seed,* and *freshly grated roots* may all be used to flavor a specific vinegar. Two or three of the spices, such as the chili and curry powders, will add zest to a vinegar used with fish and shellfish cocktails.

The process of infusion, which is the way in which herb and spice vinegars are prepared, is extremely simple. And the same method is employed whether one uses aromatic seed, fresh or dried leaves, or spices. If possible, the fresh leaves of the herbs should be used in preference to the dried, since their oil content is greater, and it is the essential oils which give the full flavors. However, there are many excellent herb vinegars which have been prepared by using the dried herbs.

Whenever a vinegar is carefully infused with herbs, either fresh or dried, it loses that sharp acidity and achieves a soft, mellow quality which we are accustomed to associating with rare old wines. As seasonings in salads and many cooked foods, herb vinegars add real gustatory goodness. If you have never used them, there is unlimited culinary pleasure in store for you.

FRESH LEAVES

To prepare herb vinegars with fresh leaves care must be taken to select the leaves just before the plants are in full bloom. The leaves should be bruised gently before they are placed in the jar, and then the vinegar is simply poured over them. Cover the jar tightly, stand it in a warm place, and shake the mixture every day. Some homemakers will allow the vinegar to stand in the sun while others have no success with this process; and one of the oldest English recipes for Thyme Herb Vinegar suggests that the jar be buried in the snow for forty days. To be absolutely safe, it is best to keep the jar in a warm spot indoors where the contents may be tasted after 10 days or 2 weeks. Then, if the flavor is sufficiently strong for the individual's taste, the vinegar may be strained and bottled without further delay. If the herb flavor is not exactly as wanted, the liquid may be strained and fresh herbs placed in it, and the same process of infusion repeated.

There are infinite varieties of herb vinegars which any homemaker may prepare. A suggested list of herbs and spices which are especially good when blended with vinegars is given later in the chapter. *If fresh leaves are used, the proportions are generally 2 cups freshly minced herb to 1 quart vinegar.* Then

Place leaves in wide-mouthed jar.
Bruise leaves slightly.
Pour only the best quality vinegar over them.
Cover jar tightly.
Allow to stand in a warm place from 10 days to 2 weeks.
Shake vigorously every day.
Taste for flavor; if not as strong as desired,
Repeat the infusion process.
Strain through fine sieve and
Cork tightly, ready for use.

Vinegars may also be flavored with a *combination of herbs.* However, using more than one or two herbs requires considerable art and a thorough knowledge of the strength and flavors of each herb. It takes a little more time to become an expert in blending combinations than it does to prepare the vinegar with but a single herb or spice. For example, it is very easy to use even a strongly accented herb, such as garlic, if the proportions and the timing are carefully regulated. But when garlic is used in combination with other herbs, greater care must be taken so that its stronger flavor does not stand out above that of the milder herbs with which it is being blended.

If too much of any strongly accented herb, such as chives, garlic, sweet basil, and tarragon, *is used in a combination with the milder herbs, the resulting vinegar will have only the flavor of the strong herb,* and the combination simply doesn't exist. Therefore, when experimenting with blends, always use half or less the amount of the strong herb so its flavor doesn't overpower all the others. For example, *too much garlic* and too long infusion in the combination Tarragon Garlic Vinegar will wreck even the flavor of an herb as strongly accented as is tarragon.

DRIED LEAVES, AROMATIC SEED, and SPICES

When using *dried herbs* and *aromatic seed* as flavoring, the infusion process is hastened if the vinegar is lukewarm or even boiling before it is poured over the herbs. This is unnecessary when one uses the fresh leaves and sprigs, though there are some blenders who always prefer to heat the vinegar at least slightly.

There are different thoughts also about straining out the herb particles, as is evidenced by some of the specially prepared blends on the market. This, too, can be a matter of personal preference. However, the majority of all herb and spice vinegars are carefully strained and filtered before being bottled; and a vinegar flavored with a powdered spice is always very carefully filtered.

The choice of vinegars which may be flavored with herbs and spices is also a wide one. In many instances *the vinegars also are blended* before the herb infusion. For example, in preparing a tarragon vinegar one may use a combination of malt and distilled vinegars, or the tarragon may be infused in a pure cider vinegar. The English prefer the malt vinegar and the French are more apt to use a red or white wine vinegar. There are many varieties of herb vinegars on the market and each one differs in its formula as do the herb blends. Here, too, the exact formulas and recipes are the specific choices of the blenders, and they all differ as do the individual tastes.

The sweet herb vinegars are growing increasingly more popular; and a *rose-petal blend* or a *rose-geranium vinegar* is

wonderfully delicious on a fruit salad. Practically any and all
the various herb vinegars may be blended with mayonnaise
or used in preparing a favorite French Dressing. The following list of those herbs and spices which are especially good in
particular and specific vinegars includes but one root herb: the
horseradish. If one is partial to any other roots, such as those
of *celeriac* or *lovage,* there's no reason why they, too, might
not be used to flavor a good cider or distilled vinegar.

Another herb vinegar which has just made its appearance
on the market is HONEY VINEGAR from Victoria, Australia. It is a vinegar which is brewed from the pure honey
secured from the blossoms of the tropical plants and wild
flowers of Australia. The color is a light golden yellow and
the flavor is epicurean. Honey vinegar is exceptionally delicious when used in fruit-salad dressings. See also chapter on
Wine Vinegars.

Herbs, Aromatic Seed, and Spices Especially Good in VINEGARS and WINE VINEGARS

Basil, purple	Curry powder	Rose geranium
Basil, sweet	Dill, fresh	Rosemary
Borage	Dill seed	Rose petals
Burnet	Fennel	Shallot
Caraway seed	Garlic	Sorrel
Cayenne pepper	Horseradish	Spearmint
Celery seed	Marjoram	Tarragon
Chives	Mint	Thyme
Coriander seed	Onion	

BASIL OR PURPLE BASIL VINEGAR: Infuse purple basil herb in
red wine, or white wine vinegars. Use *as marinade for
fish, meats, pot roasts,* or *game;* in *meat sauces, ragouts,*
and *vegetable-salad dressings.*

BASIL OR SWEET BASIL VINEGAR: Infuse sweet basil herb in
cider or red wine vinegars. Use *same as purple basil
vinegar;* also *in bean* and *tomato soups; fish* and *tomato
sauces;* also *in favorite French Dressing;* and *fruit drinks.*

BORAGE VINEGAR: Infuse borage herb in cider, distilled, or
white wine vinegars. Use *as marinade for fish* and *meats;*
also *in favorite vegetable-salad dressings.*

BURNET VINEGAR: Infuse burnet herb in distilled or white

wine vinegars. Use *same as other vinegars* in preparing *vegetable-salad dressings* and *mayonnaise.*

CARAWAY-SEED VINEGAR: Infuse caraway seed in cider or white wine vinegars. Use *as marinade for meats;* also *in fruit-salad dressings.*

CAYENNE-PEPPER VINEGAR: Infuse cayenne pepper in pure cider vinegar. Use *in fish* and *sea-food cocktails.*

CELERY-SEED VINEGAR: Infuse celery seed in cider or white wine vinegars. Use *in* preparing *French dressings for fruit salads;* also *as basting* and *marinade for fish* and *meats.*

CHIVES VINEGAR: Infuse chives herb in cider, distilled, malt, red, or white wine vinegars. Use *as marinade for roasts* and *in dressings* where tart and mild chives flavor is desired.

CORIANDER-SEED VINEGAR: Infuse in cider vinegar. Use *in fruit salad dressings.*

CURRY-POWDER VINEGAR: Infuse curry powder in distilled or white wine vinegars. Use *as basting for hamburgers* and *roast lamb;* also *in fish* and *shellfish cocktails.*

DILL VINEGAR: Infuse dill herb in cider, distilled, or white wine vinegars. Use *as basting for poultry;* also *in salad dressings.*

DILL-SEED VINEGAR: Infuse dill seed in cider, distilled, malt, or white wine vinegars. Use *as dill vinegar;* also *in favorite French salad dressings.*

FENNEL VINEGAR: Infuse fennel in cider, distilled, or white wine vinegars. Use *as marinade for fish;* also *in favorite salad dressings* and *mayonnaise.*

GARLIC VINEGAR: Infuse garlic in cider, distilled, red, or white wine vinegars. Use *in any food in which slight garlic flavor is desired;* also *as marinade for fish, game, poultry,* and *roasts;* also *in favorite salad dressings, sauces,* and *mayonnaise.*

HORSERADISH VINEGAR: Infuse grated horseradish root in distilled or white wine vinegar. Use *in fish* and *shellfish cocktails; as marinade for roasts; in vegetable-salad dressings* and *mayonnaise.*

MARJORAM VINEGAR: Infuse sweet marjoram herb in cider, distilled, and white wine vinegars. Use *as marinade for meats, poultry, game,* also *in favorite French salad dressings.*

MINT VINEGAR: Infuse mint herb in cider or white wine vinegars. Use *in vegetable soups* and *purées;* also *as mari-*

nade for lamb ragouts and *roast meats* and *ham,* and *in favorite salad dressings.*

ONION VINEGAR: Infuse onion in cider, malt, or white wine vinegars. Use *same as garlic vinegars;* also *in fish* and *horseradish sauces.*

ROSE-GERANIUM VINEGAR: Infuse rose-geranium leaves in cider or distilled vinegars. Use *in fruit punches, fruit-salad dressings, gelatine desserts,* and *mayonnaise.*

ROSEMARY VINEGAR: Infuse rosemary herb in distilled or white wine vinegars. Use *as marinade for meats* and *poultry;* also *in fruit-salad dressings* and *mayonnaise.*

ROSE-PETALS VINEGAR: Infuse rose petals in cider or distilled vinegars. Use *in sweet salad dressings;* also *same as rose-geranium vinegars.*

SHALLOT VINEGAR: Infuse shallots in distilled or white wine vinegars. Use *with all foods* and *dressings; same as chive, garlic,* and *onion vinegars.*

SORREL VINEGAR: Infuse sorrel leaves in distilled or white wine vinegars. Use *in favorite French salad dressings* and *mayonnaise;* also *in egg dishes; in sauces for roast goose, lamb,* and *roast mutton.*

SPEARMINT VINEGAR: Infuse spearmint leaves in cider or distilled vinegars. Use *as marinade for lamb;* also *in meat sauces* and *salad dressings.*

TARRAGON VINEGAR: Infuse tarragon herb in cider, distilled, malt, red or white wine vinegars. Use *as marinade for fish* and *meats;* also *in salad dressings, tartar sauce, vegetable-juice cocktails.*

THYME VINEGAR: Infuse thyme herb in cider, distilled, or red or white wine vinegars. Use *in favorite French dressings;* also *with fish* and *shellfish cocktails.*

Basic Recipe Aromatic-seed Herb Vinegar   INFUSE: 2 weeks

½ oz. preferred seed, crushed   *1 qt. selected best-quality vinegar*

Bruise seed well in mortar with pestle to release all essential oil; place seed in wide-mouthed jar.

Heat vinegar until almost boiling; pour over seed; cover jar tightly. Allow to stand in warm room 2 weeks; shake well occasionally. Filter through fine cloth or French filter paper; pour vinegar into bottles; cork tightly.

Use as desired in preparing salad dressings.

Basic Recipe Dried-leaves Herb Vinegar   INFUSE: 10 days to 2 weeks

2 tsp. dried leaves   *1 pt. selected best-quality vinegar*

Place dried leaves in wide-mouthed jar. Pour selected vinegar over leaves; cover tightly. Stand in warm place 10 days to 2 weeks; shake well at least once a day. Test for taste at the end of 10 days. If stronger flavor is desired, strain out dried leaves; replace with more leaves. Infuse 1 week longer. Strain through flannel bag or French filter paper; bottle; cork tightly.

Use as desired for flavoring and preparing salad dressings and sauces.

Basic Recipe Fresh-leaves Herb Vinegar   INFUSE: 10 days to 2 weeks

1 cup minced or bruised fresh   *1 pt. selected best-quality*
    leaves and tender stems   *vinegar*
    of selected herb

Place minced or bruised leaves in wide-mouthed jar. Pour selected vinegar over leaves; cover tightly. Stand in warm place 10 days to 2 weeks; shake well at least once a day. Test for taste at the end of 10 days. If stronger flavor is desired, strain out herb; replace with more fresh herb; repeat infusion process for another week. Strain through fine sieve; bottle; cork tightly.

Use as desired in preparing salad dressings.

Cayenne-pepper Vinegar   INFUSE: 2 weeks

¼ oz. cayenne pepper   *1 pt. cider vinegar*

Pour off ¼ cup vinegar; add cayenne pepper; cover. Allow to stand in warm place 2 weeks; shake vigorously occasionally. Filter through fine cloth or French filter paper; rebottle seasoned vinegar; cork tightly.

Use few drops to season shellfish cocktail sauces; also with raw clams and oysters.

Celery-seed White Wine Vinegar   INFUSE: 2 weeks

½ oz. celery seed, crushed   *1 qt. white wine vinegar or
cider vinegar, warmed*

Bruise seed well in mortar with pestle to release essential
aromatic oil; place seed in wide-mouthed jar. Heat vinegar
until almost boiling; pour over seeds; cover jar tightly. Allow
to stand at room temperature 2 weeks; shake well occasionally.
Filter through flannel or French filter paper; bottle; cork
tightly.

   Use in preparing salad dressings *for fish* and *vegetable
salads.*

   *Other preferred aromatic seed, such as caraway or dill, may
be used as flavoring in same way. Follow recipe.*

Curry-powder Vinegar   INFUSE: 3 to 8 days

1½ ozs. curry powder   *1 pt. distilled or white wine
vinegar*

Pour off ¼ cup vinegar; add curry powder; cover; shake well.
Allow to infuse in warm room or near heat 3 or 4 days;
shake well each day. Filter through fine cloth or French filter
paper; taste vinegar. If more pungent flavor is desired, repeat
infusion; refilter. Rebottle seasoned vinegar; cork tightly.

   Use few drops *to season sea-food cocktails* and *sauces;* also
in dressings for fish and *sea-food salads.*

Dill Herb Vinegar   INFUSE: 2 to 3 weeks

6 sprigs fresh dill   *1 qt. lukewarm white wine
vinegar or distilled
vinegar*

Fill wide-mouthed jar with several sprigs fresh dill cut into
convenient lengths. Pour vinegar or water into small saucepan
over medium flame; warm slightly. Pour lukewarm vinegar
over fresh dill; cover. Allow to stand at room temperature 2
weeks; shake occasionally. Strain or filter through fine cloth
or French filter paper. Taste. If stronger flavor is desired,
repeat infusion; refilter. Bottle seasoned vinegar; cork tightly.

   Use as desired in preparing salad dressings.

Dill-and-garlic Vinegar: Place 2 cloves halved garlic in jar
   with dill sprigs. Follow recipe. Remove garlic after 2 days.

Garlic Vinegar   INFUSE: 2 weeks

8 cloves garlic, minced   *1 qt. red or white wine vinegar*
(about 2 ozs.)   *or cider vinegar*

Peel and mince garlic with sharp knife to release flavor and essential oils. Place garlic in wide-mouthed jar.

Heat vinegar few minutes until lukewarm but not hot in small saucepan over medium flame; pour warm vinegar over garlic; cover. Allow to stand in warm place 2 weeks; shake occasionally. Strain; bottle, cork tightly.

Use *to flavor marinades* and *salad dressings,* as desired.

Herb-and-spice Wine Vinegar Française   INFUSE: 2 to 3
                                            weeks

¼ oz. dried sweet basil   *1 tsp. dill seed, crushed*
¼ oz. dried rosemary   *½ tsp. black pepper*
¼ oz. dried tarragon   *¼ tsp. allspice*
½ oz. dried marjoram   *¼ tsp. whole cloves, crushed*
¼ oz. dried curly mint   *2 qts. red wine vinegar*
4 bay leaves, crushed

Blend all herbs and spices in large wide-mouthed jar. Pour vinegar over herb-and-spice mixture (cider vinegar may be substituted if preferred); cover. Allow to stand in warm room 2 to 3 weeks; stir occasionally. Strain or filter through fine cloth or French filter paper. Pour into bottles; cork tightly.

Use 1 teaspoon to 1 tablespoon blended vinegar *in meat* and *steak sauces, roasts* and *ragouts.*

Vinegar is more fragrant when prepared with young, fresh leaves of all herbs, when available. Use 1 tablespoon fresh leaves instead of ¼ ounce dried or 2 tablespoons fresh leaves instead of ½ ounce dried herb.

Horseradish Root Vinegar   INFUSE: 2 weeks

4 tbs. freshly grated horse-   *1 qt. distilled vinegar*
radish root   *⅛ tsp. cayenne pepper*
1 oz. minced shallot

Wash and scrape root clean; grate; measure out 4 tablespoons. Peel and mince shallots. Place grated horseradish, minced shallot, and cayenne pepper in wide-mouthed jar; blend well by stirring. Pour distilled vinegar over herbs; cover. Allow to stand in warm place 2 weeks; shake occasionally. Strain; bottle; cork tightly.

Use as desired to flavor salad dressings.

Marjoram Vinegar   INFUSE: 2 weeks

Sprigs of fresh marjoram   *1 qt. white wine vinegar or distilled vinegar*

Place 6 or 7 sprigs fresh marjoram crushed slightly to release essential oils in wide-mouthed jar.

Heat vinegar to lukewarm only in small saucepan over medium flame; pour warm vinegar over leaves; cover. Allow to stand in warm room 2 weeks; shake occasionally. Strain through very fine sieve or filter. Pour into bottles; cork tightly.

Use as desired in salad dressings and meat sauces.

To prepare with dried marjoram, use 2 tablespoons crushed herb. Follow recipe. Repeat infusion before bottling if stronger flavor is preferred.

Minted Sweet Vinegar   TIME: 15 minutes

2 cups chopped fresh mint   *1 cup sugar*
                                   1 qt. cider vinegar

Select fresh young leaves and tender stems; wash thoroughly under cold running water; dry on absorbent paper. Chop leaves and stems finely with sharp knife. Pour vinegar into heavy saucepan over medium flame. Bring to boiling point. Add sugar and mint leaves, stirring well. Boil gently 5 minutes. Remove from heat. Quickly strain through very fine sieve. While still very hot, pour seasoned vinegar into hot sterilized bottles; cork tightly.

Use when preparing *mint sauce for lamb* and *mutton;* also *to flavor fruit salads* and *punches.*

Spearmint Sweet Vinegar *may be prepared in same way. Use same amount chopped fresh leaves. Follow recipe.*

Rose-geranium Vinegar   TIME: 15 minutes

2 cups minced rose-geranium leaves   *1 cup sugar*
                                        1 qt. cider vinegar

Select fresh young leaves. Wash thoroughly under cold running water; dry on absorbent paper. Mince leaves finely with sharp knife. Pour vinegar into heavy saucepan over medium flame; bring to boiling point; add sugar and rose-geranium leaves, stirring well. Boil gently 10 minutes. Remove from heat. Quickly strain through very fine sieve. While still very hot, pour seasoned vinegar into hot sterilized bottles; cork tightly.

Use when preparing *fruit punches* and *fruit-salad dressings*.

Rose-petal Vinegar *may be prepared in same way. Select fresh, fragrant petals. Follow recipe.*

Shallot Vinegar INFUSE: 2 weeks

¼ lb. shallots *1 qt. white wine vinegar or distilled vinegar*

Peel and chop shallots; place in wide-mouthed jar. Pour over them vinegar; cover. Allow to steep two weeks. Strain through fine sieve; pour seasoned vinegar into bottle; cork tightly.

Use to flavor dressings for vegetable salads.

Small sweet white onions may be used instead of shallots. To prepare **Onion Vinegar,** *follow recipe.*

Tarragon-garlic Vinegar INFUSE: 2 weeks

2 cups fresh tarragon leaves *2 whole cloves, crushed*
1 pt. white wine vinegar or *1 clove garlic, halved*
distilled vinegar

Select fresh young leaves. Wash thoroughly under cold running water; dry on absorbent paper. Crush leaves slightly to release essential oils. Place leaves in jar; pour over vinegar; add crushed cloves and halved garlic. Allow to stand in warm room 24 hours. Remove garlic. Allow to stand at room temperature 2 weeks; shake occasionally. Strain through fine sieve; pour seasoned vinegar into bottles; cork tightly.

Tarragon-garlic Malt Vinegar: Heat and combine 1 cup distilled vinegar with 1 cup malt vinegar. Follow recipe for Tarragon-garlic Vinegar. If desired, garlic may be omitted.

Tarragon-garlic Red Wine Vinegar: Heat and infuse herb with 1 cup red wine vinegar. Follow recipe for Tarragon-garlic Vinegar. If desired, garlic may be omitted.

Tarragon-shallot Vinegar: Also called **Tarragon Eschalot.** Use 2 cloves minced shallot instead of garlic. Follow recipe for Tarragon-garlic Vinegar.

CHAPTER THIRTEEN

Wines and

Wine Vinegars

WINES AND HERBS

Wines and herbs have a natural affinity, and no book on herbs and spices could be quite complete without mentioning wines, if only in passing.

Vermouth, one of the main appetizer wines, for example, is prepared from selected pure white wines which are flavored with many herbs and aromatic substances. Each label or brand name is the result of the producer's secret formula which has been developed by his chemist through months and sometimes years of experimentation. These chemists are artists in their work, and their knowledge of herbs and flavors is far beyond the average. Leaves, stems, seed, and sometimes the barks of special herbs are used; and some vermouth formulas contain as many as fifty different herbs. The two types of vermouth are the *dry* or French type and the *sweet* or Italian type. In the former the more pungent and bitter herbs predominate; in the latter the sweeter herbs.

In ancient Greece, centuries before vinification had developed into an art, herbs and spices were used to preserve the flavor of the fermented grape juice and to arrest its further fermentation and spoilage. The Greeks discovered that ordinary pitch or resin would prevent wines from turning sour, so they experimented with it until they secured a palatably flavored beverage. The resulting resin-flavored wine is still among the favorite Greek wines and is called *retsina*.

The old European tradition of serving both red and white wines at mealtimes is still a charming one. It bespeaks a warm graciousness and hospitality. It also allows the individual to enjoy the wine of his choice, regardless of the former idea that red wines are to be served only with certain dark meats and the white wines with fish, poultry, and shellfish.

However, even though there are unusual personal preferences, there remain certain flavors which are complementary to each other; and the suggestions offered here take into consideration that balance of goodness in those flavors. For example, chicken prepared with curry is equally delicious when accompanied by a glass of either white or red wine, because chicken may be cooked in either *sauterne* or *claret*. And the wines used in cooking a specific food are the wines which also may be served with that food. But curry dishes in general taste very much better if a *demi-sec* (medium-dry) white wine is served with them. And whether or not the foods have been cooked with wines, it is still wise to consider the flavor of the wine as a complement to that of the food. If so, then one will always serve a medium-dry *Riesling, sauterne,* or *Rhine wine;* or a *sparkling vouvray* to add just the right balance to the sweet spiciness of the curry.

When foods have been seasoned with the sweet herbs, such as celery, parsley, borage, or burnet, the dry white wines accent the herb flavor. And one might choose a real dry Rhine wine to serve with a mushroom soup which has been seasoned with parsley or burnet; or when the menu includes any of the sweet vegetables.

All of the less sweet white wines, such as California *chablis, moselle, Riesling,* and *sauterne,* are excellent with paprika dishes. And nothing is quite so delicious as a Hungarian chicken or veal *paprikash* accompanied by a chilled *chablis.* Either beef, game, or venison, which has been marinated in spices and red wine vinegar, is something set apart when a fruity *claret* or *burgundy* is served with it.

Cloves, cinnamon, mace, ginger, allspice, and nutmeg are being used more and more to season vegetables, salads, sauces, and meats, in addition to their well-known uses in flavoring pies, cakes, and desserts of every description. The accompanying wine with these new seasoning uses could be a problem, but it need not be, for the homemaker may serve any one of the many fruity, sweeter wines with the foods which have been seasoned with these sweeter spices. Choose the sherry to your individual taste, either a sweet one or a dry cocktail sherry. The same choice can be yours when serving port; use either the regular sweet ports (red and white) or the less sweet tawny port.

Other dessert wines which are perfect with spicy pies, cakes, custards, and fruit salads are *muscatel, tokay,* and *angelica.* The sparkling wines, too, are always deliciously correct with any dessert: all the *champagnes, sparkling burgundy, sparkling moselle, sparkling rosé, sparkling sauterne, sparkling vouvray,* and *sweet madeira.*

But more and more many of the old traditions are giving way to personal tastes; and if your choice takes you experimenting, it can be very rewarding at times. Generally speaking, there are four very simple suggestions to remember:

With foods flavored with the *sweet herbs* and *condiments,* choose a dry or medium-dry wine, such as *burgundy, cabernet, chablis, Grâves, Rhine wine, Riesling, sauterne, white burgundy, white chianti,* and *zinfandel.*

With foods flavored with the *strong herbs* and *spices,* choose a dry wine, such as *burgundy, cabernet, claret, dry chablis, Grâves, Rhine wine, Riesling, sauterne,* and *semillon.*

With foods flavored with *pungent spices,* such as cayenne and curry powder, choose a medium-sweet wine, such as *bordeaux blanc,* a *sweet chablis, haut barzac, haut sauterne,* and *sparkling vouvray.*

With foods flavored with the *sweet spices,* such as cloves, cinnamon, ginger, allspice, and nutmeg, choose a sweet or any of the sparkling wines. A suggested list includes *angelica,* all the *champagnes, muscatel,* and *all the sparkling wines* in addition to the champagnes: *sparkling burgundy, sparkling moselle, sparkling rosé, sparkling sauterne,* and *sparkling vouvray; also sweet madeira* and *tokay.*

AGED WINE VINEGARS

Wine vinegars are extremely well liked by many chefs and homemakers. In fact, the majority of European chefs prefer wine vinegars to the exclusion of all the other vinegars, using both the red wine and white wine vinegars in marinades, sauces, and salad dressings. No one will deny that the wine vinegars are unusually delicious, and they are often less acid than the fruit and distilled vinegars.

Both the red and the white wines are used in the manufacture of wine vinegars. Here again, as in spice and herb blends, the exact formulas and processes are trade secrets of each manufacturer.

Pure wine is selected, and a process of acetic acid fermentation is set up which produces the final product. The delicious flavor is the result of the individual manufacturing processes, plus very careful aging. Wine vinegars are wonderfully satisfactory to use in preparing herb vinegars. See also chapter on Herb Vinegars.

CHAPTER 14

Fresh Spices

Spices, the same as dried herbs, should be of the purest grade possible, and always fresh. (See also Using Herbs and Spices.) The true flavor and potency of a spice are dependent upon the amount of the natural volatile oil which it contains. In order to preserve the full flavor and aroma each spice should be kept tightly covered at all times. If carelessly exposed to the air, the spice will lose its flavor quickly.

It is always wise to purchase spices often and in small quantities. The delicate fragrance and aroma will disappear with the flavor if the spice is kept standing for too long a time after it has been harvested. This is true of either whole or ground spice. Let your nose be your guide on this. If the spice has lost its fresh, natural, pungent aroma, *don't use it*. It is far more economical to purchase a fresh supply than it is to ruin perfectly good food by attempting to use the stale spice as a seasoning. It just can't be done.

The amount of spice which you choose to use in any recipe can be a matter of your individual taste. The amount will have no effect upon the actual chemistry of the food. However, the same rule holds for spice as with any other seasoning. *Too much isn't good*. The amounts shown in most recipes are considered the correct amounts to use for the average taste. As you grow more familiar with the spice flavors you may wish to increase the amount of one or decrease the amount of another. But no matter how you experiment, *never use so much spice that it smothers the food flavor.*

Simply enumerated, these additional suggestions on using spices are

Always use a high-quality fresh spice.
Renew spices several times a year.
Purchase often and in small quantities.
Test aroma by smelling before using.
Destroy spices which have stood too long.
Keep spices tightly covered at all times.
Use too little rather than too much, until familiar with exact flavors.

ALLSPICE, *Pimenta officinalis*

Ground in 1¼ ounce containers at groceries and markets; also from herb dealers.
Whole in 1 ounce containers at groceries and markets; also from herb dealers.

Allspice is also called PIMENTO, JAMAICA PIMENTO, and JAMAICA PEPPER. It is the dried, unripe fruit of a very beautiful evergreen tree, the *Pimenta karst,* which belongs to the myrtle, *Myrtaceae,* family.

The trees grow from 20 to 40 feet high, and are native to the islands of the West Indies and to Central America. They are extensively cultivated on the island of Jamaica, and that is why the fruit or berry is sometimes called by the popular names Jamaica pepper and Jamaica pimento. Mexico cultivates allspice for export also, but the fruit is not of such high quality as that grown in the West Indies. Attempts to grow the trees in the East Indies have failed; so allspice remains the one major spice produced exclusively in the Western Hemisphere.

This dried, hard berry has a fragrant, aromatic, pungent taste like a mixture of cloves, cinnamon, and nutmeg. It is this combination of flavors which gave the spice its popular name of *allspice.*

Using: Ground allspice is used to flavor cakes, canned foods, catsup, chutneys, jams, jellies, mincemeat, pickles, puddings, relishes, and spiced fruits. It is also an ingredient in practically all blended spice combinations. Its aromatic fragrance lends flavor to many different sausage seasonings and to practically all pastry and poultry blends. The popular West Indian cordial, *Pimento Dram,* is allspice flavored. Many cake and pie recipes call for allspice, but it is also an unusually delicious flavoring for eggs, meats, and vegetables. Both the ground and the whole allspice may be used. Many persons enjoy the scent of allspice in sachets and moth preventives also.

The whole allspice gives a wonderful tang to pea soup if just 2 or 3 berries are added to the ingredients. When steaming or boiling fish and shellfish, 3 or 4 berries tied in with a bouquet garni of parsley, thyme, and bay leaves will add a most intriguing flavor. Sauces, meats, game, and certain sweet vegetables, such as carrots and eggplant, become something extraordinary when flavored with allspice. The whole berries are also used to flavor vinegars, and most of the pickling spices contain them. See also Cinnamon, Cloves, Nutmeg, and Spiced Recipes and Blends.

CAKES AND COOKIES: Use as suggested in familiar recipes, from ¼ to ½ teaspoon is average amount.

EGGS: See recipe Spicy Pickled Eggs.

FISH: *Boiled, steamed.* Add 3 whole allspice to bouquet garni while cooking.

MEATS: *Beef.* See recipe Spiced Beef à la Mode.
Beef loaf. Add ¼ teaspoon allspice to other seasonings.
Ham, baked. Sprinkle ham with 1 teaspoon ground allspice before baking with cloves and brown sugar.
Hamburgers. Blend in ½ teaspoon allspice with 1 pound meat before broiling.
Lamb. See recipe Eggplant and Lamb Orientale.

PIES: *Fruits,* especially *apple, apricot, banana, cherry,* and *peach.* Add ¼ to ½ teaspoon ground allspice to other seasonings, or sprinkle fruit lightly with allspice just before baking.

SALADS: *Fruits,* especially *apple, banana, cherry, grapefruit,* and *orange.* Lightly sprinkle fruit with allspice before serving.

SOUPS: *Purée of green pea.* Add 3 whole allspice to soup while cooking.

VEGETABLES: *Carrots, red cabbage, tomatoes,* buttered. Add ¼ teaspoon ground allspice to hot butter before pouring over vegetables.

For 4 servings use approximately:

¼ to 1 teaspoon ground allspice.
3 to 6 whole allspice.

Eggplant and Lamb Orientale   TIME: 1 hour

1 large eggplant	*⅛ tsp. allspice*
1½ lbs. lean lamb shanks	*⅛ tsp. cinnamon*
1 tbs. bacon grease or fat	*½ tsp. caraway seed*
3 small onions, minced	*½ cup lukewarm water*
½ tsp. salt	*1 No. 2 can tomatoes*
⅛ tsp. black pepper	*1 clove garlic, halved*

Wash, peel, and cut eggplant into 2-inch cubes. Set aside.
Have lamb meat cut into 2-inch cubes. (If lamb shanks are
not available, shoulder cut may be substituted, but have all
fat removed.) Set aside.

Heat bacon grease in large, deep, heavy skillet or Dutch
oven over medium flame; add lamb pieces; brown quickly by
stirring 3 minutes; add minced onions; brown 3 minutes; add
eggplant; brown 2 minutes. Stir in salt, pepper, allspice, cinnamon, and caraway seed; add water, tomatoes, and garlic.
Bring to boil over high flame; cover; lower flame. Simmer
gently 45 minutes, or until lamb is tender; stir occasionally to
prevent sticking. Serve piping hot over steamed rice. Serves 4
generously.

California Spiced Cake au Vin   TIME: 1 hour

1½ cups white flour	*¼ tsp. mace*
½ cup seeded raisins	*½ tsp. nutmeg*
½ cup chopped walnuts	*½ cup butter*
½ tsp. baking powder	*1 cup brown sugar*
½ tsp. baking soda	*1 egg, well beaten*
¼ tsp. salt	*½ cup sherry wine*
½ tsp. cinnamon	*½ tsp. cloves*
½ tsp. allspice	

Blend raisins and nuts in small mixing bowl; sift small quantity
flour over them so they are well coated.

Sift remaining flour, baking powder, soda, salt, and spices
in separate bowl.

Cream butter and sugar with spoon until light cream color
and fluffy in large mixing bowl; gradually blend in egg; gradu-

ally stir in flour mixture alternately with sherry wine, beating vigorously until mixture is smooth. Finally stir in coated raisins and nuts. Pour mixture into buttered floured square 8-inch cake pan. Bake in preheated moderate oven (350° F.) 40 minutes. Remove from oven. Allow cake to cool in pan at room temperature. While cake is cooling, blend

Sherry Wine Icing

1½ cups confectioners' sugar   *3 tbs. sherry wine*
2 tbs. soft butter

Cream sugar and butter; gradually add sherry wine to make thick icing. While cake is still lukewarm spread generously with icing. When cool and ready to serve, cut into squares of desired size.

Spiced Beef à la Mode   TIME: 2½ to 3 hours
                                   Marinate 2 days

4 lbs. beef, bottom round   *6 whole allspice*
1 large onion, sliced   *1½ cups cider vinegar*
1 carrot, sliced   *3 tbs. butter or margarine*
3 cloves   *6 small white onions*
¾ tsp. salt   *6 small potatoes*
6 peppercorns   *6 small carrots*
1 qt. vegetable stock   *½ cup sherry, optional*

Purchase large, square piece bottom round. Wipe lightly with damp cloth. Place beef in deep, extra-heavy aluminum saucepan; add sliced onion, carrot, cloves, salt, peppercorns, allspice, and vinegar; cover tightly. Set aside in cool place for 2 days; turn meat occasionally.

When ready to cook, remove meat from saucepan. Set aside. Strain the vinegar into small pan over medium flame; add vegetable stock; bring to boil.

Meanwhile, melt butter over low flame in saucepan in which beef marinated; when butter is very hot, turn up flame; return beef to saucepan and brown each side 2 minutes. Add vinegar and vegetable stock liquid; bring to boiling point; lower flame to medium; cover. Simmer 2 hours, or until meat is almost done. (Time depends upon cut of meat; some beef is more tender than others.) Add white onions and potatoes. If necessary, add small amount boiling water. Cook vegetables 10 minutes, then add carrots; cook 10 minutes more.

When ready to serve, place meat on slicing board for easy handling. If thick gravy is desired, remove vegetables also. Stir in 1 tablespoon flour; cook 5 minutes, stirring constantly. Add ½ cup sherry to sauce if desired. Allow to simmer 2 minutes while slicing meat.

Place slices in preheated deep serving dish; arrange carrots, onions, and potatoes around slices; pour boiling hot sauce over' all. Serve piping hot. Serves 6 to 8.

Vegetable Stock   TIME: 30 minutes

1 large bunch celery, tops	*1 whole allspice*
and outer stalks only	*2 peppercorns*
2 sprigs parsley	*½ tsp. salt*
4½ cups cold water	*1 bay leaf*

Cut fresh leaves and outer stalks from 1 large bunch celery. Rinse thoroughly under cold running water to remove all sand; wash parsley sprigs. Pour cold water into large saucepan placed over medium flame; add celery, parsley, allspice, peppercorns, salt, and bay leaf; bring to boiling point; cover; lower flame; continue boiling gently 25 minutes. Remove from flame. Strain liquid. Yield: 1 quart.

Use as needed. (If desired, 1 small onion may be added to ingredients; follow same instructions.)

Spicy Pickled Eggs   TIME: 20 minutes
                                    Marinate 4 weeks

1 doz. eggs	*½ tsp. allspice*
1 qt. cider vinegar	*½ tsp. ginger*
¼ tsp. cayenne pepper	*½ tsp. black pepper*

To prevent shells cracking, allow eggs to stand at room temperature before cooking. Place eggs in rapidly boiling water; when water resumes boiling, cook eggs 10 minutes. Remove from heat; place in cold water. Shell eggs by tapping hollow end of egg so shell may be taken off in large pieces. Arrange eggs in small stone crock.

While eggs are boiling, prepare spicy liquid by pouring vinegar into heavy saucepan over medium flame; add spices; boil 10 minutes. Strain through very fine sieve. Pour hot liquid over eggs. Allow to cool at room temperature. When cool, cover tightly; wrap crock well with paper. Stand in very cool place 4 weeks.

To serve: Slice eggs in half lengthwise; arrange on lettuce leaves; garnish with water cress and *sweet* bread-and-butter sandwiches. Serves 6 to 12.

CASSIA, *Cinnamomum cassia blume*

Buds in bulk at herb dealers.
Ground in 1½ ounce and 4 ounce containers (labeled cinnamon) at groceries and markets; also from herb dealers.
Quills or sticks in 1½ ounce containers at groceries and markets; also in bulk from herb dealers.
See also Cinnamon or True Cinnamon.

Cassia is usually called *cinnamon* because its flavor resembles the true Ceylon cinnamon. Cassia bark, however, is obtained from an entirely different botanical plant. Cassia is from the evergreen tree, *Cinnamomum cassia blume,* which is native to Burma and China.

The tree, widely cultivated in *South* China, belongs to the laurel, *Lauraceae,* family; and the cassia bark from this southern section is called CHINA CASSIA. The ground bark of China cassia is a light reddish brown and its flavor is warm and sweet, like the true cinnamon.

The cassia cultivated in *North* French-Indo China is from the evergreen tree called the *Cinnamomum loureirii Nees.* This cassia, called SAIGON CASSIA, has a sweet, pungent aroma and its taste is highly agreeable. The ground spice from the thin bark is a light brown while that from the thicker bark is a much darker brown. The Saigon cassia has the best flavor of all the cassias which reach our markets.

The BATAVIA CASSIA is native to the islands of the Dutch East Indies and is widely cultivated in Java and on the island of Sumatra. But since it is shipped from the port of Batavia, it is known as Batavia cassia. The bark is reddish brown and quite smooth, and varies from $\frac{1}{32}$ to $\frac{3}{16}$ inch in thickness.

CASSIA BUDS are the dried, unripe fruit of both the *Cinnamomum cassia* and the *Cinnamomum loureirii.* The tiny, grayish-brown buds vary in size from ¼ to ½ inch in length and are about ¼ inch wide at the crown. The bud consists of a tiny brown seed held within a little cup-shaped calyx. If a seed has dropped out and the calyx is empty, it looks like a miniature wineglass without a base. It takes more than 400 whole buds (the seed and calyx) to make a single ounce.

Using: The cassia buds are used whole in pickling, and sometimes they are chewed to sweeten the breath. Those who like spices in potpourris often include cassia buds, since they contain a goodly amount of oil.

The various species of whole cassia quills or sticks have many different uses. The larger, fancier grades are used in tall drinks of hot tea and hot wines. The shorter quills are used as flavoring in preserves, puddings, and stewed fruits, such as pears, peaches, apricots, also in sweet pickles.

Ground cassia, like the ground true cinnamon, flavors cakes, candies, cookies, fruit pies, and salads. It is extensively used by bakers, and many of the blended spice mixtures contain ground cassia. Some curry-powder blends utilize this ground spice also. Since cassia and cinnamon are used in conjunction with allspice, cloves, nutmeg, and ginger, please see also those spices for specific uses and recipes.

CAYENNE, *Capsicum*

Dried whole pods in bulk at groceries and markets; also from herb dealers.

Ground in ½ ounce and 1½ ounce containers at groceries and markets; also from herb dealers.

See also Chili Powder, Paprika, Red Pepper.

CAYENNE, or CAYENNE PEPPER, is the ground product of the dried ripe fruit of several different species of small-fruited *Capsicum* plants, which are commonly called *chilies* or *red peppers*.

There are more than 200 species of the genus *Capsicum*, which vary in flavor, color, size, and shape, and all of them belong to the potato or *Solanaceae* family. The larger species are known both as chilies and red peppers. Among two of the species which are dried and ground to produce cayenne pepper are the *Capsicum frutescens,* or *spur pepper,* and a variation of the same species which is called *Capsicum baccatum.*

Capsicum plants of all varieties are grown in all the southern zones of the world: in Africa, Asia, the East Indies, Hungary, India, Italy, Japan, Mexico, South America, southern United States, Spain, and on the island of Zanzibar. The Zanzibar varieties are very pungent and are considered among the best of all the chilies.

The color of all the chilies varies from a bright orange red to a deep dark red, but the seed are all a bright yellow. The sizes of the dried peppers used in preparing cayenne vary in length from less than ½ inch to 2 inches; and all are less than ½ inch wide. They are round at the base and taper to a point. Many of the best ground cayenne peppers are the products of small African chilies. Their taste is very pungent and biting, but *the aroma of the ground pepper is sweet* and *almost like that of a violet.*

The chili grown in Louisiana is called the *Louisiana Sport Pepper.* Its color varies from a bright orange red to a beautiful shade of deep red. It grows from 1 inch to about 2¼ inches long, and the taste is extremely pungent.

Using: Just a dash of cayenne pepper will add zest to many a flat flavor; even a pinch of cayenne in a sweet soufflé will point up the flavor. Since the pepper is so strong, it needs to be used with real caution and judgment. Many canned meats are flavored with cayenne, and condiments are made more interesting by its use. Curry sauces and other sauces for fish, meats, and shellfish may be seasoned with a few grains of cayenne. Barbecue sauces are especially delicious when a little cayenne has been added. Cottage cheese, cream cheese, and even butter may be ever so lightly flavored with cayenne and used as canapé spreads. See also Condiments, Curry Blends, and Herb Vinegars.

CHEESES: Soft, mild cheese, such as *cottage* and *cream cheese.* Blend ⅛ teaspoon cayenne pepper with ¼ pound cheese. Use as canapé spread.

SALAD DRESSINGS: Use ⅛ teaspoon cayenne pepper instead of other peppers or paprika in ingredients.

SAUCES: *Barbecue, cream, fish, meat.* Use ⅛ teaspoon cayenne in addition to ⅛ teaspoon regular pepper in ingredients. See also Celery Golden Sauce.

SHELLFISH: *Clam* and *oyster stew.* Sprinkle few grains of cayenne over stew just before serving.

For 4 servings use approximately:

¼ to ⅛ teaspoon ground cayenne.
1 small whole chili in sauces; remove chili before serving.

CHILI POWDER, *Chile ancho,* var. *acuminatum*

Sold in bottles, shaker-top cans, and glass jars of various sizes from 2 ounces to 8 ounces and more.
See also Cayenne, Paprika, and Red Pepper.

Chili powder is a hot, a sweetly hot, or a sweetly mild blend of the ground dried fruits of varieties of Mexican chili peppers with or without several herbs or spices. Most blends, however, contain Mexican *orégano.*

The hot and sweetly hot blends are prepared from several species of the small chilies of the genus *Capsicum.* The milder chili powders are blends of the ground dried fruit of the larger, less acrid peppers.

The small Mexican chilies are all a bright orange red with smooth, shiny skins, and they grow from ¼ to ½ inch in length. These varieties of tiny fiery fruits are called the *Mexican Chiltepin,* the *Chilepiquine,* the *Chili piquin,* and the *Chile petine.*

The larger, moderately pungent chilies grow from 3 to 4½ inches long and are about 2½ inches wide at the top. They are a beautiful dark red and when dried, almost a maroon color.

Each manufacturer of chili powder has particular blends to suit every taste, and *the judicious use of every blend can add a deliciously new appeal to many foods.*

Using: Mexican, South American, and Spanish cookery have all taught us much about the use of this warmly aromatic, staple spice. *None of these households are ever without chili powder.* And as we learn to make more use of the delightful seasoning qualities of this powder, many a daily menu can be lifted out of the usual into the unusual.

Meats, soups, vegetables, and sauces may all be lightly seasoned with chili powder in place of the usual black or white pepper; the peppery pungency of the chili powder will be intriguingly different. The South Americans will add a smidgeon of cinnamon to their chili dishes, or a bit of ground cumin seed. This takes away the sharpness and gives a flavor and aroma to the food which is deliciously different.

Chili powder is a wonderful seasoning for any sweet vegetable, such as corn or eggplant. The latter vegetable, when sliced and boiled for a few minutes, then rolled in flour seasoned with ½ teaspoon chili powder and fried in deep fat, is a wonderfully tasty and satisfying food.

Chile con Carne, which means Chili with Meat, is native to the Western Hemisphere. The Aztecs taught the Spaniards how to prepare the dish when Cortez conquered Mexico in 1519; and the Spaniards have been devotees of the nutritious *con carne* ever since. For those who are under the impression that the dish is too hot for American palates, a recipe for Chili con Carne Mildly Sweet is included as an introduction to the taste of a truly delicious and unusual spice flavor. A glass of white wine, which is not too dry, such as a *chablis* or *sauterne,* will add to the enjoyment of chili.

EGGS: *Boiled, scrambled.* Season lightly to taste with chili powder just before serving.

MEATS: *Beef, pork. Chops* and *steaks.* Marinate 1 hour in herb vinegar seasoned with 1 teaspoon chili powder, ¼ teaspoon ground cumin, 1 clove garlic, and ¼ teaspoon salt. Drain and broil.

RICE: *Spanish rice.* Season with ½ teaspoon chili powder instead of pepper.

SAUCES: *Cocktail, cream, tomato.* Season sauces with ½ teaspoon to 1 teaspoon chili powder instead of pepper.

SHELLFISH: *Clam, oyster, shrimp,* cocktail. Sprinkle with few grains chili powder.

SOUPS: *Meat, thick vegetable.* Lightly sprinkle few grains chili powder over each portion at time of serving.

VEGETABLES: *Sweet* vegetables, such as *carrots, corn, celery, cauliflower, eggplant, peas;* especially when *baked.* Season lightly with chili powder instead of pepper before cooking.

For 4 servings use approximately:

Few grains as flavoring in cocktails and soups.
½ teaspoon to 1 tablespoon, depending upon recipe and spiciness desired.

Vegetables Baked South American   TIME: 30 minutes

1 cup chopped raw spinach	*½ tsp. ground cumin seed*
1 green pepper, chopped	*¼ tsp. salt*
1 cup chopped celery	*½ cup tomato juice*
1 small onion, minced	*2 tbs. dry bread crumbs*
1 tbs. raisins	*½ cup grated tangy cheese*
½ tsp. sugar	*2 tbs. butter*
1 tsp. chili powder	

Mix first 4 raw vegetables with raisins in casserole. Blend sugar, chili powder, cumin seed, and salt in cup; season vegetables by mixing well; moisten vegetables with tomato juice. Sprinkle dry bread crumbs over top; spread grated cheese over; dot with dabs of butter. Bake in preheated hot oven (375° F.) 20 minutes, or until vegetables are tender but not soft. Serve piping hot from casserole. Serves 4.

Chili con Carne Mexicano with Tortillas   TIME: 3 hours

*1 lb. dried Mexican pinto
    beans or red kidney
    beans
3 pts. cold water
1½ tsp. salt
4 tbs. suet
2 medium-sized onions, sliced
3 cloves garlic, halved
2 tbs. chili powder
3 tbs. flour*

*2 lbs. beefsteak, chopped
    coarse
3 cups canned tomatoes with
    liquid
1 cup chopped celery
1½ tsp. salt, extra
1 tsp. sugar
⅛ tsp. cayenne pepper
1 tsp. dried marjoram
½ tsp. ground cumin
Tortillas*

Wash beans; drain well. Pour cold water into heavy saucepan; add beans to cold water; add salt. Heat to boiling over high flame; reduce flame; cover. Simmer gently 1½ hours, or until beans are soft but not mushy. Remove from heat. Allow beans to cool in liquid; when cool, measure liquid; if less than 1 cup, add enough cold water to make 1 cup.

Melt suet in large, deep skillet or Dutch oven over medium flame; add onions. Sauté 5 minutes, or until golden brown; add garlic; sauté 5 minutes more. Remove suet and garlic; stir in chili powder. Flour meat lightly; place in skillet; brown 10 minutes by stirring constantly; cover meat with canned tomatoes and liquid; add all seasonings. Cover; turn down flame. Simmer gently 30 minutes, or until meat is tender; add beans and liquid; heat thoroughly. Serves 8 to 10.

Serve piping hot with tossed-green salad and *tortillas.*

To save time, use 1 No. 2 can kidney beans. Add as suggested.

Tortillas   TIME: 1 hour

*1 cup yellow corn meal
1 cup enriched flour*

*¾ tsp. salt
Lukewarm water*

Mix corn meal, flour, and salt thoroughly in mixing bowl; gradually add only enough lukewarm water to make a stiff dough. Chill dough in refrigerator 30 minutes. Wet hands lightly in cold water; mold dough into small balls about 1½ inches in diameter; gently pat into paper-thin cakes. Bake on lightly greased griddle over medium flame 10 minutes on each side, or until rich brown color. Yield: 12 tortillas.

Chile con Carne Mildly Sweet   TIME: 50 minutes

3 tbs. beef suet, chopped	2 tbs. flour
coarse	Boiling hot tomato juice
1 medium-sized onion, sliced	¾ tsp. salt
thin	½ tsp. dried marjoram
2 garlic cloves, halved	½ tsp. ground cumin
2 tsp. chili powder	½ tsp. sugar
1½ lbs. beefsteak	

Have beefsteak chopped coarse, or have it sliced very thin and cut into 1-inch pieces.

Melt suet in large skillet over medium flame; add onion. Sauté 5 minutes, or until golden brown; add garlic; sauté 5 minutes more. Remove suet and garlic; stir in chili powder. Flour meat lightly; place in skillet; brown 10 minutes by stirring constantly; cover meat with boiling hot tomato juice (about 1 cup); add salt, marjoram, cumin, and sugar; cover; turn down flame. Simmer gently 30 minutes, or until meat is tender. Serve piping hot with steamed rice or noodles. Serves 4.

CINNAMON or **TRUE CINNAMON,** *Cinnamomum zey-lanicum Nees*

> Ground in 1½ ounce to 4 ounce containers at groceries and markets; also from herb dealers.
> Quills or sticks in 1½ once containers at groceries and markets; also in bulk from herb dealers.
> See also Cassia.

Cinnamon or true cinnamon comes only from the island of Ceylon and the Malabar coast of India.

The flavor is sweet and very delicate; when ground, cinnamon is a bright light-brown color, almost yellowish. The spice which is usually called cinnamon is really cassia: the *dried ground bark* of any species of the evergreen tree, the *Cinnamomum,* which belongs to the laurel, *Lauraceae,* family. Practically all the cinnamon used in the United States is cassia, which has the stronger flavor and is a rich reddish-brown.

It is the inner bark which is ground into the highest-grade spice. As the quills dry, they curl to form the familiar cinnamon sticks about 1 inch in diameter.

Using: The uses of ground cinnamon are almost too well known to enumerate. We know the warm, sweet taste of cinnamon on and in bread, buns, cakes, toast, stewed fruits, relishes, cold and hot milk drinks, pies, puddings, dumplings, and desserts. But *one of its newest and most delicious uses is in the flavoring of ice cream.* Meats, too, may be lightly sprinkled with cinnamon to bring out a new flavor, especially lamb and pork chops. Salt pork and ham are perked up by a dash of cinnamon, especially when cloves are included. Meat stews and boiled smoked shoulders are more than delicious when cinnamon is added while they are cooking. Squash baked with butter and cinnamon is far less flat than just plain squash.

Quills and sticks of cinnamon are almost as popular in cooking as is the ground cinnamon. Catsup, pickles, pickling vinegars, relishes, stewed fruits, chocolate drinks, hot herb teas, mulled wines, and even coffee are now flavored with this delicious spice. See also Allspice, Cloves, Ginger, Nutmeg, Herb and Spice Sauces, and Spiced Recipes.

BEVERAGES: *Coffee, herb teas, mulled wines.* Use 1 small piece quill in each serving.
Chocolate, chocolate milk, cold or *hot milk.* Shake dash of ground cinnamon over top of each serving.

BREAD, BUNS, COFFEECAKES: Mix ground cinnamon in batter and in topping.
Cinnamon toast: Blend ground cinnamon with butter and sugar; also sprinkle generously over top.

DESSERTS: *Junkets* and *puddings.* Lightly sprinkle top with ground cinnamon just before serving.

FRUITS: *Baked, stewed. Apples, apricots, cranberries, peaches, pears, pineapples.* Season generously with cinnamon and sugar before cooking.

MEATS: *Ham* and *salt pork.* Sprinkle with ground cinnamon before cooking.
Lamb and *pork chops.* Lightly sprinkle with ground cinnamon before broiling.

Lamb Stew. Add ¼ teaspoon ground cinnamon while cooking.

PICKLES: *Sweet gherkins* and *fruits.* Season with 1 small quill cinnamon in each pint jar.

PIES: *All fruits.* Sprinkle cinnamon over top of fruit before covering and baking. *Also* blend cinnamon and sugar *as topping for piecrust.*

PRESERVES: *Conserves* and *jams.* Use as directed in familiar recipes.

PUDDINGS: *Rice, tapioca.* Season with ½ teaspoon cinnamon.

SAUCES: *Dessert sauces.* Use as directed in recipes. See also recipe Cinnamon Fudge Sauce.

SOUPS: *Scotch broth.* Add ¼ teaspoon ground cinnamon to regular recipe.

VEGETABLES: *Beans, pumpkins,* and *squash, baked.* Sprinkle ground cinnamon over vegetable before baking.

For 4 servings use approximately:

¼ teaspoon to 1 teaspoon ground cinnamon.
4 small quills or sticks.

Cinnamon Frozen Mousse TIME: 30 minutes
Freeze 3 hours

¼ cup unsulphured molasses *2 egg whites, beaten stiff*
3 tbs. sugar *1 tsp. cinnamon*
¼ cup water *1 cup heavy cream, whipped*
⅛ tsp. salt

Set refrigerator control at coldest point 30 minutes before preparing mousse.

Pour molasses into heavy saucepan placed over low flame; add sugar and water; blend well; cook 15 minutes, or until syrup makes a soft ball when a teaspoonful is dropped into cold water. (Soft-ball stage is 234° F.)

Break egg whites into large mixing bowl; add salt; beat until stiff but not dry; add cinnamon; beat well; add hot syrup; continue beating 10 minutes, or until cold. Fold in whipped cream; blend well. Pour mixture into freezing tray; place in freezing unit until frozen—3 to 4 hours. This mousse has a soft, velvety texture and does not freeze so hard as ice cream. Serves 6.

Ginger Frozen Mousse: Use ¾ teaspoon ground ginger and ¼ teaspoon allspice instead of cinnamon. Follow recipe.

Cinnamon Ice Cream à la Minute　　TIME: 10 minutes

1 pt. vanilla ice cream　　　1½ tsp. ground cinnamon
½ pt. chocolate ice cream

Purchase ice cream; allow to soften slightly; whip or blend with powdered cinnamon, using electric mixer. Refreeze blended ice cream in freezing compartment of refrigerator. Yield: 1½ pints.

May also be made with prepared ice-cream mixes. For the 1-quart size, follow first freezing process as indicated on package but do not add flavoring. Instead, mix thoroughly 3 tablespoons chocolate syrup and 1½ tablespoons ground cinnamon; add to ice-cream mix; put in refrigerator; freeze; serve.

Cinnamon Pumpkin Crisps　　TIME: 30 minutes

½ cup cooked pumpkin,　　　1 tsp. ground cinnamon
   thick　　　　　　　　　　¼ tsp. salt
1 cup seedless raisins　　　　1 tsp. baking soda
½ cup butter　　　　　　　　½ tsp. ground ginger
1 cup sugar　　　　　　　　¾ tsp. ground nutmeg
1 egg　　　　　　　　　　　¼ tsp. ground cloves
1¾ cups sifted flour　　　　　1 tsp. vanilla
½ cup chopped walnuts

Mix seedless raisins and nuts in small bowl; flour lightly.

Cream butter and sugar thoroughly in large bowl; add egg; stir vigorously until well blended; stir in pumpkin.

Sift flour, cinnamon, salt, soda, ginger, nutmeg, and cloves in separate bowl; add to creamed mixture; stir in vanilla, raisins, and nuts. Drop mixture by small spoonfuls on greased cooky sheets. Bake in preheated moderately hot oven (375° F.) 12 to 15 minutes. Yield: 2½ dozen cookies.

Cinnamoned Acorn Squash　　TIME: 1 hour

2 acorn squash　　　　　　¼ tsp. nutmeg
2 tbs. butter　　　　　　　¼ tsp. sugar
Salt　　　　　　　　　　　¼ cup hot water
½ tsp. cinnamon

Select perfect squash. Wash thoroughly by scrubbing under cold running water. Cut squash in half lengthwise; remove seed and pulp. Salt centers lightly; place ½ tablespoon butter in each half.

Blend cinnamon, nutmeg, and sugar; place ¼ teaspoon blended spice in center of each half squash. Arrange squash in baking dish with cover; carefully pour hot water into bottom of dish; cover. Bake in preheated hot oven (400° F.) 25 minutes; remove cover; bake 20 minutes more, or until tender but not overdone. Serve piping hot with more butter if desired. Serves 4.

Cinnamoned Pumpkin: Pare and cut 2 pounds pumpkin into small cubes; arrange pieces in shallow casserole; sprinkle lightly with salt; spread blended spices over top; dot with butter. Bake uncovered in preheated, moderately hot oven (375° F.) 45 minutes, or until tender but not overdone. Serves 4.

Cinnamoned Winter Squash: Pare and cut 2 pounds winter squash into small cubes. Proceed as for pumpkin. Serves 4.

Compote Apple Pielet Fried   TIME: 1 hour

2 large tart apples	*2 cups sifted flour*
¼ cup honey	*3 tsp. baking powder*
¼ cup sugar	*1 tsp. salt*
¼ tsp. cinnamon	*¼ cup shortening*
1 cup sugar, extra	*½ cup milk*
4 tsp. cinnamon, extra	*Butter or margarine*

Wash, peel, core, and slice tart apples. Prepare as compote by placing sliced apples in shallow baking dish. Mix honey, sugar, and cinnamon; pour over apples; cover. Bake in preheated moderate oven (350° F.) 20 minutes, or until apples are soft but not mushy.

Sift and blend flour, baking powder, and salt in large mixing bowl, then cut in shortening; gradually add sufficient milk to make soft dough. Knead dough gently on lightly floured board 5 minutes; roll out very thin. Cut circles of dough about 3½ inches in diameter (use a saucer and sharp knife if large cooky cutter is not handy); place in ½ circle of the dough 3 tablespoons apple compote; fold other half over top, forming a semicircle pielet; moisten and seal edges with fingertips, making fluted design.

Prepare sugar and cinnamon coating by blending 1 cup sugar and 4 teaspoons cinnamon on cooky sheet or in flat pan; set aside.

Melt sufficient butter or margarine in heavy skillet to provide fat 1½ inches deep. When hot (350° F.), fry pielet 3 minutes, or until golden brown on one side; turn with spatula; brown on other side; drain on absorbent paper. Quickly dip pielet into sugar and cinnamon coating. When well coated on both sides, serve while piping hot, with Cinnamon Ice Cream, or whipped cream. Yield: 8 pielets.

CLOVES, *Caryophyllus aromaticus L.*

Ground in 1¼ ounce containers at groceries and markets; also from herb dealers.

Whole in 1 ounce and 2 ounce containers at groceries and markets; also from herb dealers.

Cloves are the unopened flower buds of one of the most beautiful and stately evergreens in all nature—the clove tree. It is a member of the myrtle, *Myrtaceae,* family, and was first found growing on the Molucca Islands, an archipelago of the Dutch East Indies.

The Dutch call the clove the *kruidnagel.* Literally, it means *herb nail* or *spice nail.* The word clove is derived from the French word for nail: *clou,* and the Latin *clavus.* The reddish-brown dried bud resembles a round-headed nail which measures from ½ to ¾ inch long. Four points at the end of the calyx hold the tiny round head or crown tightly in place. The aroma of the dried flower buds is delightfully strong and pungent. The taste is aromatic and almost hot.

Using: The ground clove powder is used to flavor brown breads, gingerbreads, spice cakes, chili sauce, baked meat loaves, and is an important ingredient in many sweet pickles, fruit preserves, and mincemeats. Ground clove is often used in combination with a bay leaf, or ground cinnamon, ginger, and nutmeg; but since the clove flavor is so strong, it is always best to be conservative until you become familiar with its effects upon flavors. Some homemakers will sprinkle a few grains of powdered cloves over baked fish just before serving it. Cranberry juice loses its New England plainness when a few grains of ground clove are sprinkled over the top of each serving. Soups and vegetables are also intriguing when ground clove is added to the other ingredients. This is especially true of beets, potatoes, and sweet potatoes.

The uses of the whole cloves are even more numerous and familiar. They range from flavoring beverages and condiments to soups and desserts. Whole cloves added to the water in which vegetables are boiled or steamed will give a wonderfully warm taste to them, and a clove pomander is one of the sweetest and spiciest of scents. See also Cinnamon, Ginger, Nutmeg, and Spiced Recipes and Blends.

APPETIZERS: *Cranberry juice.* Sprinkle a dash of ground cloves over each serving.

BEVERAGES: *Mulled wines, hot* or *iced tea.* Season each serving with 1 or 2 whole cloves.

BREADS, BUNS, CAKES: Flavor with ¼ to ½ teaspoon ground cloves.

DESSERTS: *Junkets, puddings.* Sprinkle top with ground cloves instead of nutmeg or cinnamon; or blend with cinnamon, using ⅓ amount cloves, ⅔ amount cinnamon.

FRUITS: *Baked, preserved, spiced, stewed.* Season *all fruits* with 6 to 8 whole cloves while cooking. See also Spiced Recipes.

MEATS: *Ham, smoked meats, tongue.* See also recipes in clove section.

PICKLES: *Sweet gherkins, fruits.* Season with 2 or 3 whole cloves in each pint jar.

PIES: *Apple, mince.* Add ¼ teaspoon ground clove to ingredients of familiar recipe.

PRESERVES: *Apples, cranberry, crabapples, peaches, pears, prunes, watermelon.* Add whole cloves as suggested in recipes.

PUDDINGS: *Fruit, rice, tapioca.* Blend ¼ teaspoon ground cloves with cinnamon as added seasoning.

SAUCES: *Chili, cream.* Flavor with dash of cloves and nutmeg.
Tomato, basic sauce. Add ¼ teaspoon ground cloves to ingredients.

SOUPS: *Bean, beef, beet, mulligatawny, potato, creamed pea, creamed tomato,* and *creamed potato.* Add ¼ teaspoon ground cloves and 1 bay leaf to soups while preparing.

VEGETABLES: *Beans, beets, squash, sweet potatoes, boiled* and *baked.* Season each serving with hot butter and light sprinkling of ground cloves.

For 4 servings use approximately:

⅛ to ½ teaspoon ground cloves.
1 to 2 whole cloves in beverages.
Variable amounts, both ground and whole cloves, in preserves and roasts.

Canton Berne Pepper Nuts
*As prepared in the canton
of Berne in Switzerland.*

TIME: 30 minutes
Chill overnight

2 cups sifted flour
1 tsp. baking powder
1 cup sugar
1 tsp. ground cinnamon
1½ tsp. ground ginger
¾ tsp. ground mace
¼ tsp. ground allspice

1½ tsp. ground cloves
Grated rind of 1 lemon
1 tbs. citron, minced
3 tbs. chopped walnuts
2 eggs
1 egg yolk, extra
1 egg white, extra

Sift flour, baking powder, sugar, and all spices in large mixing bowl; mix well. Add lemon rind, citron, and nuts; mix well again.

Beat 2 eggs and 1 egg yolk, extra, in small bowl until foamy; gradually add to flour mixture in large bowl; blend well; cover bowl. Chill dough in refrigerator overnight. (The Bernese bury the bowl of dough in the snow overnight.) In the morning shape dough into long rolls about 1 inch in diameter; cut about ½ inch thick; mold into small balls like walnuts.

Beat egg white lightly; brush over tops of pepper nuts. Bake on lightly floured cooky sheet in preheated moderate oven (350° F.) 30 minutes, or until done. Allow to cool at room temperature. Place in cooky jar. Yield: 36 cookies.

Spicy Baked Ham

TIME: Variable

1 whole tenderized ham
Cold water
1 pt. cider vinegar
1 cup molasses
5 bay leaves
1 tbs. mustard seed

*1 tbs. whole black pepper-
    corns*
1 bunch celery with leaves
1 cup sugar
½ cup yellow corn meal
2 tbs. whole cloves

Select firm, tenderized (not cooked) ham, preferably boned. Place ham in large kettle with cold water only sufficient barely to cover; add vinegar, molasses, bay leaves, mustard seed, peppercorns, and celery. Bring to boiling point over high flame; turn down flame. Simmer gently until tender, allowing approximately 15 minutes per pound. (For ½ tenderized ham allow approximately 25 minutes per pound.) Remove from heat; leave ham in liquid to cool, then skin.

Blend sugar and corn meal; roll ham in mixture; stick whole cloves into ham. Place in baking dish in preheated moderate oven (350° F.) 20 minutes, or until golden brown. Serve piping hot with Horseradish Herb Jelly Sauce. Allow ¼ to ½ pound for each serving.

CURRY POWDER

Ground, blended spice, in 2 ounce to 4 ounce bottles at fancy groceries and markets; also from herb dealers.

Curry is not a single spice but a blend of a number of spices.

There are as many different formulas as there are manufacturers and grinders. Each one has its own particular series of blends or combinations of blends, such as mild, mildly sweet, hot, mildly hot, and so on down the list.

A curry powder may contain as many as sixteen different spices. Among them are allspice, black pepper, red pepper, cayenne, ginger, cinnamon, cardamom seed, coriander seed, mustard seed, nutmeg, saffron, and turmeric.

Curry powder is one of the world's oldest seasonings, and has come to us from the Parsees and the East Indians. Both the aroma and the flavor are hauntingly exotic; and when the powder is used in small quantities, the most subtle seasoning is given to many foods. This golden-yellow blend has been called the "salt of the Orient," for it is used so constantly. And *a curry*, any dish prepared with curry powder, is the national dish of India, if a country can be said to have one particular dish.

Many who have lived in India and the Far East tell us that curry is valued in those tropical climates for its effect upon the body temperature. The Indians use it so constantly because it makes them feel more comfortable in the heat. The American curry blends are prepared from formulas that are more suited to American palates, and these blends are not so pungent and hot as those used in the Orient.

Using: The intriguing and exotic flavor of curry powder is equally delicious with eggs, fish, game, meats, and vegetables.

Always served with rice, the mild curries should be the first ones given to the uninitiated. For those who are accustomed to the more highly seasoned combinations any curry blend will be relished.

A curry consists of the main dish accompanied by steamed rice and a series of several relishes. Some mix the relishes and sauce with the rice; others prefer to eat them from many little side dishes which surround the main plate. The first two relishes which are really absolutely necessary to make a curry authentic are a *hot, mango chutney* and *grated fresh coconut.* If the fresh coconut is not available, then shredded coconut will take its place. Also among the relishes should be some *Bombay Duck,* which is *not* duck at all, but shredded, cured, dried East Indian *fish.* The fish has been treated with a Persian or East Indian fetid gum resin which has a strong odor and a slight taste of garlic. (A few shreds of this is quite enough for even a well-seasoned palate.)

Other more simple relishes may also accompany the curry. These usually include salted nuts, chopped hard-boiled egg whites, sweet pickles, and both red and green peppers, either shredded or chopped fine, and several more varieties of chutneys. It is quite usual to be served with more than one chutney in India and Persia.

In favorite and familiar recipes the amount of curry powder used can vary from 1 teaspoon to as much as 1 or 2 tablespoons, according to personal tastes. The list of suggestions which follows is intended as a guide to some of the appetizingly different flavors which may be achieved by using small amounts of curry powder.

BISCUITS AND MUFFINS: Season favorite recipe with ½ teaspoon curry powder to each cup flour used.

CHEESES: *Cottage, cream, soft cheeses.* Blend ¼ teaspoon to ½ teaspoon curry powder with each ¼ pound cheese. Use as canapé.

EGGS: Use ¼ teaspoon curry powder instead of mustard in deviled eggs.

FISH: *Baked, broiled.* Season lightly with curry powder instead of pepper before cooking.

FRENCH DRESSING: Use curry powder instead of dry mustard in ingredients.

MEATS: *Beef, lamb, pork, veal.* See recipe Curry of Lamb East Indian.

POULTRY: *Chicken, duck, squab, turkey.* See recipe Curry of Duck with Mushrooms.

SAUCES: Prepare familiar cream sauce. Season with 1 teaspoon curry powder. See also Herb Curry Sauce.

SEA FOODS: Prepare Basic White Sauce. Season with ½ to 2 teaspoons curry. Pour over *steamed fish* and *shellfish*.

SOUPS AND STEWS: *Meat* and *poultry.* Season with ½ teaspoon curry to 4 cups broth, while cooking.

VEGETABLES: *Lentils, dried;* also *dried peas.* See recipe for Dahl East Indian.

For 4 servings use approximately:

1 teaspoon curry powder for mild flavor.
2 teaspoons to 1 tablespoon for more pungent flavors.

Curried Lobster Mousse   TIME: 30 minutes
                                     Chill 4 hours

1 envelope unflavored gelatine   *¾ cup milk*
¼ cup cold water   *3 tbs. garlic vinegar*
1½ tsp. flour   *1½ tbs. butter*
2 tsp. curry powder   *1½ cups minced cooked*
1 tsp. salt   *lobster*
⅛ tsp. black pepper   *⅔ cup heavy cream, whipped*
2 eggs, beaten

Soften gelatine in cold water.

Blend flour, curry powder, salt, and black pepper in top section double boiler; gradually stir in beaten eggs; mix until smooth; add milk and vinegar. Place over lower section double boiler half filled with boiling water over high flame; cook 10 minutes, stirring constantly; when very smooth, add butter and softened gelatine; stir until dissolved; add lobster. Pour into bowl; cover. Chill in refrigerator 1 hour, stirring once or twice during that time. When slightly thickened, fold in whipped cream. Turn into mold which has been rinsed in cold water. Chill in refrigerator 3 hours, or until firm. When ready to serve, unmold on lettuce leaves. Serve with favorite dressing or mayonnaise. Serves 6.

Curried Halibut Mousse: Use finely flaked halibut instead of lobster. Follow recipe.

Curried Shellfish Mousse: Use any preferred cooked shellfish instead of lobster. Follow recipe.

Curried Tuna Mousse: Use finely flaked canned tuna instead of lobster. Follow recipe.

Curried Deviled Eggs East Indian   TIME: 30 minutes

4 hard-boiled eggs
½ cup minced onion
2 tsp. minced green pepper
1 tsp. butter, softened
¼ tsp. dry mustard
½ tsp. curry powder

½ tsp. salt
⅛ tsp. red pepper
⅛ tsp. sugar
1 tsp. lemon juice
2 tsp. minced chives

Cut hard-boiled eggs in half lengthwise; remove yolks. Mash yolks in small bowl; blend with onion, green pepper, soft butter, mustard, curry powder, salt, red pepper, sugar, and lemon juice. Lightly refill whites; garnish with minced chives. Serve well chilled on lettuce leaves with mayonnaise. Serves 4.

Curry Blend English Style   TIME: ½ hour

3 ozs. coriander seed,
    powdered
⅛ tsp. cayenne pepper
¾ oz. turmeric
¼ oz. ground cloves

¾ oz. fenugreek seed,
    powdered
¼ oz. cardamom seed,
    powdered
¾ oz. cumin seed, powdered

All spices should be thoroughly powdered; blend well in small mixing bowl. Store in tightly covered jar ready for use. Yield: 5½ ounces.

Curry Blend Spicy   TIME: 45 minutes

4 ozs. ground turmeric
4 ozs. ground coriander seed
2½ ozs. black pepper
¼ oz. ground red pepper
¼ oz. ground ginger
¼ oz. cayenne pepper

½ oz. ground mace
½ oz. ground cinnamon
1 oz. ground cardamom seed
½ oz. ground cloves
½ oz. ground fenugreek seed
¼ oz. ground cumin seed

Purchase only the best quality and exceedingly fresh herbs and spices which are ground fine. Blend thoroughly by mixing long and well in large mixing bowl—at least 45 minutes. Pack in bottle; cork tightly; use as desired. Yield: 13 ounces.
   If hotter curry is preferred, add more cayenne pepper.

Curry Blend Mild   TIME: 1 hour

1½ cups coriander seed   *¼ cup cumin seed*
⅓ cup dried chilies   *¼ cup mustard seed*
¼ cup poppy seed   *½ cup saffron*
2 tsp. garlic powder   *4 tbs. salt*

Have seed and chilies pounded to powder. Blend all ingredients well by stirring vigorously. Pack into bottles or jars; seal tightly, ready for use. Yield: 1 pint.

Curry Chicken Broth Iced   TIME: 25 minutes
                                                  Chill 3 hours

1 tbs. butter   *1 cup light cream*
1 tsp. flour   *2 egg yolks, beaten*
2 tsp. curry powder   *⅛ tsp. ground ginger*
3 cups chicken broth   *1 tbs. chopped chives*

Melt butter in heavy saucepan over medium flame. Remove from heat; add flour and curry powder by stirring constantly until smooth; add chicken broth to butter mixture; return to medium flame. Bring to boiling point. Allow to simmer gently 10 minutes.

In top section double boiler combine cream and egg yolks; when smooth, gradually stir in hot broth. Place over lower section double boiler half filled with boiling water; cook over high flame 10 minutes, or until thickened, stirring constantly. Stir in ginger. Pour into jar. Chill in refrigerator 3 hours, or until thoroughly jellied. Serve ice cold in chilled bouillon cups. Garnish each serving with freshly chopped chives or favorite minced herb. Serves 4.

Curry of Duck with Mushrooms   TIME: 1½ hours

1 duck, 4 lbs.   *1 tsp. curry powder*
1 tbs. butter   *1 cup Basic White Sauce*
1 small onion, minced   *½ cup heavy cream*
1 clove garlic, halved   *½ lb. mushrooms, sliced*
1 tsp. salt   *1 tbs. butter, extra*
¼ tsp. black pepper   *Salt and pepper to taste, extra*
¾ cup warm water   *Shredded coconut*

Have all excess fat removed from duck; cut into serving pieces.
Melt butter in large, heavy skillet over medium flame; add

onion and garlic. Sauté 3 minutes only. Remove garlic; add duck pieces; season with salt and pepper; brown lightly on all sides by turning with fork. Add warm water; cover. Simmer gently 1 hour, or until duck is tender but not soft.

Meanwhile prepare Basic White Sauce. Sauté mushrooms 10 minutes in 1 tablespoon butter melted in heavy saucepan; season with salt and pepper to taste.

When duck is tender, remove pieces from skillet; keep duck warm over steam. Quickly stir in curry powder, Basic White Sauce, and cream into sauce in which duck has been simmering; add sautéed mushrooms; add duck pieces; heat thoroughly. Serve piping hot with steamed rice and chutney. Garnish each serving with shredded coconut. Serves 4 to 6.

Curry of Fried Chicken   TIME: 1 hour

1 broiling chicken, 3 lbs.
2 tsp. salt
1 tsp. curry powder
½ tsp. paprika
¼ tsp. ginger
¼ tsp. white pepper
½ cup flour
¼ cup butter

2 cups minced tart apple
1 small onion, minced
½ cup chopped fresh or
  shredded dry coconut
¼ cup flour, extra
½ tsp. curry powder, extra
2 cups chicken broth or water
½ cup cream

Have chicken cut into serving pieces; wipe dry with towel.

Blend salt, curry powder, paprika, ginger, white pepper, and flour in small mixing bowl. Pour seasoned flour into a paper bag; place 1 piece chicken in bag; close; shake vigorously; this will coat chicken with seasoning; continue process until all pieces are coated.

Melt butter in large skillet over high flame; add chicken; brown evenly by turning with fork; lower flame; cover. Cook gently 30 minutes, or until chicken is tender. Remove chicken from skillet; keep hot while preparing gravy. Add apple, onion, and coconut to skillet drippings; cook 5 minutes, or until onion is transparent. Meanwhile blend ¼ cup flour, curry, and chicken broth in small bowl; when smooth, add to ingredients in skillet; stir well; add cream; continue stirring. Cook 5 minutes, or until sauce is thickened. Replace chicken pieces; heat thoroughly. Serve piping hot with steamed rice and relishes. Serves 4 generously.

Curry of Lamb East Indian   TIME: 1½ hours

1½ lbs. lean lamb
2 tbs. butter
3 small onions, minced
1 tbs. curry powder
1 clove garlic
1 tart apple, chopped

3 tomatoes, peeled and
  chopped
2 cups chicken broth or water
1 tsp. salt
⅛ tsp. white pepper
3 tbs. flour

Have lamb cut into 1-inch cubes.

Melt butter in large skillet over medium flame; add lamb and onions. Sauté 5 minutes, or until golden brown. Add curry powder, garlic, apple, and tomatoes; add broth, salt, and pepper; stir well. Cover. Simmer gently 1 hour, or until lamb is tender. Remove lamb; keep hot over steam. Quickly strain sauce through coarse sieve; thicken with flour mixed to paste with little cold water. Cook 5 minutes, or until smooth, stirring constantly. Return lamb to sauce; heat thoroughly. Serve piping hot with steamed rice and relishes. Serves 4.

Prepare Curry of beef, pork, poultry, veal in same manner.

Dahl East Indian   TIME: 1½ hours
Soak lentils 10 hours

Dahl is the common name given to all kinds of vegetables prepared with curry sauce, and *is used especially to define* Curried Purée of Lentils.

1½ cups dried lentils
1 pt. cold water
1 clove garlic, minced
1 small onion, minced
3 tbs. olive oil

1 tbs. curry powder
⅛ tsp. cayenne pepper
¼ tsp. salt
Juice of ½ lemon

Wash lentils; place in heavy saucepan; cover with cold water; allow to soak overnight. When ready to cook, add sufficient water to cover lentils with 1 inch water over the top. Place over medium flame; cover partially. Boil 1 hour, or until lentils are tender.

Meanwhile, sauté garlic and onion 3 minutes in olive oil in heavy skillet placed over medium flame; stir in curry powder and cayenne pepper. Simmer gently 5 minutes, stirring constantly.

When lentils are tender, add curry seasoning from skillet; mix well; season with salt and lemon juice. Simmer gently 30 minutes, or until lentils may be easily mashed with fork and Dahl becomes a thick sauce. Serve piping hot over steamed rice. Serves 6.

Dahl, over rice, may be served with or without other curry dishes. It is delicious when served with broiled chicken or veal.

Vegetarian Curry Ghandi   TIME: 45 minutes

½ cup rice	*¾ tsp. curry powder*
2 qts. boiling water	*¼ tsp. salt, extra*
1 tsp. salt	*⅛ tsp. turmeric*
1 cup minced onion	*4 tbs. butter*
1 cup diced carrots	*2 tsp. Worcestershire sauce*
1 cup diced celery	*4 tbs. shredded coconut*
1 cup shelled fresh peas	*4 tbs. chutney*

Cook rice 20 minutes in 2 quarts rapidly boiling water to which 1 teaspoon salt has been added in large saucepan over high flame. Drain in colander; rinse with hot water. Allow to stand over steam until grains of rice become separate.

Meanwhile, cook vegetables 10 minutes in heavy saucepan with only enough boiling water barely to cover them; when tender but not mushy add curry powder, salt, turmeric, butter, and Worcestershire sauce; mix gently but well.

Form a ring of steaming hot rice on preheated hot platter; fill center with curried vegetables. Serve piping hot with 1 tablespoon shredded coconut and 1 tablespoon chutney at side of each portion. Serves 4.

GINGER, *Zingiber officinale Roscoe*

Ground in ½ ounce, 1 ounce, and 2 ounce containers and larger at groceries and markets; also from herb dealers.

Root *crystallized, dried,* and *sugared,* in 8 ounce and 1 pound tin boxes at fancy groceries and markets; also from herb dealers and confectioners.

Root *preserved in syrup* in jars of varying shapes and sizes at fancy groceries and markets; also from herb dealers and confectioners.

Root *whole dried* in 1 ounce and 2 ounce containers at groceries and markets; also in bulk from herb dealers and some druggists.

See also Turmeric.

Ginger is the washed and dried root of the colorful tropical and semi-tropical herb which belongs to the ginger, *Zingiberaceae,* family.

Native to tropical Asia, ginger is extensively cultivated in Africa, China, the Dutch East Indies, Hindustan, India, Japan, and the West Indies; especially Jamaica and Puerto Rico. The plant has recently been introduced in the subtropical section of southern Florida and it is perhaps the only region in the continental United States where the climate is at all favorable for its cultivation. In the experiments to date the yield is only about half that obtained per acre in Jamaica.

African ginger root is somewhat yellowish and is used chiefly for grinding and blending with other gingers where color is not the important factor. Its flavor is extremely pungent and the aroma is not so delicate as that of the Jamaica ginger.

Both the Chinese and Japanese ginger roots are very irregular in shape. Most of the Chinese root reaches our markets as "preserved ginger"; and the flavor combined with the sweet syrup is interestingly pungent. The Japanese root looks like the Cochin ginger but is not so aromatic or flavorful. It reaches our markets dried and limed, i.e., peeled, bleached, and coated with calcium carbonate, ready for grinding.

The three best grades and flavors of ginger are the roots which reach us from Africa, India, and the West Indies. The root from India is grown chiefly along the Malabar coast. The two chief areas of production are Calicut and Cochin. These gingers, especially the COCHIN GINGER, are important ingredients of all the delicious Indian chutneys. The pieces are very irregular in size and shape. The color is a pale brown, and both the flavor and aroma are delightfully pungent.

JAMAICA GINGER is the best quality of all the gingers. The root pieces are a very light buff color and they are clean and free from any corkiness. Both the taste and the aroma are intensely agreeable.

The sugared, dried ginger is the boiled rhizome which has been dried and then sugared. Most of our preserved and sugared ginger reaches us from Canton and Hong Kong.

Using: Ginger's spicy-sweet pungency has pleased the palate of mankind since antiquity. Its uses are so infinite in number that only a few of them can possibly be suggested in these paragraphs. The food products of bakers, confectioners, spice grinders, canners, and the meat packers all contain this perfect flavoring. If there is any flavoring in the world that could possibly make a filet mignon taste better than it does with just plain salt and pepper, it is ground ginger. Try blending ½ teaspoon of this pungent spice with the salt-and-pepper seasoning for steaks, then simply rub the meat on both sides before broiling and experience one of the biggest taste thrills of your life.

Poultry and pot roasts are delicious when lightly sprinkled or dredged with flour and ginger before cooking. All meat loaves are pepped up with a bit of ginger added, especially when the loaf contains corned beef. Gingerbread, cakes, and cookies are the old standbys, and most of us have had a "gingerbread man" for Christmas eating ever since we can remember. These are but a few of the ways in which ginger became a favorite spice. Applesauce, chutneys, stewed fruits, puddings, condiments, jellies, and pickles all make use of the sweet tanginess of ground ginger.

The whole root gives that wonderful spiciness and tang to ginger ale and ginger beer. Even rum is flavored with it; and an old-time eighteenth-century recipe says that ginger root tea is a healthy drink for those who have been imbibing too freely and eating too heavily.

In all events, ginger has been the one commercial spice which has held its own with pepper through all the phases of history. In England, long before the Norman Conquest, a pound of ginger was worth the price of a good fatted sheep. Today we may not trade our ginger for sheep, but we season our sheep with it, as well as beef, chicken, turkey, and veal. See recipe for Gingered Lamb Pyramids. See also Allspice, Cinnamon, Condiments, Curry, Nutmeg, and Spiced Recipes. See also familiar recipes for exact amounts in using.

BEVERAGES: See recipe for Ginger Beer.

BREADS, CAKES, COOKIES: See familiar recipes.

Toast: Blend ground ginger and sugar; serve on buttered brown-bread toast at teatime.

DESSERTS: *Ice cream, puddings.* Use minced preserved ginger and syrup as sauce over desserts. Approximately 1 teaspoon for each serving.

FRUITS: *Baked, stewed, preserved.* Season with ¼ teaspoon ground ginger and 2 teaspoons preserved or crystallized ginger, minced.

MEATS: *Beef, lamb, veal, broiled* or *chopped.* Sprinkle

lightly with ginger before broiling. Blend ¼ to ½ teaspoon ground ginger with chopped meats.

PICKLES: See Spiced Recipes and Blends.

PIES: *Custard, fruits.* See familiar recipes.

POULTRY: Lighty sprinkle inside and out with ground ginger before roasting.

PRESERVES: See Spiced Recipes.

PUDDINGS: *Fruit, rice.* Sift 1 teaspoon ginger with sugar in recipe; prepare as usual. Also use ½ teaspoon ginger and ½ teaspoon cinnamon instead of all ginger.

SAUCES: See Herb and Spice Sauces.

VEGETABLES: See Gingered Buttered Beets.

For 4 servings use approximately:

¼ to 1 teaspoon ground ginger.

1 tablespoon to 4 tablespoons minced preserved ginger as sauce.

Variable amounts in recipes given.

Gingered Lamb Pyramids   TIME: 20 minutes
                                   Chill 1 hour

2 cups ground cooked lamb   *½ cup flour*
1 cup Basic White Sauce   *1 egg, beaten*
1 tsp. chopped fresh parsley *1 tbs. milk*
½ tsp. onion salt   *½ cup dry bread crumbs*
½ tsp. celery salt   *Margarine or cooking oil*
½ tsp. ground ginger

Prepare Basic White Sauce; stir in lamb, parsley, onion salt, celery salt, and ginger; blend well. Chill mixture in refrigerator 1 hour. When ready to fry, shape mixture into small pyramids. Roll each in flour, then dip in beaten egg which has been mixed with 1 tablespoon milk; finally roll in bread crumbs. Fry in frying basket in deep, hot (365° F. to 385° F.) margarine or cooking oil 3 minutes, or until golden brown and heated through. Serve piping hot with Mustard Sauce Épicé or other favorite sauce or condiment. Yield: 10 small pyramids.

Gingered Beef Pyramids. Use 2 cups cooked chopped beef. Follow recipe.

Gingered Chicken Pyramids. Use 2 cups cooked minced chicken. Follow recipe.

Gingered Corned Beef Pyramids. Use 2 cups cooked minced corned beef. Follow recipe.

Gingered Turkey Pyramids. Use 2 cups cooked minced turkey. Follow recipe.

Gingered Veal Pyramids. Use 2 cups minced roast veal. Follow recipe.

Old-fashioned Staffordshire Ginger Beer   TIME: 30 minutes
Allow to stand overnight before bottling

1½ ozs. bruised dried ginger   *3 gallons boiling water*
Rind and juice of 2 lemons   *2 tbs. thick, fresh brewers'*
2½ lbs. loaf sugar   *yeast*
1 oz. cream of tartar

Peel lemons; squeeze out juice; pour juice into large crock; add lemon rind, ginger, cream of tartar, and sugar; mix well. Pour boiling water over ingredients. Allow to stand at room temperature until lukewarm. While still warm, add yeast, which must be perfectly fresh. Stir contents well; cover crock with cloth. Allow liquid to stand in warm place overnight. Next day skim off all yeast; slowly pour liquid into another container, allowing all sediment to remain in original crock. Bottle liquid immediately; seal with corks securely tied down to bottles. Set aside in cool place for 3 days. Ginger beer is then ready for use. Serve chilled as desired. Yield: 3 gallons.

Two tablespoons brewers' yeast equals 1 ounce compressed yeast, or 1 cake of dry yeast.

Gingered Buttered Beets   TIME: 20 minutes

¾ tsp. ground ginger   *1½ cups sliced cooked beets*
½ cup sugar   *2 tbs. butter*
1½ tbs. cornstarch   *1 tbs. chopped parsley*
½ cup cider vinegar

Blend ginger, sugar, and cornstarch in heavy saucepan; gradually add vinegar; stir until smooth. Place saucepan over medium flame. Cook 5 minutes, stirring constantly. Add beets and butter; lower flame. Simmer gently 10 minutes, stirring occasionally. Serve piping hot garnished with chopped parsley. Serves 4.

Gingered Buttered Carrots. Use half-cooked carrots. Follow recipe.

Gingered Sweet Potatoes. Use 1½ cups sliced cooked sweet potatoes instead of beets or carrots. Follow recipe.

Tropical Snowballs   TIME: 10 minutes

1 qt. vanilla ice cream   *2 cups shredded coconut*
3 tbs. chopped preserved
    ginger

Have chilled shallow dessert bowls ready. Spread coconut on wax paper or cooky sheet. Dip a ball of ice cream with a large, round scoop. Quickly roll ball in coconut; place in bowl; top with chopped preserved ginger. Serve immediately. Yield: 6 portions.

Use any preferred flavor ice cream, such as caramel, cherry, chocolate, lemon, peach, pistachio, strawberry, et cetera.

MACE, *Myristica fragrans Houtt*

Blades or whole mace dried in bulk from herb dealers.
Ground in 1¼ ounce and 2 ounce containers at groceries
    and markets; also from herb dealers.
See also Nutmeg.

Mace or TRUE MACE is the dried, ground outer shell or whole flakes of the kernel of the fruits of the beautiful evergreen nutmeg tree. The tree is described under the nutmeg chapter.

The nutmeg fruits resemble small peaches. When ripe, these luscious tropical fruits split open to reveal one of nature's most handsome combination of colors. The first layer or cover is a vivid green, the next a bright orange, and the third layer is the brilliant scarlet aril which protects the nutmeg kernel. This is the covering which is dried and ground to produce the spice called mace. It requires more than 400 pounds of nutmeg kernels to supply enough coverings to make 1 pound of mace.

Like the other spices, all maces take their particular name from the districts from which they originate and are exported. So we have *Amboyna* mace, *Banda* mace, *Granada* mace, and *Penang* mace among the true maces.

Using: Mace, like nutmeg, is used in combination with cinnamon, cloves, allspice, and ginger, as well as alone. *The*

flavor is much stronger than that of nutmeg and the other spices; and when mace is used in combinations, the proportion of it should be considerably less. Mace is delicious with potatoes, either creamed, mashed, or hashed; and sweet vegetables, such as carrots and cauliflower, are far more palatable when just a bit of mace has been added to them as seasoning. One blade of finely minced mace will season fruit jellies, biscuit doughs, fruit salads, and Welsh rarebit with an interesting and delicious flavor. One teaspoon of ground mace in a pint of whipped cream gives it a beautiful golden color and adds an intriguing taste which cuts the cloying oiliness of the unflavored cream and increases its delicacy. All chocolate dishes are far more tasty if a dash of ground mace is added to them just before bringing them to the table.

A few grains of ground mace sprinkled over a serving of oyster stew will make everyone who tastes its deliciousness sit up and take notice. The use of mace as flavoring for cakes, biscuits, preserves, and condiments is so well known that it is only necessary to mention them. Many bakery products are prepared from sweetened doughs which have been flavored with mace. Many formulas for blended ground spices include maces. Spices such as the poultry seasonings, prepared meat and sausage seasonings used by the meat packers, prepared mustard sauces, Worcestershire sauce, Yorkshire relish, and Cambridge sausage all contain aromatic golden grains of mace. See also Jellies, Nutmeg, and Spiced Recipes and Blends.

APPETIZERS: *Tomato juice.* Sprinkle with a dash of mace just before serving.

BISCUITS, CAKES, COOKIES: *Sweet spiced doughs.* Add ¼ teaspoon ground mace to batter, especially to doughnuts, light fruitcakes, and pound cakes, then sprinkle with cinnamon and sugar after baking.

CHEESE: *Welsh rarebit.* Add 1 small blade mace to rarebit while cooking. Remove spice blade before serving.

FISH: *Any sweet-meated fish, scalloped.* Add ¼ teaspoon ground mace to ingredients while baking.

MEATS: *Meat loaf.* Flavor with ¼ teaspoon ground mace. Add to other ingredients before baking.

Chops. See recipe Penang Mace Veal Chops.

PRESERVES: Use ½ mace and ½ nutmeg instead of all nutmeg in fruit preserves which call for nutmeg.

PUDDINGS: *Apple, chocolate, cottage,* and *custard.* Add a

dash of mace, about ⅛ teaspoon, to the ingredients before preparing.

SALADS: *Fruits.* Add 1 small blade mace, finely minced,
to fruits before mixing.

SAUCES: *Cream, fish, meat.* Flavor sauce with ⅛ to ¼ teaspoon ground mace and ¼ teaspoon onion salt and ¼
teaspoon celery salt.
Custard. Add ⅛ to ¼ teaspoon mace and cinnamon.

SHELLFISH: *Stews*, especially *clams* and *oysters*. Sprinkle
each serving with few grains of ground mace for a new
and delicious flavor.

SOUPS: *Chicken, consommé,* and *cream soups.* Sprinkle
each serving lightly with few grains of ground mace
just before serving. A wonderful change from nutmeg.
See also Soup Sumatra.

VEGETABLES: *Carrots, cauliflower, potatoes, creamed,
mashed,* or *hashed;* also *spinach* and *succotash.* Add ⅛
to ¼ teaspoon ground mace to creamed and hashed
vegetables. Sprinkle boiled or steamed vegetables with
few grains of ground mace after vegetables have been
buttered.

For 4 servings use approximately:

⅛ to ½ teaspoon ground mace.
1 small whole blade, broken or crushed.

Penang Mace Veal Chops   TIME: 15 minutes
Marinate 2 hours or more

4 loin veal chops   *½ tsp. ground mace*
½ cup olive oil   *1 tsp. minced parsley*
2 tbs. tarragon vinegar   *½ small onion, minced*
½ tsp. dried thyme   *1 tsp. grated lemon rind*
1 cup bread crumbs   *¼ tsp. salt*
¼ cup minced raw mush-   *⅛ tsp. cayenne pepper*
* rooms*   *2 ozs. butter*

Have veal chops sliced 1 inch thick; wipe with damp cloth.
Blend olive oil, tarragon vinegar, and thyme in large shallow
bowl. Marinate chops in seasoned liquid from 2 to 4 hours,
as time permits.

Blend thoroughly all other ingredients except butter in large
mixing bowl. Dip marinated chops in seasoned bread crumbs.

Melt butter in heavy skillet; brown chops quickly over high flame to seal in juices; lower flame. Fry 5 minutes on each side, or until well done. Serve piping hot with favorite mushroom sauce or condiment. Serves 4.

Penang Mace Lamb Chops. Purchase loin or shoulder chops; marinate. Follow recipe.

Penang Mace Mutton Chops. Purchase loin or shoulder chops; marinate 4 hours or overnight. Follow recipe.

MUSTARD, *Brassica sinapis,* or DRY MUSTARD

Dry (flour) in 1¼ ounce, 2½ ounce, 4 ounce, and 8 ounce containers at groceries and markets; also from herb dealers and druggists.

See also Mustard Plant and Mustard Seed.

Dry, ground mustard or MUSTARD FLOUR is the resulting spice obtained when the whole mustard seeds are crushed, ground, and sifted.

The mustard seed is the fruit of the mustard plant described in the chapters on the herb. For years England and America imported most of their mustard seed from India and Russia; but today the plant is cultivated in England and to a great extent in Santa Barbara County in California and also in Montana. Domestic production has been as much as 73,000,000 pounds of mustard seed in one year.

The pure, dry mustard flour is a pale yellow, and if the color is brighter, it indicates that turmeric has been added or blended with it in the milling processes. Dry mustard, however, is always graded for quality, and the labels on the containers show the various degrees: the letters DSF mean that the mustard is Double Superfine, Pure No. 1; the letters EF indicate Extra Fine, Pure No. 2.

Using: Dry mustard or mustard flour, though prepared from the herb seed, is generally referred to as a spice; and in its variously prepared forms it becomes a condiment. As such it is doubtless the most popular condiment in the United States.

More foods than could possibly be enumerated here are made extraordinarily palatable and agreeable by the frequent and judicious use of dry mustard. Every degree of pungency of flavor can be secured by using either very little or much mustard, whichever the individual taste may demand.

Both the dry and the prepared mustards may be used to

flavor appetizers, cheeses, fish, French dressings, game, meats, poultry, salads, sauces, shellfish, and vegetables. See also condiments; Herb and Spice Butters, Herb and Spice Salad Dressings, and Herb and Spice Sauces and Stuffings.

> APPETIZERS: *Cottage, cream,* and *soft cheeses.* Flavor lightly with dry mustard and onion salt. About ⅛ teaspoon each to ¼ pound cheese.
>
> CHEESES: *Melted; Welsh rarebit.* Add ½ to 1 teaspoon dry mustard to ingredients before cooking.
>
> EGGS: *Deviled.* Mix ¼ teaspoon mustard with 4 yolks.
>
> FISH: *Croquettes, scalloped, stuffed.* Add ⅛ to ¼ teaspoon dry mustard to ingredients before cooking.
>
> FRENCH DRESSINGS: Use from ⅛ to ½ teaspoon, according to pungency preferred.
>
> GAME: *Duck, venison ragout.* Add ⅛ teaspoon dry mustard to ingredients while cooking.
>
> MEATS: *Roast, steaks.* Sprinkle very lightly with mustard flour instead of pepper, using from ⅛ to 1 teaspoon, according to pungency desired; also use prepared mustard.
>
> POULTRY: *Chicken, turkey, creamed.* Add ⅛ to ¼ teaspoon dry mustard to sauce while cooking.
>
> SALADS: *Fruit.* Add a dash of ground mustard to mayonnaise served with fruit salads. A deliciously different taste.
>
> SAUCES: *Cream* sauces for *fish.* Add ⅛ teaspoon to ¼ teaspoon dry mustard to ingredients before cooking.
>
> SHELLFISH: *Crabs, deviled.* Add 1 teaspoon dry mustard to ingredients before baking.
> *Lobster, broiled.* Blend ¼ teaspoon dry mustard with 1 tablespoon butter spread over lobster before broiling.
>
> VEGETABLES: *Baked beans, beets, succotash.* Add ¼ to ½ teaspoon dry mustard while cooking. Amount depends upon pungency desired.

For 4 servings use approximately:

¼ teaspoon in salads and dressings.
Variable amounts, according to pungency desired, in other foods.

| **Mustard Savory Ripe Olives** | TIME: 10 minutes |
| | Chill 24 hours |

1 pint can ripe olives   *¼ cup cider vinegar*
4 tsp. dry mustard

Drain olives from can; save liquid; pour into mixing bowl; add vinegar.

Place mustard in separate cup; make smooth, thin paste by gradually stirring in small quantity liquid from mixing bowl; add mustard paste to balance of liquid; blend well; pour seasoned liquid into small saucepan placed over medium flame. Bring liquid to boiling point; add olives. Simmer very gently 5 minutes. Remove from heat. Allow olives to cool in liquid at room temperature. Pack olives in glass jar; pour liquid over. Place in refrigerator to chill 24 hours. *Serve* very cold *with cheese, cold cuts, meats,* and *sea-food salads.* Yield: 1 pint.

Piquant Deviled Crab Meat   TIME: 30 minutes

1 lb. fresh crab meat	*¾ cup milk*
¼ lb. butter	*1½ tsp. dry mustard*
1 scallion, minced,	*⅛ tsp. cayenne pepper*
or very small onion	*½ tsp. Worcestershire sauce*
3 tbs. flour	*½ cup buttered bread crumbs*
¾ tsp. salt	*3 tbs. chopped fresh chervil*
¾ cup cream	*or parsley*

Select choice, chunk crab meat; remove any small shells; keep very cold until used.

Melt butter in heavy saucepan over medium flame. Sauté scallion 3 minutes but do not brown.

Blend flour, salt, mustard, and cayenne pepper in large bowl; gradually stir in cream and milk; when very smooth, gradually add liquid to butter and scallion in saucepan over low flame stirring constantly. Cook carefully until sauce thickens; add Worcestershire sauce; add crab meat; stir gently. Pour mixture into individual shells or casseroles; sprinkle crumbs lightly over top. Bake in preheated medium oven (350° F.) 10 minutes, or until crumbs are golden brown. Remove from heat. Garnish each shell or casserole with chopped fresh chervil or parsley. Serve piping hot. Serves 6.

Tangy Spiced Beets   TIME: 15 minutes

3 cups diced cooked beets	*½ tsp. dry mustard*
3 tbs. butter	*⅛ tsp. paprika*
2 tbs. cider vinegar	*1 tbs. sugar*
½ tsp. salt	*¾ tsp. Worcestershire sauce*

Blend well vinegar, salt, mustard, paprika, sugar, and Worcestershire sauce in small bowl to make smooth paste.

Melt butter in medium saucepan over low flame; add seasoned paste; blend well; add beets, stirring gently and often. Heat slowly and thoroughly about 5 minutes. *Serve* piping hot *with fish* or *roasts*. Serves 4.

Mustard Dumplings   TIME: 30 minutes

1 cup sifted flour
2 tsp. baking powder
½ tsp. salt
¼ tsp. onion salt
1 tsp. dry mustard

1 tsp. minced fresh parsley
2 tsp. butter
½ cup rich milk
¼ tsp. celery salt

Sift all dry ingredients in large mixing bowl; blend well. Cut in butter; add milk and parsley, stirring lightly and quickly to make light dough. Drop dumpling mixture by tablespoonfuls into large kettle half filled with rapidly boiling salted water. Cook gently 12 to 15 minutes, or until dumplings puff up lightly and lose all appearance of stickiness. Lift out dumplings and *serve with stews* of *beef, chicken, game,* or *veal*. Serves 4 to 6.

NUTMEG, *Myristica fragrans Houttyn*

Ground in ½ ounce and 1¼ ounce containers and larger at groceries and markets; also from herb dealers.
Whole in 1½ ounce containers at groceries and markets; also in bulk from herb dealers.
See also Mace.

Nutmeg is the dried seed of the kernel of the fruit of the nutmeg tree. This evergreen with heavy, waxy leaves like those of the rhododendron is native to the Molucca Islands in the East Indian Archipelago.

Though native to the archipelago, the tree is now extensively cultivated in the Banda Islands, Ceylon, Grenada, Java, Penang, Singapore, and Sumatra. The nutmeg belongs to the large genus of luxuriant tropical trees of the *Myristicaceae* family. They all bear beautiful white and yellow flowers and luscious tropical fruits with a hard seed enclosed in a brightly colored arillode.

The ripe, luscious fruit breaks open to reveal the bright scarlet aril which covers the hard brown kernel inside of which is the seed. It is this seed which is dried and then ground into the spice we call nutmeg.

The whole nutmegs are rather grayish brown when dried; and though hard on the surface and quite wrinkled, they are very easily grated. Most of them are oval shaped; and the largest are about 1¼ inches long and almost an inch wide. The aroma and the taste are both highly spicy and almost bitter. This aromatic bitterness is especially true of the freshly grated nutmeg.

Using: Nutmeg and mace are interchangeable in practically every instance for flavoring. Nutmeg is less pungent than mace, and because of its more delicate flavor it may be used more freely. Its many uses are perhaps better known than those of mace, though it is often used in combination with it, as well as with cinnamon, allspice, and ginger. Formulas for ground spice blends and seasonings, such as mincemeat spice, poultry seasonings, and sausage spices, all contain ground nutmeg. Bologna and frankfurter seasonings make use of it; also many condiments, such as chutney and tomato catsup.

Most of us are familiar with the spicy deliciousness which nutmeg adds to applesauce, baked apples, and pie, stewed fruits, puddings, and custard sauces. Eggnogs, jellies, and pumpkin pie are a few of the other delicacies which owe their unusual flavor to the little brown seed.

Vegetables lose all trace of flatness and monotony of flavor when they have been judiciously seasoned with ground nutmeg. Cabbage, cauliflower, kale, spinach, succotash, and sweet potatoes all have a new appeal when served either plain with hot butter and a sprinkling of nutmeg or with a cream sauce which has been flavored with ground nutmeg. See also Cinnamon, Cloves, Ginger, Mace, Spiced Recipes and Blends.

BEVERAGES: *Chocolate, egg, hot* and *cold milk drinks.* Sprinkle lightly with few grains freshly grated nutmeg just before serving.

CAKES AND COOKIES: *Spice,* especially. Use as in recipes; usually ½ teaspoon of ground nutmeg.

EGGS: *Eggnogs, scrambled.* Sprinkle each serving very lightly with few grains ground nutmeg.

FRUITS: *Apples, cherries, peaches, pears, baked, pie, stewed.* Season lightly with ground nutmeg.

MEATS: *Beef, chopped, pie, stew.* Season beef with ⅛ teaspoon ground nutmeg before cooking.

PUDDINGS: *Bread, butterscotch, chocolate, custard, rice, tapioca, vanilla.* Sprinkle lightly with freshly grated nutmeg before baking.

SALAD DRESSINGS: *Fruit salads* served *with plain mayonnaise.* Sprinkle each serving with few grains of ground nutmeg.

SAUCES: *Custard, pudding, mushroom,* and *white.* Add ⅛ teaspoon ground nutmeg to ingredients while cooking.

SOUPS: *Beef, chicken, cream, lamb broth, split pea.* Sprinkle lightly with freshly grated nutmeg just before serving.

VEGETABLES: *Carrots, cauliflower, kale, potatoes, spinach, succotash,* and *sweet potatoes.* Sprinkle lightly with few grains of ground nutmeg just before serving.

For 4 servings use approximately:

⅛ to 1 teaspoon ground nutmeg.
Few grains freshly grated whole nutmeg.

Nutmeg Golden Popovers   TIME: **1 hour**

2 cups enriched flour	*2 tsp. sugar*
½ tsp. ground nutmeg	*½ tsp. salt*
¼ tsp. ground cloves	*1¾ cups milk*
¼ tsp. ground cinnamon	*2 tsp. melted butter*
⅛ tsp. ground mace	*4 eggs, beaten until foamy*

Sift together flour, nutmeg, cloves, cinnamon, mace, sugar, and salt in large mixing bowl. Gradually stir in milk; when smooth, add melted butter; add beaten eggs. With electric or rotary beater, beat batter 2 minutes.

Heat and grease popover *pans;* fill ⅔ full with batter. Bake in preheated very hot oven (450° F.) 15 minutes; reduce heat to moderate 350° F.; bake 20 minutes more. Serve piping hot. Yield: 12 popovers.

PAPRIKA, *Capsicum annuum Linn*

Ground in ½ ounce, 1 ounce, and larger bottles and tin containers at groceries and markets; also from herb dealers.

See also Cayenne, Chili Powder, and Red Pepper.

Paprika is the ground dried fruit of several sweet varieties of the *Capsicum* plant, which belongs to the potato or *Solanaceae* family.

Native to Central America, the large sweet peppers, whose dried pods are ground to make paprika, are widely cultivated in Argentina, Bulgaria, Canada, Chile, Hungary, Portugal, Spain, and the United States.

The color, the aroma, and the taste of paprika depend upon the exact variety of the pod used and the grinding processes. *The highest-grade paprika is obtained only when the pods have been carefully graded and all stalks and stems discarded. It is really sweet to the taste* and has an agreeable, light, pleasant aroma. The color is a rich, dark red. Only the dried pericarps or walls of the pod and the seeds are ground.

The HUNGARIAN PAPRIKA, sometimes called *rose paprika,* is that which has been prepared in Hungary from choice, selected, sweet pepper pods. Its flavor is rich and sweet and its aroma warmly aromatic. The KOENIGSPAPRIKA, or *king's paprika,* is more pungent, since it contains the ground stems as well as the pods.

The Spanish and Portuguese paprikas are prepared from the peppers grown in those two countries, and the pungency and aromas of them vary with the manufacturers, formulas, and processes. There is a paprika for every palate, and the degree of flavor ranges from the sweet to the mildly pungent and pungent. The majority of Americans prefer the mild varieties. The culinary use of paprika is increasing year by year. French, Spanish, and Hungarian cookery has taught us many interesting and delicious ways of using this sweetly accented spice. *We Americans consume about 8,000,000 pounds of paprika every year,* and it is one of the principal spices used by meat packers and manufacturers of catsups, condiments, and sauces.

Perhaps the increase in American consumption of the spice can be credited to the Hungarian scientist, Dr. Albert Szent-Gyongyi. While working with the Rockefeller Foundation he discovered a new vitamin in paprika and named it Vitamin P. He proved that the spice contains more Vitamin C than any of the citrus fruits. For this scientific discovery he was given the Nobel Prize award in 1937.

Using: Paprika, as well as being unusually nourishing, is one of the most useful of all the spices. In addition to giving a sweet pungent flavor to foods, it adds color and attractiveness to many bland foods. A most simple meal can be made more appetizing and appealing by a little paprika garnish, dressing up, or decoration. Potatoes, cauliflower, cabbage, turnips, wax beans, and many other pale-colored foods respond to a touch of paprika.

Poultry, shellfish, salads, rice, fish, scrambled eggs, Welsh rarebits, macaroni, mashed potatoes, chicken stew, appetizers, meat soups, and gravies may all be flavored and garnished with this attractive, aromatic spice. Fish and cream soups take on a new taste appeal when they have been prepared with this colorful spice. See also Cayenne, and Peppers.

APPETIZERS: *Cream cheese, smoked salmon, stuffed celery.* Sprinkle canapés generously with paprika for flavor and color.

CHEESE: *Melted; Welsh rarebit.* Add ¼ to ½ teaspoon paprika to ingredients. If more pungent flavor is preferred, add 1 teaspoon paprika.

EGGS: *Scrambled.* Blend ½ teaspoon paprika with 4 eggs before beating.

FISH: *Boiled, steamed, baked, broiled.* Season generously with paprika, just before serving, after melted butter has been poured over fish. Or blend ½ teaspoon paprika with ¼ pound butter while melting.

GAME: *Duck, pheasant, venison.* Add 1 to 2 teaspoons paprika to liquid while roasting or stewing game.

MEATS: *Beef, lamb, mutton, pork* (especially *spareribs*), and *veal.* Use from 1 teaspoon to 2 tablespoons paprika, as suggested in recipes.

POULTRY: *Chicken, duck, turkey.* Season poultry by lightly rubbing inside and out with blended paprika, salt, and pepper. Use approximately twice as much paprika as salt.

SALADS: *Fruit, vegetable.* Garnish with generous sprinkling of paprika just before serving.

SAUCES: *Cream, meat, pan gravies.* Add 1 to 2 teaspoons paprika to sauce while preparing.

SOUPS AND STEWS: *Chicken, cream, fish, meat, shellfish, vegetable.* Add paprika to soup while cooking; if preferred, sprinkle each portion generously with paprika just before serving.

VEGETABLES: *Cabbage, cauliflower, corn* (fresh or canned), *kale, potatoes, turnips, wax beans.* Season vegetables with generous sprinkling of paprika after melted butter has been poured over them.

Potatoes French Fried: Dip in paprika before frying.

For 4 servings use approximately:

2 teaspoons for mild flavoring.
1 tablespoon to 2 tablespoons for more pungent flavoring.
Variable amounts as garnish.

Crusty Fried Paprika Chicken   TIME: 1 hour

1 broiling chicken, 3½ lbs.   *1 tbs. paprika*
1 cup dry bread crumbs,   *½ tsp. salt*
   sifted   *¼ tsp. white pepper*
½ cup flour   *¼ lb. butter*
1 tsp. poultry seasoning

Purchase broiling or frying chicken; have it quartered. Wipe with damp cloth.

Blend bread crumbs, flour, poultry seasoning, paprika, salt, and pepper in large mixing bowl; mix thoroughly. Sprinkle chicken pieces generously with seasoned mixture; save balance of mixture.

Melt butter in heavy skillet over high flame; brown chicken pieces quickly on all sides to seal in juices; cover; turn down flame to medium; continue frying 30 to 45 minutes, or until tender.

To make pan gravy, remove chicken pieces; place on preheated platter; keep hot over steam. Stir in balance seasoned mixture into skillet drippings; mix thoroughly. Add sufficient milk or stock to seasoned mixture in skillet to make gravy of desired consistency. Usually ½ cup to 1 cup makes a thick gravy, depending upon the amount of bread crumbs left over. Pour steaming hot gravy over chicken. *Serve* piping hot *with steamed rice* or *noodles.* Serves 4.

Chicken Paprikash Hungarian   TIME: 1¼ hours

1 broiling chicken, 3½ lbs.   *1 tbs. butter*
½ cup flour   *1 large onion, minced*
1 tsp. paprika   *1 tbs. paprika, extra*
½ tsp. salt   *½ cup hot water*
¼ tsp. white pepper   *2 tbs. flour*
1 tbs. bacon drippings   *2 cups smooth sour cream*

Have broiler cleaned and quartered. Wipe with damp cloth.
Blend flour, paprika, salt, and pepper; pour mixture into
paper bag. Coat each quarter of broiler by placing in bag, one
piece at a time, and shaking well. Chicken will be evenly
coated with seasoned flour.

Melt bacon drippings and butter in heavy skillet over high
flame; brown chicken in hot fat by frying on each side 3 minutes; push to one side of skillet, making room to brown onion
3 minutes; sprinkle 1 tablespoon paprika over chicken; add
hot water; cover skillet; turn down heat. Simmer gently 45
minutes, or until chicken is tender but not soft. Turn chicken
pieces occasionally to avoid sticking; add small quantity warm
water if necessary to prevent scorching and to keep chicken
moist.

When chicken is tender, remove from skillet; keep chicken
hot over steam. *Quickly prepare sauce* by adding 2 tablespoons
flour to pan gravy; blend well; when smooth add sour cream,
stirring constantly for 5 minutes, or until sauce is thick; cover;
simmer gently 5 minutes more over low flame. Replace hot
chicken pieces; taste; add more salt if desired; heat thoroughly.
Serve piping hot *with creamed vegetable* or *steamed rice.*
Serves 4.

Paprika Schnitzel Viennese   TIME: 20 minutes

4 veal schnitzel (leg of veal   *¼ lb. butter*
    slices ¼ in. thick)   *1 tbs. paprika, extra*
½ cup flour   *1 tbs. flour, extra*
1 tsp. paprika   *1 pt. sour cream*
½ tsp. salt   *Dutch Poppy Seed Noodles*
¼ tsp. pepper

Purchase veal from leg or shoulder. Ask dealer to slice thin
and pound with mallet, as for schnitzel. The slices may vary
from ¼ to ½ inch thick but should never be thicker.

Prepare Dutch Poppy Seed Noodles before starting
schnitzel.

Blend flour, paprika, salt, and pepper in small bowl. Dip
veal schnitzel in seasoned flour until well coated.

Melt butter in skillet over high flame (*use only butter for
genuine Viennese schnitzel);* when very hot, quickly sauté
schnitzel 3 minutes on each side; when golden brown, transfer
to hot platter; keep hot over steam. Quickly stir flour into hot

skillet drippings; blend until smooth; add paprika; blend well; gradually add sour milk, stirring 5 minutes, or until very smooth; turn down flame; cover. Simmer gently 5 minutes more; replace schnitzel; heat thoroughly. *Serve* piping hot *with Dutch Poppy Seed Noodles.* Serves 4.

Veal Paprika Casserole   TIME: 1½ hours

1 veal cutlet, 1½ ins. thick	*½ cup bread crumbs*
½ tsp. salt	*1 tbs. bacon drippings*
¼ tsp. pepper	*1 tbs. butter*
2 eggs, beaten	*1 pt. sour cream*
1 tbs. milk	*2 tbs. paprika*

Purchase 1 veal cutlet or 4 thick loin veal chops. Wipe with damp cloth. Season veal with salt and pepper. Beat eggs with 1 tablespoon milk in small bowl; brush cutlet generously with beaten eggs, then dip cutlet in bread crumbs.

Melt bacon drippings and butter in large oval casserole over high flame; when hot, add cutlet; brown each side 3 minutes, or until golden brown. Blend sour cream and paprika; pour over veal cutlet; cover. Bake in preheated moderately slow oven (325° F.) 1¼ hours, or until veal is tender and well done. *Serve* piping hot *with steamed rice* and *tossed-green salad.* Serves 4.

Beef Paprika Casserole. Purchase chuck steak; cut into squares; remove all excess fat. Follow recipe.
Chicken Paprika Casserole. Purchase broiling chicken; cut into serving pieces. Follow recipe.

Wine-jellied Beef Paprika   TIME: 2½ hours
                                              Chill 4 hours

3 lbs. beef for pot roast	*½ cup sauterne wine*
1 tsp. salt	*1 cup beef stock*
¼ tsp. black pepper	*1 tbs. unflavored gelatine*
2 tbs. drippings or butter	*¼ cup cold water*
1 bay leaf, crushed	*3 tomatoes, sliced*
4 whole cloves	*1½ cups mayonnaise*
1 carrot, chopped	*1 tsp. minced parsley*
1 small stalk celery, chopped	*1 tsp. minced chives*
1 large onion, chopped	*Lettuce leaves*
2 tsp. paprika	

Purchase bottom or top round of beef cut in uniform shape. Season meat with salt and pepper by rubbing it lightly over the surface.

Melt drippings or butter in extra-heavy saucepan over high flame; when very hot, add meat; brown on all sides about 3 minutes, or until rich brown color; add bay leaf, cloves, carrot, celery, and onion; brown lightly 3 minutes.

Place rack under meat to prevent scorching; add paprika, wine, and beef stock, stirring well.

Soften gelatine in water; add to meat; cover; lower flame. Simmer at steady heat 2½ hours. Place meat in large mold or on platter.

To save time, prepare in pressure cooker; cooking time directed by manufacturer.

Skim fat from sauce; strain through coarse sieve, pour hot sauce over meat; cool at room temperature; then chill in refrigerator 3 to 4 hours, or until jellied.

When ready to serve slice tomatoes; blend mayonnaise, parsley, and chives. Thin mayonnaise with lemon juice if thinner dressing is preferred.

If meat has been chilled in a mold, unmold on bed of lettuce leaves arranged on platter; otherwise arrange leaves around edge of platter on which meat was chilled. Garnish with tomato slices topped with seasoned mayonnaise. When serving, slice through jelly and meat with very sharp knife. Serves 6.

Zucchini Paprika Disks   TIME: 10 minutes

1 lb. zucchini squash	*1 tsp. paprika*
1 cup flour	*½ tsp. white pepper*
1 tsp. garlic salt	*1 cup milk*
Butter or margarine	*Paprika, extra*

Select firm green zucchini. Wash thoroughly under cold running water. Lightly scrape off any skin blemishes but *do not peel.* Slice zucchini crosswise, forming small disks. Set aside.

Blend thoroughly flour, garlic salt, paprika, and white pepper in mixing bowl.

Dip zucchini slices in milk, then in seasoned flour. Fry in frying basket in deep, hot butter or margarine (375° F.) 2 minutes only, or until golden brown. Drain on absorbent paper. Serve piping hot with very light sprinkling of paprika over top. Serves 4.

PEPPER or **BLACK PEPPER,** *Piper nigrum L.*

Ground in ¼ ounce, 1¼ ounce, 2 ounce, 4 ounce, and larger containers at groceries and markets, also from herb dealers.

Whole pepper or PEPPERCORNS in 1¼ ounce, 2 ounce, 4 ounce, and larger containers at groceries and markets; also in bulk from herb dealers.

See also Cayenne, Paprika, Red Pepper, and White Pepper.

Black pepper is the spice or pungent condiment which is secured by grinding the dried berry or fruit of a climbing perennial vine plant called *Piper nigrum.* The plant belongs to the *Piperaceae* family of tropical plants of which there are 9 genera and more than 1,000 species. The fruit, or whole berry with its rough outer surface, is used to produce the black pepper.

The woody vine is native to the East Indies and is widely cultivated in East India, French Indo-China, Siam or Thailand, and India. The beautiful leaves are ovate-acuminate and the minute flowers which grow in the form of a narrow spike are succeeded by brilliant red berries. These dried berries are the peppercorns.

The dried, tiny, wrinkled little globes of the black pepper range in color from a dark brown to black, depending upon the harvesting processes. They are never more than ¼ inch in diameter and it takes more than 500 whole peppercorns to weigh an ounce. The flavor is a pungent, biting one and the aroma extremely aromatic.

ALLEPPEY BLACK PEPPER comes from southern India and is shipped from Alleppey. It is a fine, clean berry with an aromatic flavor less pungent than some of the other peppers.

JAVA BLACK PEPPER is grown on the island of Java. Its berry is larger than some of the other varieties and its flavor is pungent.

JOHORE BLACK PEPPER, as its name signifies, is from the Malay state of Johore. This pepper is one of the highest grades, and it is usually labeled and shipped with Singapore Black Pepper, described in a later paragraph.

LAMPONG BLACK PEPPER, from the district of that name in the southern part of Sumatra, is one of the peppers which is dried on the ground in the sun. Because of the mineral matter it picks up when dried this way, the ground spice has a rather grayish color but is unusually pungent.

PENANG BLACK PEPPER is also sometimes called ACHEEN BLACK PEPPER. It is grown in the district of Acheen on the island of Sumatra but is shipped from Penang.

SAIGON and SIAM BLACK PEPPERS of French Indo-China seldom reach our markets. The small amounts which are exported are usually marketed in France.

SINGAPORE BLACK PEPPER may be any of several high-grade peppers grown on the Malay Peninsula and shipped from the port of Singapore. After the berry is harvested, it is dried in mats suspended over huge kettles in which the plant GAMBIER is boiled. The herb smoke turns the berry black and gives it a characteristic taste. This pepper berry is the largest, best-flavored peppercorn in commercial use. When ground, the spice is a rich, almost dark green color.

TELLICHERRY BLACK PEPPER, like the Alleppey black pepper, is from the Malabar coast in southern India in the district of South Kanara. The peppercorn has a less pungent aroma and the flavor is milder than that of the Singapore pepper. There are some who prefer the softer flavor of the Tellicherry above that of the gambier-smoked Singapore pepper. Gambier is a yellowish climbing shrub of the family *Ourouparia gambir*. The natives of the Malay Peninsula chew the berries or nuts of the gambier with the betel nut.

TRANG BLACK PEPPER comes from the Trang district on the Malay Peninsula and is usually shipped from the little island of Penang, which is directly opposite. This berry is sun-dried on the ground, and is rather grayish after grinding.

Using: Pepper is just as important in its universal use as is salt. The peppercorns are always an ingredient in prepared pickling spices; and many of the prepared spice blends for commercial uses include pepper as one of the chief seasonings. This is especially true of poultry seasonings and sausage blends.

Practically all our foods except desserts are flavored with pepper. Appetizers, with just a dash of the biting little grains; or meats and sauces with as much as half a teaspoon of pepper are all improved and made more appetizing by this most ancient of seasonings. It, too, needs careful handling and sometimes just 3 or 4 peppercorns added to a soup or a gravy will improve the flavor immeasurably and give an entire meal a completely new appeal. See also Cayenne, Paprika, Red Pepper, and White Pepper.

For suggested uses of Black Pepper with various foods, see White Pepper.

PEPPER or RED PEPPER, *Capsicum*

Crushed red pepper. The crushed pods and whole seeds in 1¼ ounce bottles and containers at groceries and markets; also in bulk from herb dealers. Also labeled *Peperone Rosso*.

Ground in 1¼ ounce, 2 ounce, 4 ounce, and larger containers at groceries and markets; also from herb dealers.

See also Cayenne, Black Pepper, Paprika, and White Pepper.

Red pepper is the crushed or ground product of the dried ripe fruit of any large species of the *Capsicum* plants which are called *chilies* or *red peppers*. (See complete description in chapters on Cayenne Pepper.)

The *Chili Ancho* or the Mexican chili pods are among the largest grown; and in recent years they have been introduced in southern California. Their color is a beautiful rich red and the enclosed seeds are a brilliant yellow. They both retain their color even when dried. The chilies may grow as long as 4 to 5 inches, and are round at the base and taper to a point. Their taste is biting and the aroma highly aromatic. A mere whiff of the crushed spice can bring tears to the eyes, but the flavor is wonderfully rich and stimulating to the palate.

The genuine Mexican chilies make the highest grade red pepper, and the product is extremely aromatic and pungent.

Using: Red pepper should not be confused with the black and the white peppers. Because of its extreme sharpness, *it needs to be used with caution and good judgment at all times;* and if so, it can do wonders to a most simple dish. Italian tomato sauces owe their great taste appeal not only to the olive oil and garlic in them but to the dash of aromatically flavored crushed red pepper, *peperone rosso*.

Often, when stewing fresh tomatoes or other sweet vegetables, I will add a small pinch of crushed red pepper to them. The resulting flavor is unbelievably good. Even though the product is crushed, I pulverize it still more by grinding it between the palms of the hands. The seeds remain whole, but the tiny flakes of dried pod disintegrate and disappear in the tomato sauce, and the only visible aftereffects are the smacking lips of those who have tasted the flavor and have exclaimed: "Ummn, isn't that good!" Whatever you do, *use crushed red pepper more sparingly than you have ever used any seasoning in your entire culinary experience.*

Ground red pepper isn't quite so pungent as the crushed pod and whole seeds, but it, too, needs to be used sparingly. Above all else, *be sure that all peppers are fresh.* They, like all other herbs and spices, lose their natural sweetness and aroma when they have been allowed to stand unused too long on a pantry or kitchen shelf. See also Cayenne, Chili Powder, and White Pepper.

GAME: *Duck, pheasant, quail, venison.* Season pan gravy with ⅛ teaspoon crushed red pepper in addition to other seasoning while cooking.

SAUCES: *Brown, tomato.* Add ⅛ teaspoon crushed red pepper or less to ingredients while cooking.

SOUPS: *Cream.* Use ⅛ teaspoon ground red pepper, or less, instead of white pepper.

Meat, vegetable. Use ⅛ teaspoon crushed red pepper with ½ the usual amount of black or white pepper.

STEWS: *Meat, poultry.* Season stews with ⅛ teaspoon, or less, crushed red pepper, in addition to regular amount white pepper.

VEGETABLES: *Corn, tomatoes.* Add ⅛ teaspoon crushed red pepper to other seasoning while cooking.

For 4 servings use approximately:

1/16 to ⅛ teaspoon crushed red pepper.
⅛ to ¼ teaspoon ground red pepper.

PEPPER or WHITE PEPPER

Ground in 1 ounce, 1¼ ounce, 2 ounce, 4 ounce, and larger containers at groceries and markets; also from herb dealers.

Whole white pepper or PEPPERCORNS in 1¼ ounce, 2 ounce, 4 ounce, and larger containers at groceries and markets; also in bulk from herb dealers.

See also Cayenne, Paprika, Black Pepper, and Red Pepper.

White pepper is procured by removing the outer and inner coatings and rough surfaces of the dried mature fruit of the *Piper nigrum,* or black pepper, and then grinding the smooth-peeled peppercorn.

Both the white and the black pepper are manufactured from

the same peppercorn. The dried fruit or berries of the black pepper are soaked and the outer surfaces are rubbed off. Most of the ground white peppers contain a small quantity of the black pepper berries, which accounts for the little specks one sometimes sees in the ground white product.

Naturally the flavor of the white pepper is not so pungent as that of the black, but its aroma is characteristically sweet and the flavor warmly aromatic. The color is a light, pale yellow, or gray.

The majority of the same districts which export black pepper also peel and prepare the peppercorns and export white pepper. The most popular are the white peppers of Java, Sarawak, Siam, Singapore, and Tellicherry.

There are limited quantities of LEGHORN WHITE PEPPER, produced in Leghorn, Italy; and the MUNTOK WHITE PEPPER is grown on the island of Banda off the southeast coast of Sumatra and shipped from the port of Muntok.

England manufactures a very special grade of DECORTICATED WHITE PEPPER. It is derived from a super grade of smooth, large, heavy berries from which two or three coatings have been removed. England supplies practically the entire world with this high-quality white pepper.

Using: White pepper may be used more freely than any of the other peppers, since it is much milder and has a less biting effect. It is a pepper to be used in and on all foods which are creamy white or light colored, and in which one does not wish to have the least speck showing, but in which one desires a pungent and appealingly stimulating result. Both black and white peppers are interchangeable, but it is good to use a trifle more of the white to secure the same peppery effect. If, however, one wishes a milder flavor, the white in the same proportion as the black will give that effect.

Both the black and the white whole peppercorns placed in pepper grinders may be used at the table instead of, or in addition to, the regulation pepper shaker. Each person grinds his own pepper while holding the grinder over the food to be seasoned. The aroma and taste of the freshly ground peppercorns is deliciously fragrant and warm. A few suggested uses for the three peppers, black, red, and white, follow.

APPETIZERS: *Cheese spreads.* Add ⅛ teaspoon *ground red pepper* to ¼ pound cheese; for greater pungency sprinkle pepper over cheese very lightly.

Vegetable Juices. Add ⅛ teaspoon *black* or *white pepper*
to juice before serving. If desired, *omit pepper in juice*
but sprinkle *few grains ground red pepper* over top of
each serving. Hot but very tasty.

EGGS: *All peppers in all forms* may be used to add delicious
pungency to all egg dishes. Colors of pepper and intensity
of flavor are matters of individual taste. *Use sparingly
but often.*

FISH: *All fish.* For appearance' sake both the *red* and the
white peppers are more attractive with fish dishes. However, *black pepper* has a flavor so good that if one doesn't
mind the tiny black specks, it is as useful as the other
peppers. (Paprika is the most decorative.)

GAME: *All game. Ground* and *whole black* and *white peppers* may be added to pan gravy while cooking. The whole
pepper is always used in the marinades. See Herb Baste
and Marinade Recipes.

MEATS: *All meats. Ground* and *whole black* and *white peppers;* also *crushed red pepper* if extra pungency is desired.

POULTRY: *Ground black* and *white peppers* usually. For
extra pungency, *ground red pepper* may be very lightly
sprinkled over poultry before roasting, but *be very cau-
tious.*

SALADS: *Fish, shellfish, vegetable. All ground peppers, black,
red,* and *white,* to taste, usually blended with the salad
dressings. *Paprika* is also an attractive addition as well as
flavorful.

SAUCES: *Cream* and *light-colored. Ground white pepper* is
preferable.
Meat and vegetable, such as *pan gravies* and *tomato*
sauces. *Crushed* or *ground red pepper* may be used.
Crushed red pepper is especially delicious *in all tomato
sauces.* Use ⅛ teaspoon or *less of the crushed pepper.*

SHELLFISH: *Broiled.* Sprinkle lightly with *any pepper desired*
before broiling. *Use cautiously,* so delicate flavor of shellfish will not be lost.

SOUPS: *Cream, light-colored. Red* and *white peppers* preferably because of appearance. *Black pepper* is just as delicious, however.
Meat, vegetable. Whole black and *white pepper* in addition to *small amount ground pepper* if extra pungency is
desired. Otherwise, omit ground pepper; use whole only.

STEWS: *Fish, game, meat, poultry. Ground white pepper* is

usually preferred because of appearance. However, both *black* and *red* are equally useful. *Use cautiously.*

VEGETABLES: *All vegetables.* Flavor with *ground black* or *white pepper* as preferred.

Corn and tomatoes, stewed. Especially delicious when ⅛ teaspoon or less *crushed red pepper* is added while cooking.

VINEGARS: For *marinades.* Use both *whole black* and *white peppercorns* as suggested in recipes. See also Herb and Spice Vinegars.

For 4 servings use approximately:

⅛ to ¼ teaspoon *ground black* pepper.
4 to 12 *whole black* peppercorns.
¹⁄₁₆ to ⅛ teaspoon *crushed red* pepper.
⅛ to ¼ teaspoon *ground red* pepper.
Few grains *ground red* pepper as garnish.
¼ to ½ teaspoon *ground white* pepper.
4 to 12 *whole white* peppercorns.
Few *grains freshly ground black* or *white peppercorns* as garnish.

SAFFRON or **SAFFRON POWDER,** *Crocus sativus*

Powder in ¼ ounce and 1 ounce bottles at fancy groceries and markets; also in bulk by the dram from herb dealers and some druggists.
See also Marigold.

Saffron or saffron powder is the rich, gold-colored powder made from the stigmas of the *Crocus sativus.* This species is a beautiful little autumn crocus with slender leaves and lovely pale purple flowers. It belongs to the iris, *Iridaceae,* family.

Native to southern Europe and Asia, it is a low-growing bulbous plant. Its delicate perfume and color-ladened stigmas have been known and used since the beginning of time. Today the plant is widely cultivated in Sicily, France, Greece, Spain, and the Far East. The Austrian saffron is highly prized for its flavor and aroma; next in preference are those of France and Spain.

It takes more than 75,000 hand-picked blossoms to make a pound of true saffron powder. Each blossom has three saffron stigmas; in turn, each one of these 225,000 delicate filaments must be picked off by hand before a single pound of saffron powder is secured.

The MEXICAN SAFFRON is not the true saffron of the iris family. It is prepared from the stigmas of one of the members of the huge family of the asteraceous plants called the *Compositae*. The particular plant cultivated in the temperate regions of central Mexico is called the *safflower*, or *Carthamus tinctorius*. It has no relation to the crocus but is a thistlelike plant with large orange-colored flower heads. Mexican saffron is often used in place of the true saffron.

Using: The flavor of this rich, reddish-yellow powder is somewhat bitter, but it is a great favorite in French, Italian, and Spanish cookery. A little goes a long way. This is most fortunate, since the true saffron is extremely expensive.

The golden color of precious saffron, as well as its oriental flavor, is a most important ingredient in many European specialties. For example, it is an absolute must in French *bouilla-baisse* (a mixture of fish and shellfish); it must also be used when preparing the Spanish *Bacalao à la Vizcaína* (Salt Cod Spanish Style), and *Arroz con Pollo* (Rice and Chicken); as well as *Risotto Milanese* (Rice Milanese) of the Italians and *Chicken South American Style* so popular in Argentina.

The mothers of some of us never baked a cake without including a few grains of the golden powder to make the cake a beautiful golden yellow; and the French bake a sweet bread flavored with saffron.

The amounts used vary from ½ teaspoon to 2 or 3 teaspoons, depending upon the recipe. See also Marigold.

> BREADS, BUNS, CAKES: ½ to 1 teaspoon is sifted with the flour.
> FISH AND SHELLFISH: *Bouillabaisse*. Recipe usually suggests about ¼ teaspoon.
> POULTRY: *Chicken*. Depending upon specific recipe, amounts vary according to nationality, from ½ teaspoon to 1 tablespoon.
> SAUCES: *Curry* sauce. Add ¼ teaspoon saffron for added flavor.

For 4 servings use approximately:

½ to 1 teaspoon in breads.
¼ teaspoon in sauces.

Sweet Saffron Bread Française   TIME: Variable

3 tsp. sugar	*¾ tsp. saffron*
1 package dry yeast	*¾ cup hot water*
¼ cup lukewarm water	*6 cups enriched flour (about)*
¼ cup butter	*½ cup seeded raisins*
¾ cup sugar, extra	*¼ cup currants*
1 tsp. salt	*¼ cup chopped peanuts*
1 cup milk, scalded	*or almonds*

Crush yeast in small bowl; blend with sugar; pour in ¼ cup lukewarm water; dissolve well.

Cream butter, extra sugar, and salt in large mixing bowl; pour milk over mixture; stir well until thoroughly smooth.

Dissolve saffron in ¾ cup hot water; allow to stand 10 minutes; strain through fine sieve; add saffron-flavored water to milk mixture. When mixture is lukewarm, add yeast mixture; blend well. When smooth, gradually sift in 3 cups flour, stirring constantly.

Blend 1 cup flour with raisins, currants, and nuts in small bowl; add to dough; mix well. When smooth, sift in sufficient flour to make soft dough. Knead with hands until very smooth and elastic. Place dough in large pan; cover lightly with waxed paper. Allow to stand in warm place 2 hours, or until the dough is double in bulk. Cut dough in half; knead gently on lightly floured board; form into two loaves; place each in buttered pan; stand in warm place 1 hour, or until dough has again doubled in bulk. Bake in preheated moderate oven 45 minutes. Remove from pans. Allow to cool gradually at room temperature. Yield: 2 loaves.

Chicken South American Style   TIME: 1½ to 2 hours

1 young fricassee chicken,	*½ tsp. salt*
from 3½ to 4 lbs.	*¼ tsp. cayenne pepper*
¼ lb. butter	*¼ tsp. white pepper*
1 medium onion, minced	*Boiling water (about 2 qts.)*
1 hot red pepper, minced	*2 cups rice*
1 green pepper, minced	*½ lb. mushrooms*
1 No. 2 can tomatoes	*Salt and pepper, extra*
1 clove garlic, halved	*1 tbs. butter, extra*
2 bay leaves	*1 No. 2 can chick-peas*
1 tbs. saffron	*drained*

Have chicken cut into small pieces as for fricassee.

Melt butter in heavy skillet over medium flame; add chicken; brown lightly 10 minutes. Remove chicken from hot butter and place in large fireproof casserole at back of stove; cover to keep hot. Place onion and peppers in butter in which chicken was browned; cook over low flame 10 minutes; add tomatoes, garlic, bay leaves, saffron, salt, cayenne, and white pepper; mix well; cover. Simmer gently 10 minutes. Pour mixture over chicken; replace casserole over medium flame. Pour sufficient amount of boiling water over chicken to cover it well; replace cover. Cook ½ hour, or until chicken is almost tender.

Meanwhile, peel, wash, and slice mushrooms; melt 1 tablespoon butter in saucepan; add mushrooms; season with salt and pepper to taste; sauté gently 10 minutes; remove from flame. Set aside to keep warm.

When chicken is almost tender, again add boiling water (about 1 quart), then add washed rice, mushrooms with liquid, and drained chick peas; cover. Stir occasionally. Simmer gently over low flame ½ hour, or until rice is soft and fluffy and has absorbed all liquid. Serve piping hot on preheated hot plates with a tossed green salad at the side. Serves 6 to 8.

TURMERIC, *Curcuma longa L.*

> Ground in ½ ounce and 1¼ ounce containers at groceries and markets; also from herb dealers.
> Root in bulk from herb dealers.
> See also Curry Powder and Ginger.

Turmeric is the washed, dried, aromatic root of the brilliant tropical plant of the genus *Curcuma,* which belongs to the ginger, *Zingiberaceae,* family.

The plant is native to the East Indies and Cochin, China; also to the tropical zones of Africa and Australia. It is now extensively cultivated in China, Java, and in several districts of India; especially in Madras in the districts of Cuddapah, Kistna, and Malabar. Turmeric is also cultivated to some extent in Haiti.

Growing in China, the turmeric is a rather dull green color, but when planted in India and the East Indies and other new surroundings the spicate flowers of the plant develop into a brilliant orange. The turmeric's irregularly shaped roots or rhizomes have a mild, clean aroma yet a peculiarly bitter flavor. Generally the rhizomes are about the same size as the ginger roots: about ½ inch thick and from 1 inch to 3 inches long.

Using: Turmeric, since earliest history, has been used as a culinary spice because of its warm, sweet flavor and beautiful color. It is used very generally in East Indian cookery, not only since it is one of the chief ingredients of curry powder and condiments, but because of the sweet richness which its flavor imparts to fish and rice dishes and sauces.

Both the whole root and the ground spice are flavorings for pickles, relishes, and chowchows. Many of the prepared mustards owe their special taste appeal, and sometimes even their rich color, to the ground turmeric included in the formula.

Turmeric is also sweet enough to be used instead of saffron as coloring for cakes and cookies, and it gives a rich taste and beautiful color to rice dishes. A small amount of ground turmeric blended with dry mustard and used to flavor French dressing will add a new color and taste appeal to this old favorite.

CAKES AND COOKIES: Use ¼ teaspoon ground turmeric as coloring.

CONDIMENTS: *Prepared mustards.* See recipe for Mild Mustard Spiced.

CURRY BLENDS: See recipes.

EGGS: *Curried.* ⅛ teaspoon ground turmeric may be added to ingredients to give a slightly sweet taste and flavor.

FISH AND SHELLFISH: *Curried.* Add ⅛ to ¼ teaspoon ground turmeric to ingredients for additional sweetness and color.

FRENCH DRESSING: Add ⅛ to ¼ teaspoon ground turmeric to other ingredients.

MEATS: *Beef, lamb, mutton, curried.* Add ⅛ to ¼ teaspoon turmeric to ingredients when slightly sweeter flavor is desired.

PICKLES: *Mixed, sweet.* See familiar recipes for old-fashioned sweet pickles.

POULTRY: *Broiled, sautéed.* Sprinkle lightly with turmeric, salt, and pepper before cooking.

RELISHES: See Condiments; also recipe Sweet and Spicy Green Corn Relish.

SAUCES: *Cream, fish, meat.* Add ¼ teaspoon ground turmeric to sauce when slightly sweet taste and rich yellow color are desired.

For 4 servings use approximately:

⅛ to 1 teaspoon ground turmeric in recipes.
4 ounces ground turmeric in 13 to 16 ounces some curry blends

Sweet and Spicy Green Corn Relish   TIME: 1 hour

9 ears corn	*1 tsp. ground turmeric*
3 cups minced new cabbage	*1 tbs. dry mustard*
½ cup chopped celery	*2 tsp. celery seed*
2 small onions, minced	*¼ cup salt*
1 green pepper, minced	*2 cups cider vinegar*
1 red pepper, minced	*1 cup brown sugar*

Cook corn in rapidly boiling water 2 minutes in large saucepan. (Count time from moment water resumes boiling.) Drain; cut kernels from cob with sharp knife. Mix corn kernels with all minced vegetables in large heavy saucepan.

Blend turmeric, mustard, celery seed, and salt in large bowl. Gradually pour in cider vinegar until seasonings are well blended and turmeric and mustard are dissolved. Add to corn mixture in saucepan; stir in sugar until dissolved. Place saucepan over medium flame. Simmer gently 30 minutes, stirring frequently. Fill hot sterilized jars with hot relish; seal immediately. Yield: 5 to 6 pints.

Use as condiment *with cold cuts, fish, meats,* and *poultry.*

Turmeric Marinated Halibut Steak   TIME: 20 minutes
Marinate 24 hours

2 lbs. halibut steak or any	*1 small onion, sliced*
lean-meated fish fillets	*½ tsp. salt*
1 bay leaf	

Wipe halibut steaks with damp cloth. Place fish in shallow saucepan; cover with cold water; add bay leaf, onion, and salt; cover saucepan. Bring to boiling point over medium flame; lower flame. Simmer gently 10 minutes, or until fish is snowy white and flakes easily when tested with fork. Drain, saving half the fish stock. Set fish aside in deep dish to cool at room temperature. While fish is simmering, prepare the spicy marinade:

Spicy Golden Marinade

½ cup white wine vinegar   *½ tsp. celery salt*
½ cup fish stock   *1 slice onion*
1 tsp. curry powder   *2 tbs. sugar*
1 tsp. turmeric

Pour vinegar and fish stock into small heavy saucepan.

Blend curry powder, sugar, turmeric, and celery salt in cup; add seasoning to liquid in saucepan; dissolve by stirring well; add onion slice. Bring seasoned liquid to boiling point over medium flame; boil slowly 10 minutes; pour boiling hot liquid over fish. Allow to cool at room temperature. Cover. Marinate 24 hours in refrigerator. Serve cold marinated fish on lettuce leaves with mayonnaise on the side. Serves 4.

CHAPTER FIFTEEN

Spiced Recipes
and Spice Blends

Spice Blends Prepared. *Each spice blend is the particular secret formula of the manufacturer who prepares it. The name of the blend identifies its use.*

Sold in ¼ ounce to 4 ounce containers and larger at groceries and markets.

Apple Pie Spice
Cake Spice
Ketchup Spice
Mincemeat Spice
Mixed Pickling Spice
Pastry Spice
Pickle Spice

Pickling Spices
Pie Spice
Poultry Seasoning
Pumpkin Pie Spice Blend
Sausage Seasoning
Whole Mixed Pickling Spice

Anna's Spiced Chunk Pickles

TIME: Variable

*7 lbs. medium-sized
    cucumbers
1 pt. salt
1 gal. water*

*2 qts. water, extra
5 bay leaves
1 oz. piece alum
1 pt. cider vinegar*

To prepare cucumbers: Select firm, fresh vegetables. Wash well. Make brine by dissolving 1 pint salt in 1 gallon water. Soak cucumbers in this brine 3 days. Drain, then soak cucumbers in fresh water 3 days, changing water every day. Drain.

Cut cucumbers in chunks of desired size (1 inch square is good size). Blend 1 pint vinegar with 2 quarts water; add bay leaves and alum. Pour into large saucepan over high flame; bring to boiling point; add cucumber chunks; turn down flame. Boil chunks slowly 1½ hours. Drain. Place in stone crock.

SYRUP INGREDIENTS:

3 cups cider vinegar
3 lbs. white sugar
3 cups water
1 4-in. quill cinnamon
½ tsp. oil of cloves

1 tsp. powdered mace
1¼ tsp. caraway seeds
1¼ tsp. celery seeds
1 2-in. piece ginger root
9 cardamom seeds

To prepare syrup: Pour vinegar into large saucepan; add all other ingredients; stir well. Place over medium flame and bring to boiling point. Pour boiling syrup over cucumber chunks; cover. Allow to stand 24 hours. Drain off syrup; re-heat; pour over cucumber chunks again. Repeat this process 4 days in succession. Pack cucumber chunks in small glass jars on the fourth day; pour boiling hot syrup over them; seal tightly. Store in cool place until ready to use. Yield: 10 pints.

Spice Blend American

For *cakes, cookies, and pastries.*

1 oz. ground cloves
1 oz. mace
1 oz. ground nutmeg

1 oz. ground cinnamon
1 oz. granulated or 2 ozs.
   powdered sugar

Blend all ingredients in large mixing bowl. Pack loosely in tightly covered container. Sprinkle over *cakes, cookies,* and *pastries* before and after baking.

Spice Blend Italiana

For *cakes and cookies.*

2 ozs. coriander seed
2 ozs. ground cloves
2 ozs. cinnamon

1 oz. anise seed
1 oz. fennel seed
2 ozs. granulated sugar

Blend all ingredients in large mixing bowl. Pack loosely in tightly covered small jars. Sprinkle over tops of *cakes* and *cookies* before baking.

When sugar is omitted, mixture is called **Tamara Italiana.**

Spiced Crabapple Sweet Pickles   TIME: 2 hours

5 lbs. crabapples   *1 6-in. stick cinnamon*
3 ozs. whole cloves   *3¼ lbs. white sugar*
1 qt. cider vinegar

Select firm, tart crabapples. Wash thoroughly under cold running water. Do not remove stems. With sharp knife make tiny incision in flower end of crabapple. Insert 1 whole clove in each end of crabapple. Arrange alternate layers of crabapples, sugar, and broken cinnamon in large oven crock. When crock is filled, gently pour in vinegar at side. Place crock in cold oven; heat to slow oven (300° F.); bake 1 hour, or until crabapples are tender but not soft. Remove from oven. Cool at room temperature. Leave fruit in crock. The syrup will be jellied when cold. Store in cool place. Yield: 4 quarts.

Serve as condiment with *meats, fish,* and *game.*

Spiced Frozen Cookies   TIME: 30 minutes
     Chill overnight

2½ cups sifted flour   *½ cup butter or shortening*
1 tsp. salt   *½ cup unsulphured molasses*
¼ tsp. soda   *½ cup sugar*
1 tsp. ground cinnamon   *1 egg*
½ tsp. ground nutmeg   *1 cup shredded coconut*

Sift together first 5 ingredients.

Melt butter or shortening in large saucepan over medium flame; gradually stir in molasses and sugar; remove from heat. Allow to cool. Beat in egg; when well blended add coconut; gradually stir in sifted dry ingredients; mix well. Divide dough into 2 equal portions; mold each piece into a roll 2 inches in diameter; wrap each roll in waxed paper; place dough in refrigerator to chill overnight, or until ready to bake. With sharp knife cut dough into slices ⅛ inch thick. Arrange slices on lightly greased cooky sheets. Bake in preheated moderately hot oven (375° F.) 10 minutes. Yield: 5 dozen cookies.

Spiced Fruits Basic Recipe   TIME: Variable

1 qt. fruit, peeled   *1 4-in. stick cinnamon*
½ cup distilled vinegar   *1 tsp. lemon juice*
3 cups sugar   *1 tsp. grated lemon rind*
24 whole cloves

Pour vinegar into heavy saucepan placed over medium flame; heat vinegar slightly; add sugar, cloves, half of the cinnamon, lemon juice, and rind; stir until sugar is dissolved. Add peeled fruit of choice; boil 15 to 20 minutes, or until fruit is done but not soft. Arrange spiced fruit in hot sterilized ½ pint jars, being certain that there are cloves in each jar; place ⅓ of remaining stick cinnamon in each jar; fill to top with boiling syrup; seal tightly. Yield: 1½ pints to 1 quart.

Use any preferred fruit, such as grapes, peaches, pears, and plums.

Spiced Italian Tomatoes   TIME: 45 minutes

2 lbs. Italian tomatoes, plum   *2 small pieces ginger root*
   shaped   *2 short sticks cinnamon*
4 cups brown sugar   *(about 2 ins. each)*
1½ cups water   *1 lemon, sliced*

Purchase firm, fresh Italian or plum tomatoes. Wash thoroughly; do not peel.

Heat water in heavy saucepan over medium flame; add sugar, ginger root, cinnamon, and lemon; stir continuously until sugar is dissolved. Boil 30 minutes. Remove ginger and cinnamon. Add tomatoes. Boil 5 minutes, or until slightly tender but not soft; syrup should be slightly thick. Remove any scum with perforated spoon. Pour preserved tomatoes into hot sterilized ½ pint jars. Allow to cool at room temperature. Yield: 4 jars.

Serve as condiment with *fish, meats,* and *shellfish.*

Spiced Pears   TIME: 30 minutes

8 lbs. Seckel pears   *4 lbs. sugar*
10 2-in. pieces stick   *1 qt. cider vinegar*
   cinnamon   *1 pt. water*
2 tbs. whole cloves   *2 tbs. whole allspice*

Select firm, ripe fruit. Wash well in cold running water. Remove blossom ends only. Place pears in deep saucepan over medium flame. Cover fruit with water. Boil 10 minutes. Drain fruit; prick skins with fork.

While pears are boiling, put spices loosely in clean, thin, white cloth; tie top tightly. Pour 1 pint water into large saucepan over high flame; add spice bag, sugar, and vinegar.

Boil 5 minutes. Add pears to boiling liquid. Cook 10 minutes, or until pears are tender. Remove saucepan from flame; cover; set aside. Allow fruit to cool overnight. In the morning, remove spice bag. Drain syrup from pears and bring to boiling point over medium flame. Pack pears in clean, hot, sterile jars. Pour hot syrup over pears; fill jars to top; seal tightly. Store in cool, dark place several weeks. Use as desired. Yield: Approximately 10 pints.

Spiced Crabapples: Prepare spiced syrup and follow directions for Spiced Pears but omit cooking in unseasoned water and *do not prick skin of fruit.*

Spiced Peaches: Peel peaches and proceed as for Spiced Pears, using but 2 pounds sugar. Eight pounds peaches yield about 6 pints.

Spiced Sautéed Mexican Hash

TIME: 45 minutes

1½ lbs. chopped beef
1 small onion, minced
1 clove garlic, minced
2 firm tomatoes, cubed
¼ cup raisins
2 tbs. olive oil

¼ tsp. ground cloves
¼ tsp. black pepper
⅛ tsp. ground cumin
1½ cups bouillon
4 slices toast

Pour 1 tablespoon oil into heavy skillet placed over medium flame; add chopped beef, stirring constantly for 3 minutes, or until meat is lightly browned. Remove skillet from flame. Stir in minced onion, garlic, tomatoes, raisins, and other tablespoon oil; blend well. Season with cloves, pepper, and cumin; blend well. Stir in bouillon. Replace skillet over medium flame; cover. Simmer gently 30 minutes. Serve piping hot over plain or buttered toast. Serves 4.

Spiced Shrimp Tidbits

TIME: 30 minutes
Marinate 2 days

2 lbs. shrimp
1 qt. water
1 tsp. salt
1 bay leaf
6 peppercorns
3 cups cider vinegar

6 whole cloves
2 tsp. whole allspice
12 cocktail onions
1 cup shrimp stock
1 pimiento, cut small

Select large fresh shrimp; peel raw, then clean and split shrimp in half lengthwise.

Pour water in saucepan over high flame; add salt, bay leaf, and peppercorns; bring to boil; add shrimp. Cook 3 minutes only, or until pink. Drain. Save 1 cup stock. Set aside.

Pour vinegar and shrimp stock into saucepan over high flame. Tie spice in small cheesecloth square; add to liquid; boil gently 10 minutes over low flame.

Arrange shrimp halves, cocktail onions, and pimiento pieces in small hot, sterilized jars; leave space of 1 inch at top. Pour boiling hot spiced vinegar over; seal tightly. Allow to cool at room temperature. Marinate 2 to 3 days before using. Serve as *hors d'oeuvre*. Yield: 3 pints.

Other shellfish, such as *mussels, prawns,* and *lobster* pieces may be spiced in same manner.

Sweet Pickled Peaches   TIME: 45 minutes

2 qts. peaches   *12 whole cloves*
2 cups cider vinegar   *2 2-in. sticks cinnamon*
4½ cups white sugar   *2 sticks cinnamon, extra*

Select firm but ripe peaches. Remove skins by scalding; insert 3 or 4 cloves in each peach. Set aside.

Pour vinegar into large preserving kettle; add sugar and stick cinnamon. Bring to boiling point; boil 5 minutes. Drop peaches into boiling syrup a few at a time. Boil 5 minutes, or until peaches are tender and slightly transparent looking. Pack peaches carefully into hot sterilized jars; place 1 stick cinnamon in each jar; pour boiling hot syrup over them; seal tightly. Allow to cool at room temperature. Yield: 4 pints.

Serve as condiment with *hot* or *cold poultry* and *roasts.*

Pears and pineapple may be pickled in same way. Boiling time 5 to 10 minutes.

Spiced Watermelon Pickles   TIME: Variable
                                        Soak overnight

4 lbs. watermelon rind, peeled   *2 tbs. whole allspice*
    and trimmed   *10 2-in. sticks cinnamon*
2 qts. cold water   *1 qt. cider vinegar*
1 tbs. calcium oxide   *1 qt. water, extra*
2 tbs. whole cloves   *4 lbs. sugar*

Purchase calcium oxide at drugstore.

Peel rind of firm ripe watermelon; trim off all pink flesh.

Weigh out 4 pounds of trimmed rind; cut into squares, diamonds, or other desired shapes.

Combine 2 quarts cold water and calcium oxide in large enamel kettle; add rind pieces; soak in liquid 1 hour. Drain. Cover with fresh water. Cook over medium flame 1½ hours. Add more water as needed. Drain.

Tie spices tightly in thin muslin or cheesecloth square; place in kettle; add vinegar, 1 quart water, and sugar. Bring to boiling point; add rind. Boil gently 2 hours. Remove spice bag; pack rind in hot sterile jars; fill to top with hot syrup; seal tightly. Allow to cool at room temperature. Yield: 6 pints.

Spiced Veal Rolls Swedish Style   TIME: 1½ hours

3 lbs. veal cutlets	6 whole allspice
¾ tsp. salt	2 tomatoes, chopped
¼ tsp. white pepper	3 small onions, minced
2 dill pickles, sliced	3 tbs. flour
2 tbs. minced parsley	2½ cups consommé
3 tbs. butter	1 cup sour cream
2 stalks celery, minced	½ tsp. celery salt
2 carrots, sliced thin	⅛ tsp. white pepper, extra
2 bay leaves	Paprika

Have veal cutlets sliced very thin; cut into oblong sizes convenient for rolling. Wipe veal with clean, moist cloth; season veal lightly with salt and pepper. Sprinkle dill pickle slices with minced parsley; wrap veal around each piece pickle; fasten rolls with thread or toothpicks.

Melt butter in flameproof casserole over medium flame; when hot but not smoking add veal rolls. Sauté 10 minutes, or until golden brown on all sides. Remove rolls. Set aside. To butter in casserole add celery, carrots, bay leaves, allspice, tomatoes, and onions; stir constantly 10 minutes, or until vegetables are tender but not soft; gradually stir in flour; when smooth, gradually pour in consommé; stir constantly 3 minutes, or until very smooth. Allow to come to boil. Add veal rolls; cover. Cook slowly over medium flame 40 minutes, or until meat is tender. Remove veal rolls; keep hot in preheated serving dish; quickly strain sauce through fine sieve; heat sauce in casserole; gradually stir in sour cream; add celery salt and pepper. Heat to boiling. Pour steaming hot sauce over rolls. Sprinkle lightly with paprika. Serve piping hot. Serves 6.

CHAPTER SIXTEEN

Herb and Spice Condiments and Popular Prepared Sauces

A-1 Sauce: Sold in 5 ounce bottles at groceries and markets. Contains tomato purée, herbs, spices, herb vinegar, orange marmalade, and raisins. Use with *cheese, cold cuts, chops, fish, game, gravies, hash, meats, poultry, salads, shellfish cocktails, roasts,* and *tomato juice.*

Barbecue Sauce: Sold in 6 ounce and 12 ounce bottles at groceries and markets. Contains tomatoes, catsup, green peppers, onions, herbs, and spices. Use piping *hot* or *cold with fish, roast meats,* and *shellfish.*

Barbecue Sauce à la Minute   TIME: 30 minutes

2 tbs. butter
1 medium onion, minced
3 tbs. red wine vinegar
1 tbs. lemon juice
1 cup water
1 cup chili sauce

½ tbs. dry mustard
1 tsp. chili powder
⅛ tsp. cayenne pepper
2 tbs. Worcestershire sauce
2 tbs. brown sugar
½ cup minced celery

Melt butter in large, heavy saucepan over medium flame; add onion. Simmer gently 3 minutes. Gradually stir in all remaining ingredients. Simmer gently 20 minutes, or until sauce is thick. Stir occasionally. Yield: 1 pint.

Serve piping *hot with roast beef;* or allow to cool; bottle. *Use cold* as desired *with fish* and *meats.*

Barbecue Sauce de Luxe   TIME: 40 minutes

¾ cup catsup	*¼ tsp. celery salt*
½ cup olive oil	*¼ tsp. garlic salt*
½ cup red wine vinegar	*½ tsp. salt*
2 tbs. garlic vinegar	*¼ tsp. mustard seed*
1 tbs. tarragon vinegar	*¼ tsp. celery seed*
½ cup water	*¼ tsp. ground cloves*
1 tbs. Worcestershire sauce	*1 tsp. chili powder*
1 small onion, minced	*1 tsp. orégano*
2 tsp. brown sugar	*1 small bay leaf, crushed*

Pour 7 liquids into heavy saucepan over medium flame; stir well.

Blend all dry seasonings in mixing bowl; add to liquid; stir vigorously until well blended; lower flame. Simmer gently 25 minutes. Taste. If more salt is preferred, add celery salt. Stir occasionally to prevent sticking. Remove from flame. Serve sauce *piping hot as condiment with fish, roasts,* and *steaks.* Yield: 1 pint.

Béarnaise Sauce: Sold in 5 ounce bottles at fancy groceries and markets. Contains butter, eggs, oil, salt, tarragon vinegar, pepper, herbs, and spices. Especially good *with fish.*

Caper Sauce: Sold in 6 ounce and 10 ounce jars at fancy groceries and markets. Contains capers, Spanish sauce, black pepper, and grated nutmeg. Use piping *hot with fish, shellfish,* and *steaks.*

Catsup: Sold in 6 ounce to 12 ounce bottles at groceries and markets. Contains tomatoes, vinegar, sugar, herbs, and spices. Use in *sauces* and *soups;* also with *fish, game, meats,* and *shellfish.*

Tomato Catsup Mild   TIME: 2 hours

4 qts. firm tomatoes	*½ tbs. mace*
1 qt. cider vinegar	*½ tbs. celery seed*
1 cup sugar	*1 tbs. cinnamon*
½ tbs. cayenne pepper	*⅛ cup salt*

Select firm, ripe, medium-sized tomatoes. To peel easily, dip each tomato separately into boiling water 1 minute only, then peel and chop. Pour vinegar into large, deep saucepan; add sugar and salt; stir well.

Place all spices loosely in clean, thin white cloth; tie top tightly; add spices to vinegar. Place saucepan over high flame; bring vinegar to boil; lower flame; add tomatoes; cover. Boil slowly 1½ hours, or until mixture is reduced to half original volume. Remove mixture from flame. Take out spice bag. Strain tomato mixture through very fine sieve.

Reheat mixture over medium flame, stirring constantly to prevent sticking. Pour hot mixture into clean, hot, sterile jars. See Chili Sauce Spicy. Fill jars to top; seal tightly; store in cool, dark place. Use as desired. Yield: Approximately 4 pints.

Tomato Catsup Spicy   TIME: 2 hours

2½ qts. medium-sized   *1 cup cider vinegar*
   tomatoes (about 17   *½ cup sugar*
   tomatoes)   *1¼ tsp. salt*
¾ cup chopped onion   *1 tsp. paprika*
1 3-in. piece stick cinnamon   *⅛ tsp. cayenne pepper*
1 large clove garlic, chopped   *1 tsp. whole cloves*

Select firm, ripe tomatoes. Cut into cubes. Place tomatoes and onion in large saucepan over medium flame. Simmer gently 30 minutes. Remove from flame. Strain through fine sieve. Place tomato mixture in top section double boiler placed over lower section half filled with boiling water. Boil mixture rapidly 1 hour, or until it is half original volume.

Meanwhile, place cinnamon, garlic, and cloves in clean, thin white cloth; tie tightly. Pour vinegar into small saucepan over medium flame; add spices. Simmer 30 minutes. Remove spices.

After tomato mixture has boiled sufficiently, add spiced vinegar, sugar, salt, paprika, and cayenne pepper to tomato mixture. Boil rapidly 10 minutes, or until slightly thickened. Pour into clean, hot sterile jars; fill jars to top; seal tightly. Store in cool, dark place until ready to use. Yield: Approximately 2 pints.

Chili Pepper Sauce: Sold in 5 ounce shaker-top bottles at groceries and markets. A vinegar flavored with hot chili peppers, sugar, and spices. Use on *fish* and *shellfish cocktails*.

Chili Sauce: Sold in 12 ounce bottles at groceries and markets. Contains tomatoes, sugar, salt, onions, vinegar, and spices. Use as condiment *with chops, fish, game, roast meats,* and *steaks;* also as base for *sea-food cocktail sauce.*

Chili Sauce Spicy
TIME: 3 hours

28 medium-sized tomatoes
2 cups chopped sweet red
    pepper
1 hot red pepper, chopped
2 cups minced onion
2 tbs. celery seed
1 tbs. mustard seed
1 bay leaf

1 tsp. whole cloves
1 tsp. ground ginger
1 tsp. ground nutmeg
2 3-in. pieces stick cinnamon
1 cup firmly packed brown
    sugar
3 cups cider vinegar
2 tbs. salt

Select firm, ripe tomatoes. To peel easily, dip tomatoes singly into boiling water 1 minute. Cut tomatoes into small pieces. Remove seeds from peppers; chop finely. Combine tomatoes, peppers, and onion in large kettle. Stir well.

Place celery seed, mustard seed, bay leaf, cloves, ginger, nutmeg, and cinnamon sticks loosely in thin white cloth; tie top tightly. Add to tomato mixture. Boil mixture about 2 hours over medium flame, until half original volume. Stir frequently. Remove spice bag. Then add sugar, vinegar, and salt. Boil rapidly 5 minutes, stirring constantly. Pack into clean, hot, sterilized jars; fill jars to top; seal tightly. Keep in cool, dark place until ready to use. Yield: Approximately 3 quarts.

To sterilize jars and lids, place in warm water; heat to boiling, and continue boiling for 20 minutes before packing.

Chili Powder Tomato Sauce
TIME: 45 minutes

1 No. 2 can tomatoes
1 large bottle catsup (8 ozs.)
1 tbs. chili powder

1 medium onion, minced
2 tsp. salt

Blend catsup, chili powder, minced onion, and salt in large mixing bowl.

Mash canned tomatoes to a pulp; add to catsup mixture; blend well. Pour mixture into heavy saucepan over medium flame. Bring to boil; cook 30 minutes, stirring constantly to prevent scorching. Allow sauce to cool at room temperature. Bottle and cork tightly. Yield: 1½ pints.

Chop Suey Sauce: Sold in 5 ounce bottles at groceries and markets. Contains sugar, salt, herbs, and spices. Use with *Chinese dishes* and *rice.*

Chutneys: Sold in 8 ounce, 10 ounce, and 17 ounce bottles at fancy groceries and markets. All East Indian chutneys have the tropical mango fruit as the base. They also contain other fruits, sugar, vinegar, herbs, ginger root, and other spices. All of them have a tangy, fruity, and rather hot flavor. Some formulas are very hot and spicy to the taste. *The best chutneys are those which come from Bombay, India.* Some of the better-known formulas are sold under these brand names:

CHUTNUT: A blend of selected tropical fruits, herbs, spices, and nuts.

COL. SKINNER'S: An unusual, pungent flavor, not so highly seasoned as many chutneys.

J. K. BRAND: A dark, rich combination.

MAJOR GREY'S: A sweet, rather hot blend, especially well liked by the Americans and English.

MANGO CHUTNEY: A rich blend of mango and passion fruits with Cochin ginger.

SWEET LUCKNOW: A medium hot, sweet blend, rich in fruit.

TAMARIND: A very dark, rich, fruity chutney.

Chutneys are served with all curry dishes; also as a condiment with cold cuts, game, hors d'oeuvre, roast meats, fish, chops, and steaks.

Apple-Tomato Chutney Cooked   TIME: 2 hours

*1½ qts. firm tomatoes (about
    10 medium sized)
1½ qts. tart apples (about
    6 or 7 medium sized)
½ cup chopped green pepper
1½ cups minced onion
1 cup seedless raisins*

*2 tsp. salt
2 cups firmly packed brown
    sugar
2 cups cider vinegar
¼ cup whole mixed pickling
    spices*

Select firm, ripe tomatoes and tart apples. To peel easily, dip each tomato into boiling water 1 minute only, then peel and cut into cubes.

Peel and core apples; cut into quarters.

Combine tomatoes, apples, pepper, onion, raisins, salt, sugar, and vinegar in large kettle.

Place spices loosely in clean, thin white cloth; tie top tightly. Place spice bag in tomato mixture. Bring to boil over high flame; lower flame; cover. Simmer gently 1½ hours, stirring frequently. Remove spice bag. Pack chutney into clean, hot sterilized jars; fill jars to top; seal tightly. Keep in cool dark place. Use as desired. Yield: Approximately 3 pints.

Spicy Fruit Chutney with Ginger   TIME: 3 hours

1 doz. sour apples	*1 tsp. ground cloves*
1 doz. medium-ripe tomatoes	*1 tsp. ground ginger*
8 medium-sized onions	*4 tbs. preserved ginger*
1 pt. cider vinegar	*(optional)*
2 cups dark brown sugar	*¼ tsp. cayenne pepper*
1½ tbs. salt	*1 cup seeded raisins*
1 tsp. dry mustard	

Peel and core apples; cut into quarters. Peel and quarter tomatoes and onions. Chop apples and onions fine; mix well and place them in large saucepan over medium flame; add tomatoes; watch carefully; stir constantly so fruit does not scorch. Cook 10 minutes or until onion is tender but not soft. Add vinegar, sugar, and salt; stir constantly until sugar is completely dissolved; watch carefully.

Mix mustard, cloves, ginger, and cayenne in cup; dissolve with little of hot vinegar from saucepan; stir into mixture; add raisins. Lower flame. Cook slowly 1½ hours, stirring occasionally. Add chopped preserved ginger, if desired; mix well; taste mixture. If needed, add little salt. Cook ½ hour longer, or until of desired consistency (usually as thick as chili sauce). Pour into hot, sterilized small jars or wide-mouthed bottles; seal tightly as for canned fruit. Cool and store in cold, dark place until needed. Yield: Approximately 3 quarts, depending upon exact sizes of apples, tomatoes, and onions.

Cocktail Sauce: Sold in 6 ounce and 9 ounce bottles at groceries and markets. Contains tomatoes, onions, vinegar, herbs, and spice. Use as condiment *with fish* and *shellfish; also as base for sea-food cocktails.*

Cocktail Tangy Sauce   TIME: 10 minutes

1 cup chili sauce   *1 tsp. Worcestershire sauce*
1 tsp. lemon juice   *¼ tsp. tabasco sauce*
1 tbs. prepared horseradish

Blend well lemon juice, horseradish, Worcestershire sauce, and tabasco sauce in small bowl. Add chili sauce; mix well. Serves 4 to 6. Serve *with sea-food cocktails.*

Escoffier Sauces: Made in England; sold in 7 ounce bottles. **Diable Sauce** contains tomatoes, vinegar, oil, wine, chili pods, and spices. Use with steaks, chops, and cold cuts. **Robert Sauce** contains tomatoes, vinegar, sugar, pimientos, and spices. Use as desired condiment.

French Dressings: Sold in 4 ounce, 6 ounce, 8 ounce, and 12 ounce bottles at groceries and markets. Contains olive oil, cider or herb vinegars, sugar, herbs, and spices. See also Salad Dressings.

Hollandaise Sauce: Sold in 5 ounce bottles at fancy groceries and markets. Contains butter, eggs, vinegar, lemon juice, and spices. Use *with fish* and *vegetables.* See also recipe.

Horseradish, prepared: Sold in 4 ounce and 6 ounce bottles at groceries and markets. Contains horseradish root, distilled vinegar, and salt. Use as condiment *with eggs, fish, game, roasts,* and *steaks;* also *as base for sea-food cocktail sauces.* See also Horseradish.

H. P. Sauce: Sold in 6 ounce bottles at groceries and markets. Contains herbs, spices, vinegar, other seasonings, and water. Especially good *with cheese, curries, chops, fish, gravies, meats, steaks,* and *shellfish.*

Mexican Sauces:

   ENCHILADA SAUCE: Sold in 15 ounce cans at fancy groceries and markets. Contains red peppers, tomato purée, water, flour, oil, garlic, and salt.
   CHAPINGO SAUCE: Sold in 5 ounce bottles. Consists of a chili sauce mixed with vinegar, olive oil, and herbs.
   PIPIAN SAUCE: Sold in 6 ounce tins. A chili sauce prepared

with ground chilies, sesame oil, celery, vinegar, salt, and spices.

RANCHERA SAUCE: Sold in 6 ounce tins. Contains chopped green chilies, onion, garlic, salt, and spices.

TLAMOLE SAUCE: Sold in 6 ounce and 12 ounce tins. A liquid mole sauce prepared with ground chilies, sesame oil, pimiento, salt, garlic, onion, and orégano.

Use Mexican sauces as condiments with chicken, eggs, meats, tortillas, and preferred Mexican dishes.

Mint Sauce: Sold in 6 ounce bottles at fancy groceries and markets. Contains chopped mint, sugar, pure malt, and distilled vinegars. Use as condiment *with lamb, chicken,* and *veal;* also *as base for blended sauce.* See also Sauces and Stuffings.

Mushroom Sauce: Sold in 6 ounce bottles. Contains mushrooms cooked in malt vinegar with soy, salt, spices, and blended flavorings. Use as condiment, either *hot* or *cold;* use *to flavor chops, steaks,* and *roast meats* while cooking.

Mustard Flavored with Herbs: Basic Recipe   TIME: Variable

4 ozs. dry mustard	*Garlic vinegar or*
2 tbs. flour	*cider vinegar*
2 tsp. salt	*2 tsp. freshly minced basil*
2 tbs. sugar	*or ½ tsp. crushed dried basil*

Blend dry mustard, flour, salt, and sugar in mixing bowl. Stir vigorously until well blended. (The secret of a smooth herb mustard lies in the perfect blending of the dry ingredients.)

When dry ingredients are well blended, gradually add sufficient herb vinegar to make a smooth paste of desired consistency. Gradually stir in minced leaves of preferred herb; cover. Allow to stand overnight. Bottle or place in small jars; cover tightly; keep in refrigerator. Yield: 7 ounces.

Serve cold as desired condiment. Use also to flavor chopped meats. Add 1 teaspoon herb-flavored mustard to meat loaves and hamburgers before cooking.

See also recipes; Prepared Mustard Tips.

Mustards Flavored with Herbs:

WITH BASIL: Sold in 2½ ounce jars at fancy groceries and some herb farms. Contains mustard flour, flour, herb vinegar, and dried or fresh basil herb. Especially good *with eggs, cold cuts, game,* and *roast meats.*

WITH HORSERADISH: Sold in 2½ ounce jars at groceries and markets; also at some herb farms. Contains mustard flour, flour, herb vinegar, mustard seed, sugar, turmeric, and grated horseradish root. Mild, tangy flavor. Especially good *with roast beef, ham, steaks,* and *chops.*

WITH LOVAGE: Sold in 2½ ounce jars at fancy groceries and some herb farms. Contains mustard flour, flour, herb vinegar, seasonings, and dried or fresh lovage leaves. Especially good *with roast ham* and *pork.*

WITH MARJORAM: Sold in 2½ ounce jars at fancy groceries and some herb farms. Contains mustard flour, flour, herb vinegar, seasonings, and dried or fresh marjoram leaves. Especially good *with cheese* and *egg dishes.*

WITH ORÉGANO: Sold in 2½ ounce jars at fancy groceries and some herb farms. Contains mustard flour, flour, herb vinegar, seasonings, and dried or fresh orégano leaves. Especially good *with fish* and *shellfish.*

WITH PARSLEY: Sold in 2½ ounce jars at fancy groceries and some herb farms. Contains mustard flour, flour, herb vinegar, seasonings, and dried or fresh parsley leaves. Especially good *with fish* and *shellfish.*

WITH ROSEMARY: Sold in 2½ ounce jars at fancy groceries and some herb farms. Contains mustard flour, flour, herb vinegar, seasonings, and dried or fresh rosemary leaves. Especially good *with poultry, pork,* and *veal.*

WITH SAGE: Sold in 2½ ounce jars at fancy groceries and some herb farms. Contains mustard flour, flour, herb vinegar, seasonings, and dried or fresh sage leaves. Especially good *with cheese dishes* and *pork.*

WITH TARRAGON: Contains mustard flour, flour, herb vinegar, seasonings, and dried or fresh tarragon leaves. Especially good *with fish* and *shellfish.*

WITH THYME: Sold in 2½ ounce jars at fancy groceries and some herb farms. Contains mustard flour, flour, herb vinegar, seasonings, and dried or fresh thyme leaves. Especially good *with cold cuts, game, pork,* and *ham.*

Mustards, Prepared:

BAHAMIAN STYLE: Sold in 6 ounce bottles at fancy groceries and markets. Contains mustard flour, flour, vinegar, sugar, herbs, and spices. *Very hot,* this blend is especially good *with eggs, cold cuts, steaks, chops, roast meats,* and *game.*

ENGLISH STYLE: Sold in 5 ounce jars at fancy groceries and markets. Contains mustard flour and water only. Use when an unusually *sharp and pungent* effect is preferred.

FRENCH STYLE, or DIJON: Sold in 5 ounce jars at fancy groceries and markets. Contains mustard flour, flour, sugar, herbs, spices, and white wine. This French blend is *unusually pungent* but has a *very smooth* flavor. Especially good as flavoring *in soups, eggs,* and *rabbits;* also *as a condiment with cold cuts, roasts, steaks, chops,* and *fish.*

HOLLAND STYLE: Sold in 5 ounce jars at fancy groceries and markets. Contains mustard flour, sugar, vinegar, herbs, and spices. *Delightfully sharp.* Especially good as a flavoring and a condiment. *Use as preferred.*

Basic Mild Tomato Aspic	TIME: 20 minutes
with Prepared Mustard	Chill 2 to 4 hours

3½ cups tomato juice	*1 tbs. any preferred*
2 envelopes unflavored	*prepared mustard*
gelatine	*½ tsp. onion salt*
¾ tsp. salt	*⅛ tsp. white pepper*
½ tsp. celery salt	*½ cup cold water*

Pour tomato juice into heavy saucepan; add salt, celery salt, mustard, onion salt, and white pepper. Heat tomato juice over low flame. Simmer gently 3 minutes.

Soften gelatine in cold water. Dissolve softened gelatine in hot tomato juice. Remove from heat. Pour into 8-inch ring mold which has been rinsed in cold water. Chill in refrigerator until firm. When ready to serve, unmold on salad greens. Serve with preferred herb salad dressing or herb mayonnaise. Yield: 8 generous portions.

Tomato aspic may be half chilled if desired; then fold in 2 cups cooked chopped shellfish, such as prawns, shrimp, or lobster; finish chilling. Serve on salad greens with mayonnaise. Serves 10 to 12.

Any desired combination raw, shredded vegetables may be folded in aspic when half chilled, such as celery, cabbage, carrots, and green peppers; or any desired combination cooked vegetables, such as corn, peas, asparagus, or potato salad.

Tips on Using Dijon Style and Other Prepared Mustards:

CHEESE BISCUITS: Add ½ teaspoon prepared mustard to ingredients for extra tasty flavor.

EGGS BENEDICT: Cream ½ teaspoon prepared mustard with 2 tablespoons butter; spread on toast for Eggs Benedict.

EGGS, DEVILED: Add 2 teaspoons mustard to 6 yolks.

FISH SANDWICH SPREADS: Add 1 teaspoon mustard to 8 ounces canned or flaked fish.

JUICES: *Tomato* or *blended vegetable.* Dissolve 1 tablespoon mustard in 1 pint juice; add herb salt to taste.

MEAT LOAF: Add 2 teaspoons prepared mustard to 1½ pounds meat; gives most delicious flavor to leftover meats.

OMELET: Add 1 teaspoon prepared mustard to a 4-egg omelet.

RAREBIT: Add 1 teaspoon prepared mustard to rarebit which serves 4.

SOUP: *Black Bean.* Add ⅛ teaspoon prepared mustard to each serving.

STEAKS AND CHOPS: Spread prepared mustard over top before broiling.

Hot English Mustard   TIME: 10 minutes

¼ cup dry mustard   *2 tbs. water*

Place dry mustard in small mixing bowl; gradually add cold water, stirring constantly until mixture is like thick cream. Set aside for 10 minutes. Yield: ¼ cup. Only mix amount needed so flavor is always fresh and pungent.

Use as desired *with fish, cheese,* and *ham.*

Shrimps Marinated in English Mustard   TIME: 15 minutes
                                            Marinate 6 hours

1 lb. raw shrimp   *1 tbs. Hot English Mustard*
1 tsp. chopped chives   *⅛ tsp. black pepper*
1 tsp. chopped parsley   *¼ tsp. celery salt*
1 tsp. dried basil   *½ tsp. salt*
¼ tsp. garlic salt   *2 eggs, well beaten*

Select large, firm, shrimp; peel and clean them. Set aside.

Blend well all herbs, mustard, and herb salts in large mixing bowl. Gradually stir in well-beaten eggs; add cleaned shrimp to mixture; cover well. Marinate in cool place 6 hours. Fry in deep fat 3 minutes, or until golden brown. Serve piping hot on preheated plates with generous helping fluffy steamed rice and chili sauce. Serves 2 to 4.

Mild Mustard Spiced   TIME: 30 minutes

3 tbs. dry mustard flour   *¼ tsp. ground cloves*
½ cup white flour   *⅔ cup cider vinegar*
½ tbs. salt   *1 cup boiling water*
¼ tsp. turmeric

Thoroughly blend all dry ingredients in large mixing bowl. Gradually stir in boiling water, stirring constantly to prevent lumping. Pour mixture into top section of double boiler placed over lower section half filled with boiling water. Cook mixture 15 minutes, or until well thickened, stirring occasionally. Remove from flame. Gradually add vinegar, stirring constantly; when well blended, beat vigorously until smooth and of desired consistency. Place in small glass jar; cover tightly. Will keep indefinitely. Yield: 8 ounces.

O. K. Sauce: Sold in 9 ounce bottles at groceries and markets. Contains spices, herbs, vinegar, other seasonings, and water. Use *with cheese, curries, chops, fish, gravies, meats, steaks,* and *shellfish.*

Pickapeppa Sauce: Sold in 5 ounce bottles at groceries and markets. Contains chili pepper, herbs, spices, other seasonings, and water. Use whenever hot flavor is desired. Especially good *in shellfish cocktail sauces* and *over raw shellfish.*

Salad Dressings: See Herb and Spice Salad Dressings.

Tabasco Sauce: Sold in 2 ounce and 5 ounce bottles at groceries and markets. Derives its name from the pepper used in its preparation. The tabasco pepper is a small, very hot, red pepper about 1½ inches long and about ½ inch in diameter at the top, tapering to a point. The sauce contains herbs, other seasonings, the tabasco pepper, and water. Especially good *with fish* and *shellfish cocktails;* also *as flavoring for meats* and *poultry. Use sparingly from 2 drops to ½ teaspoon only.*

Worcestershire Sauce: Sold in 5 ounce bottles at groceries and markets. Contains sugar, salt, spices, vinegar, other seasonings, and water. Especially good *with cheese, curries, chops, fish, game, gravies, salads, soups, roast meats,* and *steaks.*

Worcestershire Beef Casserole   TIME: 45 minutes

1 lb. chopped beef	*1 tsp. curry powder*
¾ cup uncooked rice	*½ tsp. celery salt*
2 qts. boiling water	*½ tsp. onion salt*
1½ tsp. salt	*¼ tsp. salt, extra*
1 small onion, minced	*⅛ tsp. black pepper*
1 tbs. butter	*1 tbs. butter, extra*
1 No. 2 can tomatoes	*1 clove garlic, minced*
1 tbs. Worcestershire sauce	

Wash rice in cold running water. Drain. Pour 2 quarts boiling water into heavy saucepan over high flame; add salt; when boiling rapidly, add rice. Boil 20 minutes, or until tender; stir occasionally with fork to prevent sticking. Drain rice in colander; rinse with hot water.

While rice is boiling, melt 1 tablespoon butter in large skillet over medium flame; add minced onion; brown lightly 3 minutes; add chopped beef; brown 5 minutes by stirring constantly. Remove from flame.

Drain half of liquid from tomatoes. Mix balance of liquid and tomatoes with meat; add all seasonings; mix well; add cooked rice; mix well again. Pour mixture into greased casserole; top with 1 tablespoon butter. Bake in preheated moderate oven (375° F.) 20 minutes, or until golden brown. Serve piping hot with tossed-green salad. Serves 4 to 6.

101 Sauce: Sold in 5 ounce bottles at groceries and markets. Contains sugar, salt, herbs, spices, herb vinegar, tomato purée, and raisins. Use *with cheese, cold cuts, chops, fish, game, gravies, hash, meat, poultry,* and *salads.*

Index

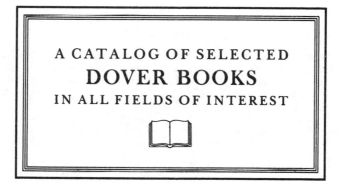

A CATALOG OF SELECTED
DOVER BOOKS
IN ALL FIELDS OF INTEREST

A CATALOG OF SELECTED DOVER
BOOKS IN ALL FIELDS OF INTEREST

CONCERNING THE SPIRITUAL IN ART, Wassily Kandinsky. Pioneering work by father of abstract art. Thoughts on color theory, nature of art. Analysis of earlier masters. 12 illustrations. 80pp. of text. 5⅜ x 8½. 23411-8 Pa. $3.95

ANIMALS: 1,419 Copyright-Free Illustrations of Mammals, Birds, Fish, Insects, etc., Jim Harter (ed.). Clear wood engravings present, in extremely lifelike poses, over 1,000 species of animals. One of the most extensive pictorial sourcebooks of its kind. Captions. Index. 284pp. 9 x 12. 23766-4 Pa. $12.95

CELTIC ART: The Methods of Construction, George Bain. Simple geometric techniques for making Celtic interlacements, spirals, Kells-type initials, animals, humans, etc. Over 500 illustrations. 160pp. 9 x 12. (USO) 22923-8 Pa. $9.95

AN ATLAS OF ANATOMY FOR ARTISTS, Fritz Schider. Most thorough reference work on art anatomy in the world. Hundreds of illustrations, including selections from works by Vesalius, Leonardo, Goya, Ingres, Michelangelo, others. 593 illustrations. 192pp. 7⅛ x 10¼. 20241-0 Pa. $9.95

CELTIC HAND STROKE-BY-STROKE (Irish Half-Uncial from "The Book of Kells"): An Arthur Baker Calligraphy Manual, Arthur Baker. Complete guide to creating each letter of the alphabet in distinctive Celtic manner. Covers hand position, strokes, pens, inks, paper, more. Illustrated. 48pp. 8¼ x 11. 24336-2 Pa. $3.95

EASY ORIGAMI, John Montroll. Charming collection of 32 projects (hat, cup, pelican, piano, swan, many more) specially designed for the novice origami hobbyist. Clearly illustrated easy-to-follow instructions insure that even beginning papercrafters will achieve successful results. 48pp. 8¼ x 11. 27298-2 Pa. $3.50

THE COMPLETE BOOK OF BIRDHOUSE CONSTRUCTION FOR WOOD-WORKERS, Scott D. Campbell. Detailed instructions, illustrations, tables. Also data on bird habitat and instinct patterns. Bibliography. 3 tables. 63 illustrations in 15 figures. 48pp. 5¼ x 8½. 24407-5 Pa. $2.50

BLOOMINGDALE'S ILLUSTRATED 1886 CATALOG: Fashions, Dry Goods and Housewares, Bloomingdale Brothers. Famed merchants' extremely rare catalog depicting about 1,700 products: clothing, housewares, firearms, dry goods, jewelry, more. Invaluable for dating, identifying vintage items. Also, copyright-free graphics for artists, designers. Co-published with Henry Ford Museum & Greenfield Village. 160pp. 8¼ x 11. 25780-0 Pa. $10.95

HISTORIC COSTUME IN PICTURES, Braun & Schneider. Over 1,450 costumed figures in clearly detailed engravings–from dawn of civilization to end of 19th century. Captions. Many folk costumes. 256pp. 8⅜ x 11¾. 23150-X Pa. $12.95

STICKLEY CRAFTSMAN FURNITURE CATALOGS, Gustav Stickley and L. & J. G. Stickley. Beautiful, functional furniture in two authentic catalogs from 1910. 594 illustrations, including 277 photos, show settles, rockers, armchairs, reclining chairs, bookcases, desks, tables. 183pp. 6½ x 9¼. 23838-5 Pa. $9.95

AMERICAN LOCOMOTIVES IN HISTORIC PHOTOGRAPHS: 1858 to 1949, Ron Ziel (ed.). A rare collection of 126 meticulously detailed official photographs, called "builder portraits," of American locomotives that majestically chronicle the rise of steam locomotive power in America. Introduction. Detailed captions. xi + 129pp. 9 x 12. 27393-8 Pa. $12.95

AMERICA'S LIGHTHOUSES: An Illustrated History, Francis Ross Holland, Jr. Delightfully written, profusely illustrated fact-filled survey of over 200 American lighthouses since 1716. History, anecdotes, technological advances, more. 240pp. 8 x 10¾. 25576-X Pa. $12.95

TOWARDS A NEW ARCHITECTURE, Le Corbusier. Pioneering manifesto by founder of "International School." Technical and aesthetic theories, views of industry, economics, relation of form to function, "mass-production split" and much more. Profusely illustrated. 320pp. 6⅛ x 9¼. (USO) 25023-7 Pa. $9.95

HOW THE OTHER HALF LIVES, Jacob Riis. Famous journalistic record, exposing poverty and degradation of New York slums around 1900, by major social reformer. 100 striking and influential photographs. 233pp. 10 x 7⅞. 22012-5 Pa. $10.95

FRUIT KEY AND TWIG KEY TO TREES AND SHRUBS, William M. Harlow. One of the handiest and most widely used identification aids. Fruit key covers 120 deciduous and evergreen species; twig key 160 deciduous species. Easily used. Over 300 photographs. 126pp. 5⅜ x 8½. 20511-8 Pa. $3.95

COMMON BIRD SONGS, Dr. Donald J. Borror. Songs of 60 most common U.S. birds: robins, sparrows, cardinals, bluejays, finches, more—arranged in order of increasing complexity. Up to 9 variations of songs of each species.
Cassette and manual 99911-4 $8.95

ORCHIDS AS HOUSE PLANTS, Rebecca Tyson Northen. Grow cattleyas and many other kinds of orchids—in a window, in a case, or under artificial light. 63 illustrations. 148pp. 5⅜ x 8½. 23261-1 Pa. $4.95

MONSTER MAZES, Dave Phillips. Masterful mazes at four levels of difficulty. Avoid deadly perils and evil creatures to find magical treasures. Solutions for all 32 exciting illustrated puzzles. 48pp. 8¼ x 11. 26005-4 Pa. $2.95

MOZART'S DON GIOVANNI (DOVER OPERA LIBRETTO SERIES), Wolfgang Amadeus Mozart. Introduced and translated by Ellen H. Bleiler. Standard Italian libretto, with complete English translation. Convenient and thoroughly portable—an ideal companion for reading along with a recording or the performance itself. Introduction. List of characters. Plot summary. 121pp. 5¼ x 8½. 24944-1 Pa. $2.95

TECHNICAL MANUAL AND DICTIONARY OF CLASSICAL BALLET, Gail Grant. Defines, explains, comments on steps, movements, poses and concepts. 15-page pictorial section. Basic book for student, viewer. 127pp. 5⅜ x 8½. 21843-0 Pa. $4.95

BRASS INSTRUMENTS: Their History and Development, Anthony Baines. Authoritative, updated survey of the evolution of trumpets, trombones, bugles, cornets, French horns, tubas and other brass wind instruments. Over 140 illustrations and 48 music examples. Corrected and updated by author. New preface. Bibliography. 320pp. 5⅜ x 8½.   27574-4 Pa. $9.95

HOLLYWOOD GLAMOR PORTRAITS, John Kobal (ed.). 145 photos from 1926-49. Harlow, Gable, Bogart, Bacall; 94 stars in all. Full background on photographers, technical aspects. 160pp. 8⅜ x 11¼.   23352-9 Pa. $12.95

MAX AND MORITZ, Wilhelm Busch. Great humor classic in both German and English. Also 10 other works: "Cat and Mouse," "Plisch and Plumm," etc. 216pp. 5⅜ x 8½.   20181-3 Pa. $6.95

THE RAVEN AND OTHER FAVORITE POEMS, Edgar Allan Poe. Over 40 of the author's most memorable poems: "The Bells," "Ulalume," "Israfel," "To Helen," "The Conqueror Worm," "Eldorado," "Annabel Lee," many more. Alphabetic lists of titles and first lines. 64pp. 5³⁄₁₆ x 8¼.   26685-0 Pa. $1.00

PERSONAL MEMOIRS OF U. S. GRANT, Ulysses Simpson Grant. Intelligent, deeply moving firsthand account of Civil War campaigns, considered by many the finest military memoirs ever written. Includes letters, historic photographs, maps and more. 528pp. 6⅛ x 9¼.   28587-1 Pa. $11.95

AMULETS AND SUPERSTITIONS, E. A. Wallis Budge. Comprehensive discourse on origin, powers of amulets in many ancient cultures: Arab, Persian Babylonian, Assyrian, Egyptian, Gnostic, Hebrew, Phoenician, Syriac, etc. Covers cross, swastika, crucifix, seals, rings, stones, etc. 584pp. 5⅜ x 8½. 23573-4 Pa. $12.95

RUSSIAN STORIES/PYCCKNE PACCKA3bl: A Dual-Language Book, edited by Gleb Struve. Twelve tales by such masters as Chekhov, Tolstoy, Dostoevsky, Pushkin, others. Excellent word-for-word English translations on facing pages, plus teaching and study aids, Russian/English vocabulary, biographical/critical introductions, more. 416pp. 5⅜ x 8½.   26244-8 Pa. $8.95

PHILADELPHIA THEN AND NOW: 60 Sites Photographed in the Past and Present, Kenneth Finkel and Susan Oyama. Rare photographs of City Hall, Logan Square, Independence Hall, Betsy Ross House, other landmarks juxtaposed with contemporary views. Captures changing face of historic city. Introduction. Captions. 128pp. 8¼ x 11.   25790-8 Pa. $9.95

AIA ARCHITECTURAL GUIDE TO NASSAU AND SUFFOLK COUNTIES, LONG ISLAND, The American Institute of Architects, Long Island Chapter, and the Society for the Preservation of Long Island Antiquities. Comprehensive, well-researched and generously illustrated volume brings to life over three centuries of Long Island's great architectural heritage. More than 240 photographs with authoritative, extensively detailed captions. 176pp. 8¼ x 11.   26946-9 Pa. $14.95

NORTH AMERICAN INDIAN LIFE: Customs and Traditions of 23 Tribes, Elsie Clews Parsons (ed.). 27 fictionalized essays by noted anthropologists examine religion, customs, government, additional facets of life among the Winnebago, Crow, Zuni, Eskimo, other tribes. 480pp. 6⅛ x 9¼.   27377-6 Pa. $10.95

FRANK LLOYD WRIGHT'S HOLLYHOCK HOUSE, Donald Hoffmann. Lavishly illustrated, carefully documented study of one of Wright's most controversial residential designs. Over 120 photographs, floor plans, elevations, etc. Detailed perceptive text by noted Wright scholar. Index. 128pp. 9¼ x 10¾. 27133-1 Pa. $11.95

THE MALE AND FEMALE FIGURE IN MOTION: 60 Classic Photographic Sequences, Eadweard Muybridge. 60 true-action photographs of men and women walking, running, climbing, bending, turning, etc., reproduced from rare 19th-century masterpiece. vi + 121pp. 9 x 12. 24745-7 Pa. $10.95

1001 QUESTIONS ANSWERED ABOUT THE SEASHORE, N. J. Berrill and Jacquelyn Berrill. Queries answered about dolphins, sea snails, sponges, starfish, fishes, shore birds, many others. Covers appearance, breeding, growth, feeding, much more. 305pp. 5¼ x 8¼. 23366-9 Pa. $8.95

GUIDE TO OWL WATCHING IN NORTH AMERICA, Donald S. Heintzelman. Superb guide offers complete data and descriptions of 19 species: barn owl, screech owl, snowy owl, many more. Expert coverage of owl-watching equipment, conservation, migrations and invasions, etc. Guide to observing sites. 84 illustrations. xiii + 193pp. 5⅜ x 8½. 27344-X Pa. $8.95

MEDICINAL AND OTHER USES OF NORTH AMERICAN PLANTS: A Historical Survey with Special Reference to the Eastern Indian Tribes, Charlotte Erichsen-Brown. Chronological historical citations document 500 years of usage of plants, trees, shrubs native to eastern Canada, northeastern U.S. Also complete identifying information. 343 illustrations. 544pp. 6½ x 9¼. 25951-X Pa. $12.95

STORYBOOK MAZES, Dave Phillips. 23 stories and mazes on two-page spreads: Wizard of Oz, Treasure Island, Robin Hood, etc. Solutions. 64pp. 8¼ x 11. 23628-5 Pa. $2.95

NEGRO FOLK MUSIC, U.S.A., Harold Courlander. Noted folklorist's scholarly yet readable analysis of rich and varied musical tradition. Includes authentic versions of over 40 folk songs. Valuable bibliography and discography. xi + 324pp. 5⅜ x 8½. 27350-4 Pa. $9.95

MOVIE-STAR PORTRAITS OF THE FORTIES, John Kobal (ed.). 163 glamor, studio photos of 106 stars of the 1940s: Rita Hayworth, Ava Gardner, Marlon Brando, Clark Gable, many more. 176pp. 8⅜ x 11¼. 23546-7 Pa. $12.95

BENCHLEY LOST AND FOUND, Robert Benchley. Finest humor from early 30s, about pet peeves, child psychologists, post office and others. Mostly unavailable elsewhere. 73 illustrations by Peter Arno and others. 183pp. 5⅜ x 8½. 22410-4 Pa. $6.95

YEKL and THE IMPORTED BRIDEGROOM AND OTHER STORIES OF YIDDISH NEW YORK, Abraham Cahan. Film Hester Street based on Yekl (1896). Novel, other stories among first about Jewish immigrants on N.Y.'s East Side. 240pp. 5⅜ x 8½. 22427-9 Pa. $6.95

SELECTED POEMS, Walt Whitman. Generous sampling from *Leaves of Grass*. Twenty-four poems include "I Hear America Singing," "Song of the Open Road," "I Sing the Body Electric," "When Lilacs Last in the Dooryard Bloom'd," "O Captain! My Captain!"—all reprinted from an authoritative edition. Lists of titles and first lines. 128pp. 5³⁄₁₆ x 8¼. 26878-0 Pa. $1.00

THE BEST TALES OF HOFFMANN, E. T. A. Hoffmann. 10 of Hoffmann's most important stories: "Nutcracker and the King of Mice," "The Golden Flowerpot," etc. 458pp. 5⅜ x 8½. 21793-0 Pa. $9.95

FROM FETISH TO GOD IN ANCIENT EGYPT, E. A. Wallis Budge. Rich detailed survey of Egyptian conception of "God" and gods, magic, cult of animals, Osiris, more. Also, superb English translations of hymns and legends. 240 illustrations. 545pp. 5⅜ x 8½. 25803-3 Pa. $13.95

FRENCH STORIES/CONTES FRANÇAIS: A Dual-Language Book, Wallace Fowlie. Ten stories by French masters, Voltaire to Camus: "Micromegas" by Voltaire; "The Atheist's Mass" by Balzac; "Minuet" by de Maupassant; "The Guest" by Camus, six more. Excellent English translations on facing pages. Also French-English vocabulary list, exercises, more. 352pp. 5⅜ x 8½. 26443-2 Pa. $8.95

CHICAGO AT THE TURN OF THE CENTURY IN PHOTOGRAPHS: 122 Historic Views from the Collections of the Chicago Historical Society, Larry A. Viskochil. Rare large-format prints offer detailed views of City Hall, State Street, the Loop, Hull House, Union Station, many other landmarks, circa 1904-1913. Introduction. Captions. Maps. 144pp. 9⅜ x 12¼. 24656-6 Pa. $12.95

OLD BROOKLYN IN EARLY PHOTOGRAPHS, 1865-1929, William Lee Younger. Luna Park, Gravesend race track, construction of Grand Army Plaza, moving of Hotel Brighton, etc. 157 previously unpublished photographs. 165pp. 8⅞ x 11¾. 23587-4 Pa. $13.95

THE MYTHS OF THE NORTH AMERICAN INDIANS, Lewis Spence. Rich anthology of the myths and legends of the Algonquins, Iroquois, Pawnees and Sioux, prefaced by an extensive historical and ethnological commentary. 36 illustrations. 480pp. 5⅜ x 8½. 25967-6 Pa. $8.95

AN ENCYCLOPEDIA OF BATTLES: Accounts of Over 1,560 Battles from 1479 B.C. to the Present, David Eggenberger. Essential details of every major battle in recorded history from the first battle of Megiddo in 1479 B.C. to Grenada in 1984. List of Battle Maps. New Appendix covering the years 1967-1984. Index. 99 illustrations. 544pp. 6½ x 9¼. 24913-1 Pa. $14.95

SAILING ALONE AROUND THE WORLD, Captain Joshua Slocum. First man to sail around the world, alone, in small boat. One of great feats of seamanship told in delightful manner. 67 illustrations. 294pp. 5⅜ x 8½. 20326-3 Pa. $5.95

ANARCHISM AND OTHER ESSAYS, Emma Goldman. Powerful, penetrating, prophetic essays on direct action, role of minorities, prison reform, puritan hypocrisy, violence, etc. 271pp. 5⅜ x 8½. 22484-8 Pa. $6.95

MYTHS OF THE HINDUS AND BUDDHISTS, Ananda K. Coomaraswamy and Sister Nivedita. Great stories of the epics; deeds of Krishna, Shiva, taken from puranas, Vedas, folk tales; etc. 32 illustrations. 400pp. 5⅜ x 8½. 21759-0 Pa. $10.95

BEYOND PSYCHOLOGY, Otto Rank. Fear of death, desire of immortality, nature of sexuality, social organization, creativity, according to Rankian system. 291pp. 5⅜ x 8½. 20485-5 Pa. $8.95

A THEOLOGICO-POLITICAL TREATISE, Benedict Spinoza. Also contains unfinished Political Treatise. Great classic on religious liberty, theory of government on common consent. R. Elwes translation. Total of 421pp. 5⅜ x 8½. 20249-6 Pa. $9.95

MY BONDAGE AND MY FREEDOM, Frederick Douglass. Born a slave, Douglass became outspoken force in antislavery movement. The best of Douglass' autobiographies. Graphic description of slave life. 464pp. 5⅜ x 8½. 22457-0 Pa. $8.95

FOLLOWING THE EQUATOR: A Journey Around the World, Mark Twain. Fascinating humorous account of 1897 voyage to Hawaii, Australia, India, New Zealand, etc. Ironic, bemused reports on peoples, customs, climate, flora and fauna, politics, much more. 197 illustrations. 720pp. 5⅜ x 8½. 26113-1 Pa. $15.95

THE PEOPLE CALLED SHAKERS, Edward D. Andrews. Definitive study of Shakers: origins, beliefs, practices, dances, social organization, furniture and crafts, etc. 33 illustrations. 351pp. 5⅜ x 8½. 21081-2 Pa. $8.95

THE MYTHS OF GREECE AND ROME, H. A. Guerber. A classic of mythology, generously illustrated, long prized for its simple, graphic, accurate retelling of the principal myths of Greece and Rome, and for its commentary on their origins and significance. With 64 illustrations by Michelangelo, Raphael, Titian, Rubens, Canova, Bernini and others. 480pp. 5⅜ x 8½. 27584-1 Pa. $9.95

PSYCHOLOGY OF MUSIC, Carl E. Seashore. Classic work discusses music as a medium from psychological viewpoint. Clear treatment of physical acoustics, auditory apparatus, sound perception, development of musical skills, nature of musical feeling, host of other topics. 88 figures. 408pp. 5⅜ x 8½. 21851-1 Pa. $10.95

THE PHILOSOPHY OF HISTORY, Georg W. Hegel. Great classic of Western thought develops concept that history is not chance but rational process, the evolution of freedom. 457pp. 5⅜ x 8½. 20112-0 Pa. $9.95

THE BOOK OF TEA, Kakuzo Okakura. Minor classic of the Orient: entertaining, charming explanation, interpretation of traditional Japanese culture in terms of tea ceremony. 94pp. 5⅜ x 8½. 20070-1 Pa. $3.95

LIFE IN ANCIENT EGYPT, Adolf Erman. Fullest, most thorough, detailed older account with much not in more recent books, domestic life, religion, magic, medicine, commerce, much more. Many illustrations reproduce tomb paintings, carvings, hieroglyphs, etc. 597pp. 5⅜ x 8½. 22632-8 Pa. $11.95

SUNDIALS, Their Theory and Construction, Albert Waugh. Far and away the best, most thorough coverage of ideas, mathematics concerned, types, construction, adjusting anywhere. Simple, nontechnical treatment allows even children to build several of these dials. Over 100 illustrations. 230pp. 5⅜ x 8½. 22947-5 Pa. $7.95

DYNAMICS OF FLUIDS IN POROUS MEDIA, Jacob Bear. For advanced students of ground water hydrology, soil mechanics and physics, drainage and irrigation engineering, and more. 335 illustrations. Exercises, with answers. 784pp. 6⅛ x 9¼. 65675-6 Pa. $19.95

SONGS OF EXPERIENCE: Facsimile Reproduction with 26 Plates in Full Color, William Blake. 26 full-color plates from a rare 1826 edition. Includes "TheTyger," "London," "Holy Thursday," and other poems. Printed text of poems. 48pp. 5¼ x 7. 24636-1 Pa. $4.95

OLD-TIME VIGNETTES IN FULL COLOR, Carol Belanger Grafton (ed.). Over 390 charming, often sentimental illustrations, selected from archives of Victorian graphics—pretty women posing, children playing, food, flowers, kittens and puppies, smiling cherubs, birds and butterflies, much more. All copyright-free. 48pp. 9¼ x 12¼. 27269-9 Pa. $7.95

PERSPECTIVE FOR ARTISTS, Rex Vicat Cole. Depth, perspective of sky and sea, shadows, much more, not usually covered. 391 diagrams, 81 reproductions of drawings and paintings. 279pp. 5⅜ x 8½. 22487-2 Pa. $7.95

DRAWING THE LIVING FIGURE, Joseph Sheppard. Innovative approach to artistic anatomy focuses on specifics of surface anatomy, rather than muscles and bones. Over 170 drawings of live models in front, back and side views, and in widely varying poses. Accompanying diagrams. 177 illustrations. Introduction. Index. 144pp. 8⅜ x11¼. 26723-7 Pa. $8.95

GOTHIC AND OLD ENGLISH ALPHABETS: 100 Complete Fonts, Dan X. Solo. Add power, elegance to posters, signs, other graphics with 100 stunning copyright-free alphabets: Blackstone, Dolbey, Germania, 97 more–including many lower-case, numerals, punctuation marks. 104pp. 8⅛ x 11. 24695-7 Pa. $8.95

HOW TO DO BEADWORK, Mary White. Fundamental book on craft from simple projects to five-bead chains and woven works. 106 illustrations. 142pp. 5⅜ x 8. 20697-1 Pa. $4.95

THE BOOK OF WOOD CARVING, Charles Marshall Sayers. Finest book for beginners discusses fundamentals and offers 34 designs. "Absolutely first rate . . . well thought out and well executed."–E. J. Tangerman. 118pp. 7¾ x 10⅝. 23654-4 Pa. $6.95

ILLUSTRATED CATALOG OF CIVIL WAR MILITARY GOODS: Union Army Weapons, Insignia, Uniform Accessories, and Other Equipment, Schuyler, Hartley, and Graham. Rare, profusely illustrated 1846 catalog includes Union Army uniform and dress regulations, arms and ammunition, coats, insignia, flags, swords, rifles, etc. 226 illustrations. 160pp. 9 x 12. 24939-5 Pa. $10.95

WOMEN'S FASHIONS OF THE EARLY 1900s: An Unabridged Republication of "New York Fashions, 1909," National Cloak & Suit Co. Rare catalog of mail-order fashions documents women's and children's clothing styles shortly after the turn of the century. Captions offer full descriptions, prices. Invaluable resource for fashion, costume historians. Approximately 725 illustrations. 128pp. 8⅜ x 11¼. 27276-1 Pa. $11.95

THE 1912 AND 1915 GUSTAV STICKLEY FURNITURE CATALOGS, Gustav Stickley. With over 200 detailed illustrations and descriptions, these two catalogs are essential reading and reference materials and identification guides for Stickley furniture. Captions cite materials, dimensions and prices. 112pp. 6½ x 9¼. 26676-1 Pa. $9.95

EARLY AMERICAN LOCOMOTIVES, John H. White, Jr. Finest locomotive engravings from early 19th century: historical (1804–74), main-line (after 1870), special, foreign, etc. 147 plates. 142pp. 11⅜ x 8¼. 22772-3 Pa. $10.95

THE TALL SHIPS OF TODAY IN PHOTOGRAPHS, Frank O. Braynard. Lavishly illustrated tribute to nearly 100 majestic contemporary sailing vessels: Amerigo Vespucci, Clearwater, Constitution, Eagle, Mayflower, Sea Cloud, Victory, many more. Authoritative captions provide statistics, background on each ship. 190 black-and-white photographs and illustrations. Introduction. 128pp. 8⅞ x 11¾. 27163-3 Pa. $13.95

EARLY NINETEENTH-CENTURY CRAFTS AND TRADES, Peter Stockham (ed.). Extremely rare 1807 volume describes to youngsters the crafts and trades of the day: brickmaker, weaver, dressmaker, bookbinder, ropemaker, saddler, many more. Quaint prose, charming illustrations for each craft. 20 black-and-white line illustrations. 192pp. 4⅝ x 6. 27293-1 Pa. $4.95

VICTORIAN FASHIONS AND COSTUMES FROM HARPER'S BAZAR, 1867–1898, Stella Blum (ed.). Day costumes, evening wear, sports clothes, shoes, hats, other accessories in over 1,000 detailed engravings. 320pp. 9⅜ x 12¼.
22990-4 Pa. $14.95

GUSTAV STICKLEY, THE CRAFTSMAN, Mary Ann Smith. Superb study surveys broad scope of Stickley's achievement, especially in architecture. Design philosophy, rise and fall of the Craftsman empire, descriptions and floor plans for many Craftsman houses, more. 86 black-and-white halftones. 31 line illustrations. Introduction 208pp. 6½ x 9¼. 27210-9 Pa. $9.95

THE LONG ISLAND RAIL ROAD IN EARLY PHOTOGRAPHS, Ron Ziel. Over 220 rare photos, informative text document origin (1844) and development of rail service on Long Island. Vintage views of early trains, locomotives, stations, passengers, crews, much more. Captions. 8⅞ x 11¾. 26301-0 Pa. $13.95

THE BOOK OF OLD SHIPS: From Egyptian Galleys to Clipper Ships, Henry B. Culver. Superb, authoritative history of sailing vessels, with 80 magnificent line illustrations. Galley, bark, caravel, longship, whaler, many more. Detailed, informative text on each vessel by noted naval historian. Introduction. 256pp. 5⅜ x 8½.
27332-6 Pa. $7.95

TEN BOOKS ON ARCHITECTURE, Vitruvius. The most important book ever written on architecture. Early Roman aesthetics, technology, classical orders, site selection, all other aspects. Morgan translation. 331pp. 5⅜ x 8½. 20645-9 Pa. $8.95

THE HUMAN FIGURE IN MOTION, Eadweard Muybridge. More than 4,500 stopped-action photos, in action series, showing undraped men, women, children jumping, lying down, throwing, sitting, wrestling, carrying, etc. 390pp. 7⅞ x 10⅝.
20204-6 Clothbd. $25.95

TREES OF THE EASTERN AND CENTRAL UNITED STATES AND CANADA, William M. Harlow. Best one-volume guide to 140 trees. Full descriptions, woodlore, range, etc. Over 600 illustrations. Handy size. 288pp. 4½ x 6⅜.
20395-6 Pa. $6.95

SONGS OF WESTERN BIRDS, Dr. Donald J. Borror. Complete song and call repertoire of 60 western species, including flycatchers, juncoes, cactus wrens, many more–includes fully illustrated booklet. Cassette and manual 99913-0 $8.95

GROWING AND USING HERBS AND SPICES, Milo Miloradovich. Versatile handbook provides all the information needed for cultivation and use of all the herbs and spices available in North America. 4 illustrations. Index. Glossary. 236pp. 5⅜ x 8½.
25058-X Pa. $6.95

BIG BOOK OF MAZES AND LABYRINTHS, Walter Shepherd. 50 mazes and labyrinths in all–classical, solid, ripple, and more–in one great volume. Perfect inexpensive puzzler for clever youngsters. Full solutions. 112pp. 8⅛ x 11.
22951-3 Pa. $4.95

PIANO TUNING, J. Cree Fischer. Clearest, best book for beginner, amateur. Simple repairs, raising dropped notes, tuning by easy method of flattened fifths. No previous skills needed. 4 illustrations. 201pp. 5⅜ x 8½.　　　23267-0 Pa. $6.95

A SOURCE BOOK IN THEATRICAL HISTORY, A. M. Nagler. Contemporary observers on acting, directing, make-up, costuming, stage props, machinery, scene design, from Ancient Greece to Chekhov. 611pp. 5⅜ x 8½.　　　20515-0 Pa. $12.95

THE COMPLETE NONSENSE OF EDWARD LEAR, Edward Lear. All nonsense limericks, zany alphabets, Owl and Pussycat, songs, nonsense botany, etc., illustrated by Lear. Total of 320pp. 5⅜ x 8½. (USO)　　　20167-8 Pa. $6.95

VICTORIAN PARLOUR POETRY: An Annotated Anthology, Michael R. Turner. 117 gems by Longfellow, Tennyson, Browning, many lesser-known poets. "The Village Blacksmith," "Curfew Must Not Ring Tonight," "Only a Baby Small," dozens more, often difficult to find elsewhere. Index of poets, titles, first lines. xxiii + 325pp. 5⅜ x 8¼.　　　27044-0 Pa. $8.95

DUBLINERS, James Joyce. Fifteen stories offer vivid, tightly focused observations of the lives of Dublin's poorer classes. At least one, "The Dead," is considered a masterpiece. Reprinted complete and unabridged from standard edition. 160pp. 5³⁄₁₆ x 8¼.　　　26870-5 Pa. $1.00

THE HAUNTED MONASTERY and THE CHINESE MAZE MURDERS, Robert van Gulik. Two full novels by van Gulik, set in 7th-century China, continue adventures of Judge Dee and his companions. An evil Taoist monastery, seemingly supernatural events; overgrown topiary maze hides strange crimes. 27 illustrations. 328pp. 5⅜ x 8½.　　　23502-5 Pa. $8.95

THE BOOK OF THE SACRED MAGIC OF ABRAMELIN THE MAGE, translated by S. MacGregor Mathers. Medieval manuscript of ceremonial magic. Basic document in Aleister Crowley, Golden Dawn groups. 268pp. 5⅜ x 8½.　　　23211-5 Pa. $8.95

NEW RUSSIAN-ENGLISH AND ENGLISH-RUSSIAN DICTIONARY, M. A. O'Brien. This is a remarkably handy Russian dictionary, containing a surprising amount of information, including over 70,000 entries. 366pp. 4½ x 6⅛.　　　20208-9 Pa. $9.95

HISTORIC HOMES OF THE AMERICAN PRESIDENTS, Second, Revised Edition, Irvin Haas. A traveler's guide to American Presidential homes, most open to the public, depicting and describing homes occupied by every American President from George Washington to George Bush. With visiting hours, admission charges, travel routes. 175 photographs. Index. 160pp. 8¼ x 11.　　　26751-2 Pa. $11.95

NEW YORK IN THE FORTIES, Andreas Feininger. 162 brilliant photographs by the well-known photographer, formerly with *Life* magazine. Commuters, shoppers, Times Square at night, much else from city at its peak. Captions by John von Hartz. 181pp. 9¼ x 10¾.　　　23585-8 Pa. $12.95

INDIAN SIGN LANGUAGE, William Tomkins. Over 525 signs developed by Sioux and other tribes. Written instructions and diagrams. Also 290 pictographs. 111pp. 6⅛ x 9¼.　　　22029-X Pa. $3.95

ANATOMY: A Complete Guide for Artists, Joseph Sheppard. A master of figure drawing shows artists how to render human anatomy convincingly. Over 460 illustrations. 224pp. 8⅜ x 11¼. 27279-6 Pa. $10.95

MEDIEVAL CALLIGRAPHY: Its History and Technique, Marc Drogin. Spirited history, comprehensive instruction manual covers 13 styles (ca. 4th century thru 15th). Excellent photographs; directions for duplicating medieval techniques with modern tools. 224pp. 8⅜ x 11¼. 26142-5 Pa. $12.95

DRIED FLOWERS: How to Prepare Them, Sarah Whitlock and Martha Rankin. Complete instructions on how to use silica gel, meal and borax, perlite aggregate, sand and borax, glycerine and water to create attractive permanent flower arrangements. 12 illustrations. 32pp. 5⅜ x 8½. 21802-3 Pa. $1.00

EASY-TO-MAKE BIRD FEEDERS FOR WOODWORKERS, Scott D. Campbell. Detailed, simple-to-use guide for designing, constructing, caring for and using feeders. Text, illustrations for 12 classic and contemporary designs. 96pp. 5⅜ x 8½. 25847-5 Pa. $2.95

SCOTTISH WONDER TALES FROM MYTH AND LEGEND, Donald A. Mackenzie. 16 lively tales tell of giants rumbling down mountainsides, of a magic wand that turns stone pillars into warriors, of gods and goddesses, evil hags, powerful forces and more. 240pp. 5⅜ x 8½. 29677-6 Pa. $6.95

THE HISTORY OF UNDERCLOTHES, C. Willett Cunnington and Phyllis Cunnington. Fascinating, well-documented survey covering six centuries of English undergarments, enhanced with over 100 illustrations: 12th-century laced-up bodice, footed long drawers (1795), 19th-century bustles, 19th-century corsets for men, Victorian "bust improvers," much more. 272pp. 5⅜ x 8¼. 27124-2 Pa. $9.95

ARTS AND CRAFTS FURNITURE: The Complete Brooks Catalog of 1912, Brooks Manufacturing Co. Photos and detailed descriptions of more than 150 now very collectible furniture designs from the Arts and Crafts movement depict davenports, settees, buffets, desks, tables, chairs, bedsteads, dressers and more, all built of solid, quarter-sawed oak. Invaluable for students and enthusiasts of antiques, Americana and the decorative arts. 80pp. 6½ x 9¼. 27471-3 Pa. $8.95

HOW WE INVENTED THE AIRPLANE: An Illustrated History, Orville Wright. Fascinating firsthand account covers early experiments, construction of planes and motors, first flights, much more. Introduction and commentary by Fred C. Kelly. 76 photographs. 96pp. 8¼ x 11. 25662-6 Pa. $8.95

THE ARTS OF THE SAILOR: Knotting, Splicing and Ropework, Hervey Garrett Smith. Indispensable shipboard reference covers tools, basic knots and useful hitches; handsewing and canvas work, more. Over 100 illustrations. Delightful reading for sea lovers. 256pp. 5⅜ x 8½. 26440-8 Pa. $7.95

FRANK LLOYD WRIGHT'S FALLINGWATER: The House and Its History, Second, Revised Edition, Donald Hoffmann. A total revision—both in text and illustrations—of the standard document on Fallingwater, the boldest, most personal architectural statement of Wright's mature years, updated with valuable new material from the recently opened Frank Lloyd Wright Archives. "Fascinating"—*The New York Times*. 116 illustrations. 128pp. 9¼ x 10¾. 27430-6 Pa. $11.95

PHOTOGRAPHIC SKETCHBOOK OF THE CIVIL WAR, Alexander Gardner. 100 photos taken on field during the Civil War. Famous shots of Manassas Harper's Ferry, Lincoln, Richmond, slave pens, etc. 244pp. 10⅝ x 8¼. 22731-6 Pa. $9.95

FIVE ACRES AND INDEPENDENCE, Maurice G. Kains. Great back-to-the-land classic explains basics of self-sufficient farming. The one book to get. 95 illustrations. 397pp. 5⅜ x 8½. 20974-1 Pa. $7.95

SONGS OF EASTERN BIRDS, Dr. Donald J. Borror. Songs and calls of 60 species most common to eastern U.S.: warblers, woodpeckers, flycatchers, thrushes, larks, many more in high-quality recording. Cassette and manual 99912-2 $9.95

A MODERN HERBAL, Margaret Grieve. Much the fullest, most exact, most useful compilation of herbal material. Gigantic alphabetical encyclopedia, from aconite to zedoary, gives botanical information, medical properties, folklore, economic uses, much else. Indispensable to serious reader. 161 illustrations. 888pp. 6½ x 9¼. 2-vol. set. (USO) Vol. I: 22798-7 Pa. $9.95
Vol. II: 22799-5 Pa. $9.95

HIDDEN TREASURE MAZE BOOK, Dave Phillips. Solve 34 challenging mazes accompanied by heroic tales of adventure. Evil dragons, people-eating plants, blood-thirsty giants, many more dangerous adversaries lurk at every twist and turn. 34 mazes, stories, solutions. 48pp. 8¼ x 11. 24566-7 Pa. $2.95

LETTERS OF W. A. MOZART, Wolfgang A. Mozart. Remarkable letters show bawdy wit, humor, imagination, musical insights, contemporary musical world; includes some letters from Leopold Mozart. 276pp. 5⅜ x 8½. 22859-2 Pa. $7.95

BASIC PRINCIPLES OF CLASSICAL BALLET, Agrippina Vaganova. Great Russian theoretician, teacher explains methods for teaching classical ballet. 118 illustrations. 175pp. 5⅜ x 8½. 22036-2 Pa. $5.95

THE JUMPING FROG, Mark Twain. Revenge edition. The original story of The Celebrated Jumping Frog of Calaveras County, a hapless French translation, and Twain's hilarious "retranslation" from the French. 12 illustrations. 66pp. 5⅜ x 8½. 22686-7 Pa. $3.95

BEST REMEMBERED POEMS, Martin Gardner (ed.). The 126 poems in this superb collection of 19th- and 20th-century British and American verse range from Shelley's "To a Skylark" to the impassioned "Renascence" of Edna St. Vincent Millay and to Edward Lear's whimsical "The Owl and the Pussycat." 224pp. 5⅜ x 8½. 27165-X Pa. $4.95

COMPLETE SONNETS, William Shakespeare. Over 150 exquisite poems deal with love, friendship, the tyranny of time, beauty's evanescence, death and other themes in language of remarkable power, precision and beauty. Glossary of archaic terms. 80pp. 5³⁄₁₆ x 8¼. 26686-9 Pa. $1.00

BODIES IN A BOOKSHOP, R. T. Campbell. Challenging mystery of blackmail and murder with ingenious plot and superbly drawn characters. In the best tradition of British suspense fiction. 192pp. 5⅜ x 8½. 24720-1 Pa. $6.95

THE WIT AND HUMOR OF OSCAR WILDE, Alvin Redman (ed.). More than 1,000 ripostes, paradoxes, wisecracks: Work is the curse of the drinking classes; I can resist everything except temptation; etc. 258pp. 5⅜ x 8½. 20602-5 Pa. $5.95

SHAKESPEARE LEXICON AND QUOTATION DICTIONARY, Alexander Schmidt. Full definitions, locations, shades of meaning in every word in plays and poems. More than 50,000 exact quotations. 1,485pp. 6½ x 9¼. 2-vol. set.
Vol. 1: 22726-X Pa. $16.95
Vol. 2: 22727-8 Pa. $16.95

SELECTED POEMS, Emily Dickinson. Over 100 best-known, best-loved poems by one of America's foremost poets, reprinted from authoritative early editions. No comparable edition at this price. Index of first lines. 64pp. 5³⁄₁₆ x 8¼.
26466-1 Pa. $1.00

CELEBRATED CASES OF JUDGE DEE (DEE GOONG AN), translated by Robert van Gulik. Authentic 18th-century Chinese detective novel; Dee and associates solve three interlocked cases. Led to van Gulik's own stories with same characters. Extensive introduction. 9 illustrations. 237pp. 5⅜ x 8½. 23337-5 Pa. $6.95

THE MALLEUS MALEFICARUM OF KRAMER AND SPRENGER, translated by Montague Summers. Full text of most important witchhunter's "bible," used by both Catholics and Protestants. 278pp. 6⅝ x 10. 22802-9 Pa. $12.95

SPANISH STORIES/CUENTOS ESPAÑOLES: A Dual-Language Book, Angel Flores (ed.). Unique format offers 13 great stories in Spanish by Cervantes, Borges, others. Faithful English translations on facing pages. 352pp. 5⅜ x 8½.
25399-6 Pa. $8.95

THE CHICAGO WORLD'S FAIR OF 1893: A Photographic Record, Stanley Appelbaum (ed.). 128 rare photos show 200 buildings, Beaux-Arts architecture, Midway, original Ferris Wheel, Edison's kinetoscope, more. Architectural emphasis; full text. 116pp. 8¼ x 11. 23990-X Pa. $9.95

OLD QUEENS, N.Y., IN EARLY PHOTOGRAPHS, Vincent F. Seyfried and William Asadorian. Over 160 rare photographs of Maspeth, Jamaica, Jackson Heights, and other areas. Vintage views of DeWitt Clinton mansion, 1939 World's Fair and more. Captions. 192pp. 8⅞ x 11. 26358-4 Pa. $12.95

CAPTURED BY THE INDIANS: 15 Firsthand Accounts, 1750-1870, Frederick Drimmer. Astounding true historical accounts of grisly torture, bloody conflicts, relentless pursuits, miraculous escapes and more, by people who lived to tell the tale. 384pp. 5⅜ x 8½. 24901-8 Pa. $8.95

THE WORLD'S GREAT SPEECHES, Lewis Copeland and Lawrence W. Lamm (eds.). Vast collection of 278 speeches of Greeks to 1970. Powerful and effective models; unique look at history. 842pp. 5⅜ x 8½. 20468-5 Pa. $14.95

THE BOOK OF THE SWORD, Sir Richard F. Burton. Great Victorian scholar/adventurer's eloquent, erudite history of the "queen of weapons"–from prehistory to early Roman Empire. Evolution and development of early swords, variations (sabre, broadsword, cutlass, scimitar, etc.), much more. 336pp. 6⅛ x 9¼.
25434-8 Pa. $9.95

AUTOBIOGRAPHY: The Story of My Experiments with Truth, Mohandas K. Gandhi. Boyhood, legal studies, purification, the growth of the Satyagraha (nonviolent protest) movement. Critical, inspiring work of the man responsible for the freedom of India. 480pp. 5⅜ x 8½. (USO) 24593-4 Pa. $8.95

CELTIC MYTHS AND LEGENDS, T. W. Rolleston. Masterful retelling of Irish and Welsh stories and tales. Cuchulain, King Arthur, Deirdre, the Grail, many more. First paperback edition. 58 full-page illustrations. 512pp. 5⅜ x 8½. 26507-2 Pa. $9.95

THE PRINCIPLES OF PSYCHOLOGY, William James. Famous long course complete, unabridged. Stream of thought, time perception, memory, experimental methods; great work decades ahead of its time. 94 figures. 1,391pp. 5⅜ x 8½. 2-vol. set.
Vol. I: 20381-6 Pa. $12.95
Vol. II: 20382-4 Pa. $12.95

THE WORLD AS WILL AND REPRESENTATION, Arthur Schopenhauer. Definitive English translation of Schopenhauer's life work, correcting more than 1,000 errors, omissions in earlier translations. Translated by E. F. J. Payne. Total of 1,269pp. 5⅜ x 8½. 2-vol. set. Vol. 1: 21761-2 Pa. $11.95
Vol. 2: 21762-0 Pa. $12.95

MAGIC AND MYSTERY IN TIBET, Madame Alexandra David-Neel. Experiences among lamas, magicians, sages, sorcerers, Bonpa wizards. A true psychic discovery. 32 illustrations. 321pp. 5⅜ x 8½. (USO) 22682-4 Pa. $8.95

THE EGYPTIAN BOOK OF THE DEAD, E. A. Wallis Budge. Complete reproduction of Ani's papyrus, finest ever found. Full hieroglyphic text, interlinear transliteration, word-for-word translation, smooth translation. 533pp. 6½ x 9¼.
21866-X Pa. $10.95

MATHEMATICS FOR THE NONMATHEMATICIAN, Morris Kline. Detailed, college-level treatment of mathematics in cultural and historical context, with numerous exercises. Recommended Reading Lists. Tables. Numerous figures. 641pp. 5⅜ x 8½.
24823-2 Pa. $11.95

THEORY OF WING SECTIONS: Including a Summary of Airfoil Data, Ira H. Abbott and A. E. von Doenhoff. Concise compilation of subsonic aerodynamic characteristics of NACA wing sections, plus description of theory. 350pp. of tables. 693pp. 5⅜ x 8½. 60586-8 Pa. $14.95

THE RIME OF THE ANCIENT MARINER, Gustave Doré, S. T. Coleridge. Doré's finest work; 34 plates capture moods, subtleties of poem. Flawless full-size reproductions printed on facing pages with authoritative text of poem. "Beautiful. Simply beautiful."–*Publisher's Weekly.* 77pp. 9¼ x 12. 22305-1 Pa. $6.95

NORTH AMERICAN INDIAN DESIGNS FOR ARTISTS AND CRAFTSPEOPLE, Eva Wilson. Over 360 authentic copyright-free designs adapted from Navajo blankets, Hopi pottery, Sioux buffalo hides, more. Geometrics, symbolic figures, plant and animal motifs, etc. 128pp. 8⅜ x 11. (EUK) 25341-4 Pa. $8.95

SCULPTURE: Principles and Practice, Louis Slobodkin. Step-by-step approach to clay, plaster, metals, stone; classical and modern. 253 drawings, photos. 255pp. 8⅛ x 11.
22960-2 Pa. $11.95

THE INFLUENCE OF SEA POWER UPON HISTORY, 1660–1783, A. T. Mahan. Influential classic of naval history and tactics still used as text in war colleges. First paperback edition. 4 maps. 24 battle plans. 640pp. 5⅜ x 8½.   25509-3 Pa. $12.95

THE STORY OF THE TITANIC AS TOLD BY ITS SURVIVORS, Jack Winocour (ed.). What it was really like. Panic, despair, shocking inefficiency, and a little heroism. More thrilling than any fictional account. 26 illustrations. 320pp. 5⅜ x 8½.
20610-6 Pa. $8.95

FAIRY AND FOLK TALES OF THE IRISH PEASANTRY, William Butler Yeats (ed.). Treasury of 64 tales from the twilight world of Celtic myth and legend: "The Soul Cages," "The Kildare Pooka," "King O'Toole and his Goose," many more. Introduction and Notes by W. B. Yeats. 352pp. 5⅜ x 8½.   26941-8 Pa. $8.95

BUDDHIST MAHAYANA TEXTS, E. B. Cowell and Others (eds.). Superb, accurate translations of basic documents in Mahayana Buddhism, highly important in history of religions. The Buddha-karita of Asvaghosha, Larger Sukhavativyuha, more. 448pp. 5⅜ x 8½.   25552-2 Pa. $12.95

ONE TWO THREE . . . INFINITY: Facts and Speculations of Science, George Gamow. Great physicist's fascinating, readable overview of contemporary science: number theory, relativity, fourth dimension, entropy, genes, atomic structure, much more. 128 illustrations. Index. 352pp. 5⅜ x 8½.   25664 2 Pa. $8.95

ENGINEERING IN HISTORY, Richard Shelton Kirby, et al. Broad, nontechnical survey of history's major technological advances: birth of Greek science, industrial revolution, electricity and applied science, 20th-century automation, much more. 181 illustrations. ". . . excellent . . ."–*Isis.* Bibliography. vii + 530pp. 5⅜ x 8¼.
26412-2 Pa. $14.95

DALÍ ON MODERN ART: The Cuckolds of Antiquated Modern Art, Salvador Dalí. Influential painter skewers modern art and its practitioners. Outrageous evaluations of Picasso, Cézanne, Turner, more. 15 renderings of paintings discussed. 44 calligraphic decorations by Dalí. 96pp. 5⅜ x 8½. (USO)   29220-7 Pa. $4.95

ANTIQUE PLAYING CARDS: A Pictorial History, Henry René D'Allemagne. Over 900 elaborate, decorative images from rare playing cards (14th–20th centuries): Bacchus, death, dancing dogs, hunting scenes, royal coats of arms, players cheating, much more. 96pp. 9¼ x 12¼.   29265-7 Pa. $11.95

MAKING FURNITURE MASTERPIECES: 30 Projects with Measured Drawings, Franklin H. Gottshall. Step-by-step instructions, illustrations for constructing handsome, useful pieces, among them a Sheraton desk, Chippendale chair, Spanish desk, Queen Anne table and a William and Mary dressing mirror. 224pp. 8⅛ x 11¼.
29338-6 Pa. $13.95

THE FOSSIL BOOK: A Record of Prehistoric Life, Patricia V. Rich et al. Profusely illustrated definitive guide covers everything from single-celled organisms and dinosaurs to birds and mammals and the interplay between climate and man. Over 1,500 illustrations. 760pp. 7½ x 10¼.   29371-8 Pa. $29.95

Prices subject to change without notice.

Available at your book dealer or write for free catalog to Dept. GI, Dover Publications, Inc., 31 East 2nd St., Mineola, N.Y. 11501. Dover publishes more than 500 books each year on science, elementary and advanced mathematics, biology, music, art, literary history, social sciences and other areas.